# THE ROLL CALL OF HONOUR

JOHN BROWN

*From a pen-drawing by*
*E. Heber Thompson*

# THE ROLL CALL OF HONOUR

*by*

## A. T. QUILLER-COUCH

("Q")

THOMAS NELSON AND SONS LTD
LONDON EDINBURGH PARIS MELBOURNE
TORONTO AND NEW YORK

*First published in this Series, November 1938*

# CONTENTS

# CONTENTS

# INTRODUCTION

THE nine names inscribed upon our *Roll Call of Honour* have not been selected at random, or merely as examples of modern heroism; they have passed certain definite tests.

In the first place, all are eminent for that self-devotion which is the pure gold of heroism. Few boys and girls will find themselves attracted by Simon Bolivar, for instance, as none can help being attracted by such a hero as Charles Gordon or such a heroine as Florence Nightingale. The characters of these are so bright and winning that they feelingly persuade us towards virtue; whereas Bolivar had none of " the beauty of holiness," and little enough beauty of any kind. One can easily prove that he was a vain man and at times very cruel. But he was disinterested, and he devoted his life to a cause. As Bunyan would say, " That which put glory of grace into all that he did was that he did it of pure love to his country;" and so he passes our first test along with Gordon and Florence Nightingale. " What is a golden deed? " asked the late Miss Charlotte Yonge in the preface of a very noble book we all read as children; and after rejecting the alloys of greed, bravado, fear of disgrace, insensibility—something unworthy in the doer or in the object sought—she rightly decided that " the true metal of a golden deed is self-devotion . . . the spirit that gives itself for others—the temper that for the sake of religion, of country, of duty, of kindred, nay, of pity even to a stranger, will dare all things, risk all things, endure all things."

So far so good, but Miss Yonge is speaking of golden *deeds* only, while we are dealing rather with golden *lives*; not with isolated actions, but sustained careers of self-devotion. Collecting examples from many books of history, Miss Yonge filled her pages with more than a hundred stories of heroism, some told briefly, some at length, and might easily have made the list up to a thousand. I find some additional scores of modern instances in *The Romance of Every Day*, a book by my sister, Lilian Quiller-Couch. If you step aside from the traffic of St. Martin's-le-Grand into the old churchyard of St. Botolph's, now converted into a small garden of rest and renamed " Postman's Park "—it almost faces our vast General Post Office—you will find a roofed shelter, along the wall of which run two rows of inscriptions, set there " to commemorate the brave deeds of a few men and women who were neither soldiers nor sailors nor persons of distinction in the social world " ; records to assure you that heroic self-devotion has not perished from the earth, or from our race, or from among the humblest ones of our race. It is not altogether to our discredit, perhaps, that we like to connect high deeds with high-sounding names and titles ; they deserve this adornment, and our poetical instinct delights in giving it. Names such as Marathon, Roncesvalles, Caerleon-upon-Usk, Château Gaillard, Ashby-de-la-Zouche reward valour, whether cheaply or not, by wrapping it in the cloak of beauty. But although Gravel Lane, S.E., be a less romantic address, and a London " general " not the likeliest heroine for " literature," it was in Gravel Lane, S.E., that Alice Ayres, domestic servant to a small shopkeeper, in April 1885 laid down her life bravely as a Roland or a Hereward, and nobly as a Philip Sidney, refusing to leap from the upper floor of a blazing house until she had rescued, one by one, her employer's three little daughters.

Now moral philosophers, from Aristotle down, will tell us—and I dare say they are right—that an isolated act of heroism, such as this of Alice Ayres, is not really isolated, but proceeds from a habit of heroism cultivated in secret, preparing itself unconsciously for the sudden call. This may well be ; yet by us the method of preparation cannot be traced. We have no data concerning Alice Ayres. Of the " lives " included in this volume, on the other hand, we can give a rational account, following them step by step as they prepare themselves for their work in the world, and as they achieve it. So we lay down as our second test that the heroism we admit to this book must be continuous and sustained.

For a third test this sustained self-devotion must be deliberate and conscious of its purpose, though unforeseeing of its precise opportunity. To meet what particular crisis Florence Nightingale is training her faculties, she knows no more than David Livingstone knows whither the Zambesi will lead him. He only knows that small rivers lead into great ones, and great ones to the sea. Pasteur only knows that he who enlarges human knowledge confers benefit on mankind and earns honour for his own country. Gordon only knows, or has faith, that by placing himself in God's hand and doing his best he will somehow be helping God's inscrutable design. " I am a chisel which cuts the wood ; the Carpenter directs it. If I lose my edge, He must sharpen me ; if He puts me aside and takes another, it is His own good will. None are indispensable to Him ; He will do His work with a straw just as well." So Gordon, too, goes forward with the rest, all pressing after the great river which somehow, somewhere, must lead to the sea.

Our fourth test is important. The object of self-devotion must be an idea, and not a person or a group of persons. Bolivar had one dream, one master passion—political liberty for South America ; John Brown one—the breaking of slavery ; Lincoln one— to save the Union ; Garibaldi one—to redeem Italy ; Livingstone one—to let in light upon Africa. The good wrought by Florence Nightingale at Scutari, and the whole reform of nursing which her example in-augurated, grew out of a single conviction that took hold of her—the conviction that women must train themselves as seriously as do men for whatever business they undertake in life. Pasteur, starting with devotion to one single idea—the enlargement of "scientific" knowledge—from 1870 onwards imposed a second upon it : that his beloved France, trampled in the dust by force and slaughter, might be rehabili-tated and restored to her proud place in Europe by peaceful discoveries triumphing over disease and death. Damien gave his life, not for this or that leper, nor for a group of men personally dear to him, but for the sake of leading in divine love to let it shine upon men of whom he knew only that they lived in misery without hope. Gordon was charitable to all poor and suffering folk he met ; but he was great through a wider charity which bade him help unseen tribes who dwelt in darkness. That, and not the smaller benefactions, in which thousands of kind-hearted Christians vie with him daily, made him " God's warrior, man's friend."

It seems a hard saying that devotion to an idea, if the idea be a noble one, will confer a thousandfold more benefits on the world than will devotion to wife, child, friend, or to any number of dear ones. But we must get that truth into our heads if we would under-stand in what true greatness consists. Tens of thou-sands of men and women, even in these islands, can and do suffer or strive heroically, week in and week out, for the sake of those whose faces they daily see, whose thanks they hear, whose loving secrets they share. To suffer or strive heroically for a conviction in your own mind; to dare all, trusting in " the evidence of things not seen," as did Columbus to discover America—*that* is the test. And to justify its claim we have only to compare the two forms of heroism in their operation. Alice Ayres saves three lives at the cost of her own. The world is the better, we hope, by those three lives; certainly the better by a golden example—and Heaven forbid that I seem to disparage the price of the example. "*This* is what we have in exchange for Beauchamp!" is the unspoken comment of two characters, at the conclusion of Meredith's fine novel, as they stare at the small gutter-snipe whom Beauchamp died to save. But of course it is not all: the value of such men as Beauchamp lies precisely in their readiness to give away self without reckoning the returns, and their example cannot, in justice to them, be discussed in terms of price. Yet it may be pointed out of Florence Nightingale that, over and above the thousands she relieved at Scutari in 1855–56, tens of thousands of sick-beds are being soothed in England to-day, as hundreds of thousands of sick folk have been saved from death because she gave all her strength to an idea; or again of John Brown that, although the negroes refused to rise at Harper's Ferry, millions of negroes are free to-day because he faithfully pursued an idea even to a point which most men accounted madness.

The world, in fact, is moved by ideas, and it is because the characters in this book devoted themselves to ideas that the influence of each has been profoundly felt in the world. They have all been *initiators*. Now there is a heroism which, equally unsparing of self, rests its devotion upon discipline or obedience—the heroism, for instance, of the Roman soldier who stood at his post at the gate of Pompeii until overwhelmed by the dust and cinders pouring down from Vesuvius; of the British soldiers who stood composedly on the deck of the sinking *Birkenhead* ; or of those others who charged down the valley of Balaklava riding to death for a blunder—

> " Theirs not to reason why,
> Theirs but to do and die."

But theirs is not the heroism which initiates ; nor, admirable as we may find it, does it happen to be the heroism with which we are concerned in this book.

For our fifth and last test the heroism must be eminent, or at least important, in result. It must not have been spent in vain, or even apparently in vain, though it miss all that the vulgar understand by success. I observe that my sister, discussing one of the heroes commemorated in " Postman's Park," maintains that his action was as splendid as though he had rescued a nation. She is speaking of a Croydon policeman who, summoned to a burning oil store, had started with one companion to roll out the intact barrels of paraffin from the cellar, when, fancying he heard a woman's cry in an upper part of the house, he left the deadly storage, that the least touch of flame would explode beneath him, and rushed up a staircase to help. As he made his way up under a hot drip of oil the fearful thing happened : the flame reached the cellarage, and the exploding casks sent up a flame that cut off all retreat. When the firemen drove it back they found him dead in an upper room —and he had died in vain. There was no woman in the house ; the cry had existed only in his imagination. We do not belittle such devotion by choosing here devotion less futile in result, any more than we belittle the heroes of medicine who of late years have fallen martyrs to the deadly X-rays when we choose for our hero Pasteur, whose death came to him in the ordinary way, and not out of the discoveries by which he has saved mankind from an amount of suffering never to be computed. Of vulgar success the heroes on our Roll Call knew little. Bolivar died in despair, outcast from the vast territories he had liberated. John Brown perished on the gallows, after seeing two sons die in agony, and uncheered by any certain prospect of the victory achieved by his mad deed. Lincoln tasted power, but power with awful dangers and responsibilities, and fell under the assassin's pistol at the moment when fate apparently freed him to enjoy the love and gratitude of his countrymen. I know of no more pathetic figure than Livingstone, in his last days, wandering half crazed under the wizardry of Africa, his mind clear enough to realize, his incurable honesty compelling him to realize, that he had been following a mirage. He died solitary, on his knees, his head bowed on his bent arms; in what bitterness of spirit who can guess? Turn from him to Gordon, beleaguered with a starving garrison, gazing day by day across the sands across which no help came, and do not accuse these pages of truckling to what the vulgar call success. Eminent results they record, but results won at cost of infinite personal suffering.

The successive tests enumerated are such as in any century (and we confine ourselves to the nineteenth) only a few of the choicest spirits could pass. I regretfully omit one or two names, which should be included in another edition if this book is ever to satisfy me. There is Nelson, who lived for an idea of patriotism —set it so high and died for it so splendidly that his name should surely be added to the Roll. But it seemed idle to re-write a life so often written. There is Yoshida-Torajiro, the Japanese patriot, concerning whom my ignorance could add little or nothing to the essay in Stevenson's *Men and Books*. And there is Tolstoy, under whose spell so much of my own life has lain that I can hardly write of him yet proportionately and without confusion. There may be two or three others—not more, I think—who between 1800 and 1900 pass all tests. Even if held to be capricious or arbitrary, they are high tests indeed which exclude Outram and Havelock.

In conclusion, I must acknowledge special indebtedness to Mr. F. Loraine Petre's *Simon Bolivar, el Libertador* (John Lane) ; Mrs. Sarah A. Tooley's *Life of Florence Nightingale* ; Mr. John Newton's *Captain John Brown of Harper's Ferry* (T. Fisher Unwin) ; Mr. Edward Clifford's *Father Damien* (Macmillan), with the *Life and Letters of Father Damien*, published by the Catholic Truth Society ; and M. Valery-Radot's *Life of Pasteur*, a translation of which by Mrs. R. L. Devonshire is published by Messrs. Constable in this country.

ARTHUR QUILLER-COUCH.

# THE ROLL CALL OF HONOUR

## BOLIVAR

VERY likely the first name on our roll call means little or nothing to most of my younger readers, and not much more to some elderly ones. Simon Bolivar,* the Liberator, had a tremendous reputation in his day; men spoke of him, of George Washington, of Napoleon, in the same breath. He did not deserve it, and, as usually happens, too much praise has ended in neglect equally undeserved. Moreover, South America is a great way off ; and the republics—Venezuela, Colombia, Ecuador, Peru, Bolivia—which he freed from Spanish misrule are connected in our minds with a misrule of their own. We have a general impression of them as of states in which revolution succeeds revolution with bewildering rapidity, and bloodthirsty street-fighting is commonly followed by the victorious party's repudiating the debts of the previous government. Indeed, towards the end of his career, Bolivar became sadly convinced that the people for whom he had fought so magnificently were unfit to work out for themselves the salvation he had brought them, and that a Washington may toil in vain unless he liberate a worthy people. He died a disappointed man. His life had been very far from stainless. But he had flung it fearlessly upon a high cause, refusing no labours, no perils. He had planted the ideal of self-

---

* The name should be pronounced Bolívar (*Boleevar*), not Bolivár.

government—less circumspectly than did Washington, and therefore less surely, but over a wider area.   He won splendid successes ; and it may help to excuse an interest in them that some were won with the help of our own countrymen fighting under him for the cause of liberty.

Simon Bolivar was born, on the 24th July 1783, at Carácas, the capital of Venezuela.   His father, Don Juan Vicente de Bolivar, a landowner and high in the state service, died when the child was scarcely three years old ; his mother when he was six ; and young Simon became ward of his maternal uncle, Don Carlos Palacio, an easy-going old gentleman, who let him grow up anyhow, more or less.

The Bolivars and their kinsfolk were descended from emigrants of good family, who had come across the Atlantic from Spain and settled in her American dominions.   These dominions, won for her by her early navigators, were vast indeed—twice the size of Europe ; and if Great Britain made a mess of governing or attempting to govern her North American colonies from Westminster, it is not surprising that decadent Spain made a worse mess from Madrid.   For at least two centuries the government, amenable to applicants at home, sent out shoals of needy adventurers to make money and earn titles in governorships and other posts from which the colonists, or " creoles," were jealously excluded, though they had better claims.   Of 754 viceroys and captains-general only eighteen were creoles.*   The result of this bad custom was that the colonists lived in a constant state of dis-

* *Simon Bolivar, el Libertador*, by F. Loraine Petre.   The word " creole," properly used, implies no admixture of dark blood. The child of a European and a negress is a " mulatto " ; the child of a European and an American Indian is a " mestizo." Creole (*criollo*, " little servant ") was merely a contemptuous name for " colonials."   " To the Spaniard coming over from Europe ' criollo ' signified a man of the pure blood of his own race, often of purer blood and higher lineage than himself, who had been born and bred in the colonies, and was domiciled there."

## SIMON BOLIVAR.

*From a pen-drawing by*
*E. Heber Thompson.*

content, and at the same time, having no motives to honourable exertion, wasted their lives in indolence or in vice. They saw how the British in North America had wrested their independence from King George III., and dreamed of copying their example ; but they lacked a leader.

In such a society young Simon Bolivar grew up—a quick-witted, wilful-tempered boy, without father or mother to correct his faults. Tutors were found for him, but he gave more time to riding and open-air exercises than to Latin, arithmetic, or history. He spent much of his time on his paternal estate in the Aragua Valley, and at the age of fourteen was appointed ensign in the Aragua militia, of which his father had been colonel. This was his only training for war, and it cannot have amounted to much.

In 1799 his uncle Carlos shipped him off to Madrid, where, under the care of another uncle, Esteban Palacio, the lad saw something of high society in the capital and the vices of the court. On one occasion (the story is his own) he was invited to play tennis with the Prince of Asturias, whom he beat. The prince turned sulky, and for some time would not go on. This young opponent was afterwards Ferdinand VII., from whom Bolivar wrested so many of his South American dominions.

He had already drunk deeply of the doctrines of the French Revolution, and hated all monarchs and priests. He paid a long visit to Paris ; and, returning to Madrid, on the eve of his departure for home, married a young girl with whom he had fallen passionately in love. Maria Teresa Rodriguez de Toro, niece of the Marquis de Toro of Carácas, was a mere child, scarcely sixteen years old ; but Bolivar, aged eighteen, owned estates worth about £160,000, while she had no fortune. This consideration no doubt helped Bolivar's ardour, and persuaded her father to allow the marriage. The couple spent their honeymoon on board a sailing vessel, which carried them from Corunna to Carácas. But their happiness was brief. The young bride had spent but a few months in her new home in the Aragua Valley when a fever carried her off after a few days' illness.

Bolivar was heart-broken. He vowed never to marry again, and kept his vow. Aragua was hateful to him, and he wished to make over the whole estate to his brother—an offer that was very nobly refused. To cure the pain of his heart, he visited Europe again, and in Madrid and Paris plunged into wild dissipation, which not only brought no peace but threatened to wreck his life. Restless of soul, in despair with God and man, he returned to Aragua again, and shut himself up with his books, varying his gloomy studies with wild rides about the rich estates that brought no joy to him.

He was saved by a new interest, which by degrees became an absorbing passion. In 1808–9 Napoleon compelled Charles IV. and his son Ferdinand to abdicate the throne of Spain in favour of his own brother Joseph. But the Spaniards rose against the French usurpation, formed a central " Junta," or committee to carry on the government, and appealed to England for help ; the result being, as every one knows, the famous Peninsular War, in which the allied troops under Wellington finally drove the French out of Spain.

Let us see how these events affected the Spanish creoles in Venezuela and other parts of South America. Their own rightful monarch, Charles, had abdicated. They had no mind to accept a Bonaparte in his place ; for the most revolutionary spirits (such as Bolivar) hated Napoleon, now that he had become a despot, in proportion as they had loved him while he was a mere general winning victories for the cause of revolutionary France, with her watchwords of " Liberty, Equality, Fraternity." As for the central or regency

Junta at home, " Why," argued some, " should we
not set up a junta of our own ? Is not this the opportunity for which we have so long been waiting, to
cut ourselves loose from the old country, have done
with governors and officials from Europe, and assert
our independence after the example of the United
States ? " Bolivar was one of those who reasoned
thus ; but for some time nothing was done. Early in
1809 there arrived at Carácas a new captain-general,
Vicente Empáran, holding appointment under the
new regency Junta. For a few weeks his rule seemed
to be peaceably accepted ; but on Thursday, April
19th (Maundy Thursday), as he was walking across
the square to attend service at the cathedral, the
agitators stopped him, and walked him back to the
municipal hall. From its balcony one of them called
down to the crowd, " Are you content with the present government ? " " No ! " they cried back ; " we
do not love it." " I love it just as little," said
Empáran, hearing their shouts, and he offered no
opposition when they proceeded to form a Venezuelan
junta and pass a resolution affirming " the right of
the provinces of America to rule themselves, in the
absence of a general government."

The regency Junta at home, on getting news of this,
promptly treated it as an act of rebellion, and decreed
a blockade of the Venezuelan ports. Bolivar, who had
hastened to tender his services to the new Junta, and
had been appointed lieutenant-colonel of his father's
old militia, thereupon suggested sending a deputation
to England (now the ally of Spain against Napoleon)
to persuade the British Government to reason with
the Spanish Regency and put a stop to hostilities.
The suggestion was well received, a deputation appointed, and Bolivar himself sent as chief negotiator.
He reached London in July 1810, and was perhaps
not greatly surprised that the British Government,
though polite, could not agree to help him in breaking

off allegiance to the mother country. But his journey had a further object. Exiled in London, there lived a veteran revolutionary, Francisco Miranda. This man had twice attempted to lead the Venezuelans in armed revolt against Spanish rule ; and though the risings had been suppressed, his name was still one to conjure with. Without consulting his colleagues on the Junta at Carácas, Bolivar persuaded Miranda to sail back with him, and they reached La Guaira, the port of Carácas, on the 5th of December.

They were at first very coldly welcomed by the Junta, which did not approve of having its hand forced in this fashion. But in the following summer (1811) the discovery of a vast Royalist conspiracy threw the new government into confusion ; and Miranda, Bolivar, and the rest of the bolder spirits seized their opportunity. Proclaiming that strong diseases required strong remedies, on July 5th they persuaded the Junta to declare complete independence of Spain ; and on the 11th they put down with bloodshed an attempted insurrection in the capital. Valencia, a town seventy or eighty miles to the southwest, gave more trouble, assembled a strong Royalist force, and defied the new government. The Marquis de Toro, Bolivar's uncle by marriage, marched out a " patriotic " force against Valencia, but was sharply repulsed at La Cabrera, where the road cuts through a dangerous defile. Every one now called on Miranda as a trained soldier to take command of the troops of the republic. Miranda somewhat superciliously consented, making no concealment of his opinion that his army was a mere rabble, and stipulating that Bolivar —with whom he had recently quarrelled—should hold no important command. Consequently, in the campaign that followed, our hero had to content himself with the post of aide-de-camp to the Marquis de Toro ; but he showed such conspicuous bravery in the assault on Valencia (which Miranda took with the loss of 800

men) that he was selected to carry back to Carácas
the dispatch announcing victory. For a time the
new government breathed freely ; but the regency in
Spain kept up, and very naturally, an implacable
resentment. " To what class do these South Ameri-
cans belong ? " " They complain of having been
oppressed for three hundred years ; they shall henceforth be oppressed for three thousand "—such was the
language used in the Spanish Cortes. Even in Venezuela the Royalists held several strong positions, and,
refusing to submit, awaited reinforcements from home.
The Republicans were arming expeditions to reduce
them, when on the 26th of March 1812 (again a
Maundy Thursday) a dreadful earthquake, heralded
by a roar louder than any thunder, swept the northern
part of Venezuela, burying within a few minutes
Carácas itself, its port of La Guaira, and many minor
towns, in heap upon heap of ruins. In Barquisimeto,
1,000 Republican troops on the march against the
Royalists were engulfed and wiped out. The barracks
to the north of Carácas subsided, overwhelming almost
all the garrison in the ruins.

While Bolivar and others were working to collect
and burn the corpses that everywhere polluted the air
—10,000 bodies lay in the streets of Carácas itself—
the clergy, mostly Royalists, were busy at the easier
task of persuading superstitious people that the earthquake was a direct visitation of God upon the new
government, and in pointing, for proof, to a church in
which everything had fallen except one pillar bearing
a shield with the royal arms of Spain.

Upon this scene of awful destruction there arrived—
and opportunely, as if he too were part of the divine
vengeance—a somewhat remarkable man, Domingo
Monteverde by name ; a Spanish naval officer, who
had arrived from the Canaries with a company of
marines to help the Royalists. Marching on Barquisimeto with 1,000 men, he dug out of its ruins seven

guns and a great quantity of ammunition, pressed on, and captured post after post from the Republicans, who fought half-heartedly, their nerves shaken by the earthquake and their superstitions. He reached Valencia and occupied it, Miranda retreating before him and encamping himself above the defile of La Cabrera, already described. There, through the treachery of a deserter, Monteverde learned of a path leading round the Republicans' right, and considered so difficult that it had been left almost unwatched. The Royalist general succeeded in climbing it, and drove Miranda back on another position, La Victoria, still covering the road to Carácas.

Just then it must be admitted that Bolivar, by an act of negligence, did much to hasten the end. Miranda, to whom he was still odious, had packed him off to command the citadel of Puerto Cabello on the coast —a magazine of arms and supplies, and a place of detention for many Spanish prisoners. It is possible that Bolivar, in his disgust at being shelved, showed some slackness in guarding these unarmed men. At any rate, they bribed Francisco Vinoni, the officer in charge, who released them in Bolivar's temporary absence ; whereupon they manned the guns of the citadel, and opened fire on the town below. At the end of five days they had battered it into surrender, and Bolivar—for once in his life outdared and out-witted—escaped with a few officers and men to La Guaira. It was fortunate for him, perhaps, that the downfall of the republic was near ; for there seems no reason to doubt that Miranda would have made little scruple of shooting him for this military blunder. But as it happened, Miranda had his hands full at La Victoria. Bolivar (who never lacked pluck), having landed at La Guaira, was proceeding to La Victoria to report himself, when the news reached him that the Republican government was at an end ; that Miranda, despairing of his position, had capitulated at La Victoria; and that Monteverde was marching unopposed on the capital.

Monteverde entered Carácas on July 30th. That same evening Miranda reached La Guaira, half dead with fatigue, and there met Casas—commandant of the port—Bolivar, and other fugitive leaders. A British corvette, H.M.S. *Sapphire*, lay in the harbour, ready to take Miranda off. They dined together, and then, the hour being late, it was agreed that the ex-general should snatch a few hours' rest, and embark in the early morning. While he slept, Bolivar, convinced that he had capitulated for Spanish gold, persuaded the others to arrest and detain him. " Since he has signed our capitulation, whether for gold or not, let him stay and see it through to the bitter end." At three in the morning, Bolivar and two companions entered his room, secured his sword and pistols, and awoke him. Half dazed with sleep, Miranda obeyed, and followed them to the castle, where he was put under lock and key. It is likely enough that he would have been shot on the morrow for a traitor ; but soon after dawn an order reached the commandant Casas from Monteverde, requiring him to stop all embarkations. The threatened fugitives dispersed in haste ; a few succeeded in getting on board the *Sapphire*, which beat out for sea. Bolivar that same evening slipped back through the enemy's posts to Carácas, where he lay in hiding, sheltered by a worthy man, Francisco Iturbe, a dear friend of his though a Royalist by conviction. As for the hapless Miranda— to get him out of the story—after languishing for months in the castle of La Guaira, he was removed to Puerto Cabello, thence to Puerto Rico, and thence shipped home to Cadiz, where the Regency Government confined him in the arsenal in chains, until, on July 14th, 1816, death released him from his sufferings.

As soon as the storm had blown over a little, the

good Iturbe besought Monteverde for a passport
enabling Bolivar to quit the country. Monteverde
reluctantly assented, stipulating, however, that the
fugitive should appear before him. " You have put
yourself," said he, " beyond the terms of the capitulation. But you did a praiseworthy deed in arresting
Miranda, and that entitles you to the king's clemency."
" I have no claim to His Majesty's clemency on that
ground," answered Bolivar fearlessly : " I arrested
Miranda as the traitor, not to him, but to my country."
Monteverde flew into a rage, and was on the point
of refusing the passport, when Iturbe flung himself
between them and, interceding, procured his friend's
liberty.

Monteverde little guessed what a formidable foe
he was loosing from under his hand. Probably he
thought little of this prisoner, who had, be it remembered, taken no prominent part in the late campaign, and moreover had bungled in his secondary
command at Puerto Cabello. He was soon to regret
that passport.

For Bolivar, making his way to Cartagena, in the
neighbouring viceroyalty of New Granada, at once
offered his services to the Republican Government
there. New Granada (now Colombia) had followed
Venezuela into revolt against Spain ; and the Republicans there were holding their own and no more.
Especially they were threatened by the Royalist
province of Santa Marta, which thrusts itself in like
a wedge between Cartagena and the western frontier
of Venezuela. So sorely pressed indeed were they by
the Royalist forces in Santa Marta, that they had
elected one Torices as dictator, and Torices, a young
man of twenty-four, had enlisted a French adventurer,
Labatut, to lead an expedition against the obstinately
" royal " province. To the Dictator Torices Bolivar
promptly offered his services, and was purposely
given by Labatut (who had met him at La Guaira) a

small post on the left bank of the river Magdalena, with strict orders to guard it, and not to budge. Hitherto, it would seem, Bolivar's title to prominence chiefly consisted in the distrust he inspired in his commanding officers. He was now at one stroke to justify that distrust and lay his claim to greatness —a claim never afterwards disputed.

Labatut had no sooner turned his back than Bolivar boldly disobeyed orders. Starting with 200 men, but getting adherents as he went, he swept up the Magdalena, driving out post after post of the Royalists, and never halting until he had cleared 300 miles of the river, driving out the Spanish garrisons, capturing their boats, and surprising whole stores of ammunition and artillery.

Labatut, on hearing of these successes, was beside himself, and ordered this venturesome lieutenant to return at once to his post. Bolivar answered, recounting his successes, not promising obedience. Labatut appealed to the Dictator Torices, demanding Bolivar's trial by court-martial. But Torices refused to grant it : the disobedience had been a brilliant success, and he could not punish a man whose exploits had made him the idol of all Cartagena. Relying on this and on the dictator's evident goodwill, Bolivar in his turn made a request. He had cleared the way to the western frontier of Venezuela. " Might he be allowed to invade his country with a small expedition, and attempt to recapture it ? " Torices gave his consent, and on the 9th of February 1813 Bolivar started eastward.

He had but 400 men ; he counted on the Venezuelans flocking to him as soon as he reached the frontier, and difficulties of commissariat forbade his carrying a large force across the intervening country. The route lay across the Eastern Cordilleras, through terrific gorges, alongside the edge of precipices, on mountain slopes swept by storms of sleet and snow. His men, dwellers on the warm plains, suffered miserably from the icy winds, the rarefied air, the strange and difficult toil of mountaineering. But the ridges were crossed at length, and the small troop descended like hawks upon the frontier town of San José de Cucuta, into which, after a four hours' fight, they marched on February 28th, driving the routed Spaniards before them. Next morning they crossed the actual frontier, and stood within the gates of Venezuela.

While this was happening in the west, a small force of exiled Venezuelans had made a swoop upon the north-east coast under the leadership of Santiago Marino, a young officer who had won distinction in the late war. Thus Monteverde, whom we left in pretty secure possession, ruling over a people cowed by earthquake and violent proscription, suddenly found himself caught between two fires. Two brief anecdotes will illustrate the spirit of the warfare that now opened as Bolivar marched forward from the frontier upon Carácas. There had been some jealousy between the New Granadans and the Venezuelans in his command, and certain of the former had withdrawn to their homes in a huff. " General," wrote Rafael Urdaneta, a Venezuelan, " if two men are sufficient to liberate our country, I am ready to go with you." Another enthusiastic Venezuelan, who had accompanied Bolivar in exile and across the mountains, having started off on a hot-headed expedition without orders, was surprised by a Spanish commander named Yanez, captured, and shot. Bolivar, on hearing the news, promptly proclaimed " war to the death "— that is to say, war without quarter ; and this ghastly edict was never revoked until Bolivar, after fighting his long way up towards Carácas, and overthrowing the Spaniards in engagement after engagement, reached Valencia, into which Monteverde, after being repulsed by Marino in the east, flung himself for a last desperate stand. But the army sent out to engage the oncoming Republicans, finding itself outflanked by Bolivar's cavalry and in danger of being cut off, retreated and broke up in a rout, and Monteverde had barely time to escape seaward to Puerto Cabello, in which fortress—to conclude the story of his career—he kept up an obstinate resistance for some time; but at length, having received a severe wound in the face, gave up the hopeless struggle and took ship for Spain.

On August 6th Bolivar rode into Carácas in triumph, the people hailing him with shouts of " Long live the Liberator ! " crowning his soldiers with wreaths of laurel and of flowers, firing salutes, waving flags, and embracing one another in wild jubilation. He at once announced the restoration of the republic, and as soon as possible convoked an assembly of the chief inhabitants to draw up the new form of government. For himself he formally declined to accept any authority but " that of leading our soldiers to danger, to save our country." There is no doubt that Bolivar's patriotism was pure, disinterested, and devoid of self-seeking. Even his popular title—though he remained *the* Liberator by general acclaim—he chose to share with the rest of the Republican leaders, founding an " Order of Liberators," and conferring its badge and ribbon on those who had eminently served their country's cause.

But although by hard fighting and marching he had won Carácas and ousted Spanish rule from the Venezuelan capital, his position and that of the new government were most insecure. Enemies surrounded him in an irregular ring, and among them, out of many incompetent commanders, there emerged one truly formidable man. José Tomas Boves, *alias* Rodriguez, was perhaps as unlovely a scoundrel as even the history of South America can present. Born in Spain and brought up as a pilot, he had emigrated to Venezuela and turned pirate; had been caught, and sentenced to imprisonment as a " sea-robber"; had joined the Republicans on his release, changing his name from Rodriguez to Boves; had quarrelled with them, and transferred his allegiance to the Royalists. In the name of the King of Spain he had raised a troop of cavalry and turned bandit, looting the country under pretence of military operations. At this game he was engaged when the almost simultaneous invasion of Bolivar on the west and Marino on the east recalled him and his marauders to something like regular service. Joining Cajigal, the Spanish commander in the east, he marched some way against Marino's forces, but contrived on the road to be left behind to collect forces among the Llaneros, or " men of the plains " north of the Orinoco.

These Llaneros were a wild race, half Spanish and half Indian, cattle-breeders by calling; horse-breeders, too, for the cattle, being practically wild, had, when required for use, to be ridden down and either lassoed or cast by a cunning twist of the tail. It followed that the Llaneros were marvellous horsemen; also that, scattered over the wide plains and dwelling in remote huts or groups of huts, they knew no politics, were absolutely illiterate, and could only be raised as a military force upon promises of plunder, as they could only be held together in any sort of discipline by a man they recognized as an even more reckless blackguard than themselves. Such a man after their own heart they found in Boves. He was ready with promises of pay; he commanded by sheer brutality. In person he resembled Attila the Hun. " Broad of chest, hideous of feature, red-haired, with lowering brow, wide nostrils, deep-sunk eyes; of massive skull, with a restless and horrible look, that wandered around like that of a tiger watching its prey . . . a man born for the destruction of the universe." He had a trick of tying his prisoners to posts after flogging them, choosing a spot in the eye of the sun and leaving them to die of hunger and thirst, while the tropical insects settled on their raw wounds. On one occasion having captured an old man with his son (neither of them combatants), he asked the boy, "Will you submit to have your ears and nose cut off to save your father's life?" The boy submitted heroically to this awful torture; it was no sooner over than Boves ordered the pair to be beheaded. For another example. Towards the close of the campaign that followed, when Boves was assailing Valencia (which, as we have seen already, was the military "key" of Carácas), two brothers came into his camp as deserters, hoping to save their lives. Boves ordered each to be adorned with bulls' horns and turned loose in a ring of horsemen, to be slowly pricked to death by lances, like bulls in a ring.

Such was the man who, having collected his Llaneros in sufficient quantities, swept them north and west against the capital. disregarding orders from his nominal commander Cajigal, or treating them with open contempt. Bolivar, too, much occupied with the framing of his new constitution and other political matters that might wisely have been deferred until his enemies were overcome, had made the mistake of splitting up his forces instead of concentrating them and overthrowing the Spanish commanders one after another. Again and again, when one of his detached armies found itself in trouble, he hastened from Carácas and restored the fortunes of the fight; and notably at Carabobo on May 28th. Marino, to whom Bolivar had sent for help, had arrived from the east and taken the field, great hopes being built on his reputation. These hopes were belied by a crushing defeat on the 17th of April on the plain of the Aroa. Bolivar hastily got together 5,000 men, and marching to the rescue, put the Royalists under Cajigal to complete rout, capturing all their artillery, with 4,000 horses, 500 muskets, and 9 standards. But again he committed the fault of dividing up his army and returning to Carácas, with the result that by the 15th of June Boves caught Marino in a hopeless position at La Puerta. Bolivar, summoned once more from the capital, took over the command and attempted to retire; but it was too late. Boves, who had concealed his strength by posting some thousands of his Llaneros in the neighbouring ravines, suddenly let them loose and swept Bolivar off the field by sheer weight of numbers, taking or destroying one-half of the Republican force. " I have," he reported to Cajigal contemptuously, " recovered the arms, ammunition, and the honour of the Spanish flag, which your Excellency lost at Carabobo."

Boves massacred all his prisoners. It was a hideous war. Already the Spanish prisoners in Carácas had been put to death by Bolivar's orders; and this is the gravest blot on the Liberator's memory, his only excuse—which is no excuse—being that, having captured some correspondence of a Spanish general Rosete, he had found amongst it a plan for a rising of these prisoners; and from such a rising Bolivar had once before, as we know, suffered severely enough. This same Rosete carried with him a branding-iron and used it to burn the letter P (for Patriot) on the faces of captured Republicans.

After the disaster of La Puerta nothing remained but flight; and on the 6th of July, abandoning Carácas, Bolivar and Marino, with 2,000 troops and an immense throng of unarmed folk—including women and children fleeing in terror of Boves—marched out eastwards to escape to the Republican town of Barcelona. They had twenty days' start; for Boves, after entering Carácas on the 16th, spent ten days in pillaging and murdering, and did not take the road in pursuit until the 26th. The poor fugitives needed all this advantage; for their march—the Emigration of 1814, as it is called—was one of untold horrors. The roads, at the height of the rainy season, were mere rivers of slush; the rain fell pitilessly day after day. Through this, with no covering at night, no fire, and on starvation victuals, soldiers, children, delicate women, strove to hurry, always with the dread of Boves at their heels. It is said that mothers, unable to nourish or even carry their infants, flung them over precipices rather than abandon them to die by the roadside.

They reached Barcelona at length, only to find that the chief inhabitants meant to open their gates to the Spaniards; and therefore pressed on for Cumaná, still farther eastward on the coast. There they took ship, and escaped in various ways, Bolivar and Marino sailing for Cartagena; and the second Venezuelan republic was at an end. As for Boves, he perished in the last action of the campaign, being pierced with a lance just as his men were dispersing some 3,000 Republicans who had gathered together for a last stand.

Bolivar, landing at Cartagena on September 25th, 1814, at once offered his services to the Republican Government of New Granada, and was entrusted with 1,800 men and the task of reducing Santa Fé (afterwards called Bogotá), which had set itself up as an independent state. This he did after a short siege, and was promptly dispatched to coerce Santa Marta, the one Royalist stronghold remaining on the New Granadan coast. There was a province of Santa Marta as well as a fortress. Having cleared the province, Bolivar prepared to reduce the fortress, and for that purpose turned aside to collect arms and munitions from Cartagena. To his infinite disgust, an old enemy of his, one Castillo, had been intriguing against him in the town, and had persuaded the inhabitants not only to refuse the supplies, but to hinder his march. Bolivar in a fury marched his troops up to storm Cartagena into a better sense of what was due to their common cause; and the citizens, equally incensed by Castillo against the Venezuelan intruder, and unable to hold their outworks against him, were actually poisoning the wells around the city by throwing rotten hides into them (against such dissensions had South America to win its freedom!), when the foe against whom they should have been united to strive stepped in amid their folly, and for a while destroyed them both. By this time, thanks to Wellington and his armies, Ferdinand VII. was back on his throne in Madrid, and almost his first thought there was to equip an expedition to suppress the revolted American colonies. In mid-February 1815 it sailed from Spain —one large battleship, three frigates, forty smaller war-vessels, and sixty to seventy transports, carrying 10,600 soldiery, with a siege train, the whole under command of Don Pablo Morillo. Early in April this fleet reached Venezuela, and finding it already subdued, sailed on for New Granada. Already the Royalists there, gaining heart, had pushed in and cut Bolivar off from communication with the Republican seat of government while he quarrelled with Castillo. On the 7th and 8th of May Bolivar dispersed his troops, and sailed away for Jamaica, leaving Cartagena to its fate. This fate fell on it in the autumn, when Morillo arrived and laid siege so severe that the garrison, looking in vain for a ship bringing relief, with sentries dying of starvation at their posts, evacuated the town, and escaped on shipboard. The Spaniards entered a city of which the streets were strewn with men dying on the pavements of hunger, and intermixed with corpses polluting the air. Spain was triumphant, and in a few weeks the republic of New Granada had crumbled to nothing, even as the Venezuelan republic had twice crumbled.

If ever a man had a right to despair of life, it was Bolivar in 1816. Every hope on which he had built lay prostrate; he was an exile, and almost penniless; and in Jamaica, whither he first fled, he could gain no promise of assistance. Here indeed his career was nearly ended by a negro assassin, who crept into his chamber one night and stabbed to death, by mistake, an officer named Amestoy, to whom the Liberator had temporarily given up his sleeping quarters. It must ever stand to Bolivar's credit that in these darkest days he never lost hope, and never remitted his exertions; like the famous Roman, he "never despaired of the republic." From Jamaica he made his way to Aux Cayes in Hayti, the president of which —Alexandre Pétion, a mulatto—received him with sympathy, and helped him to fit out (with a number of fugitive Republicans who had escaped to Hayti from Cartagena) yet another expedition to relieve his country. Pétion demanded one promise only—that the freedom of all slaves in Venezuela should be proclaimed as soon as the expedition landed.

Ships and arms were contributed by Luis Brion, a Dutch merchant of Curaçoa, who devoted his life and large fortune to the cause of liberty; and the expedition sailed on March 31, 1816. On May 3rd it reached the island of Margarita, off the Venezuelan coast. The first descent on the mainland was mishandled, and proved a fiasco. Still undaunted, Bolivar went back to Hayti for reinforcements, returned, and on December 31, 1816, landed for the last time on the soil of South America, never to quit it until his time came to die. The new year was to turn the tide of his fortunes.

The tide turned very slowly at first. A great part of the year was wasted in confused operations against the Spanish commander Morillo. But by degrees Bolivar learnt the secret of success, which was to neglect the exhausted hill country near the coast, and fix his base in the rich plains alongside the Orinoco and its tributary rivers. Here he could always fall back with a certainty of finding food in plenty; and this, too, was the country from which his enemy Boves had collected the invincible Llaneros. The

Llaneros cared nothing for this government or that ;
they would fight on any side that held out fair promise of plunder ; and José Antonio Paez—himself a
Llanero, as illiterate as his fellows, and only unlike
them in having definite Republican convictions—persuaded them to join Bolivar, now settled in headquarters at Angostura on the Orinoco, which river,
with the aid of gunboats supplied by his faithful
admirer Brion, he now held clear to the sea.  Besides
the Llaneros, there came to him (1817–19) yet more
useful help in contingents of British volunteers—
Peninsular veterans, "out of work" at home, and
neglected by Wellington now that the struggle against
Napoleon was over.  Some 220 of these soldiers of
fortune arrived in 1817 ; by 1819 their numbers had
grown to close upon 6,000 ; and in the spring of that
year Bolivar, tired of aimless marchings and counter-
marchings, conceived the idea of a feat which not only
proved a high success in strategy, but for its daring,
and the desperate courage with which it was carried
through, may rank with the few most famous military
exploits in history, even with Hannibal's passage of
the Alps.

Indeed Bolivar's exploit, in conception as in per-
formance, challenges Hannibal's at many points.  In
New Granada, on the western side of the Andes, the
Republican general Santander still kept up the fight
for liberty.  If Bolivar could only pierce the mountain
range, considered impassable, and unite with Santander—leaving behind sufficient strength to hold his
already strong positions on the Orinoco—the united
forces could reconquer all the fertile centre and south
of New Granada, and their enemies would have
nothing left but the northern hills and retreat to the
sea.

It was a tremendous adventure upon which he set
out on February 27, 1819.  Morillo, though little
dreaming of his situation, stood in his path, blocking

the way. But a brilliant cavalry action by **Paez**
opportunely drove Morillo northwards to seek better
quarters, deeming that the campaign was over, since
the season of heavy rains was at hand. Leaving **Paez**
with some cavalry to screen his movements, Bolivar
struck westward, concealing his intention even from
his own men—though, as it leaked out, the Llaneros
deserted in large numbers. The route of this heroic
march led at first across the broad open plains which
lie at the base of the Eastern Cordilleras, and are
threaded by the upper waters of the Apure, the
Arauca, and other tributaries of the Orinoco. In the
dry season the hard muddy track led through waving
stretches of grass, between rivers withered in their
beds and knolls crowned with palm trees diversifying
the long levels. But with the rains all this flat
country is flooded, every stream turns to a torrent,
the knolls are islands, and the soil underfoot is liquid
mud. Through such a country Bolivar's men waded
day after day, knee-deep in water and at times waist-
deep, rain beating down on them most of the time.

"At night they camped on the nearest eminence
where they could obtain, not dry ground indeed, but
ground not covered deeply by water. Day after day
they had to ford a dozen streams, or to swim or ferry
themselves across in boats constructed of hides.
Swimmers were always exposed to terrible risks from
alligators, electric eels, and the dreaded caribe fish.
The men, badly fed, were unable to find any shelter at
night, and with difficulty kept their provender dry in
the torrential rain. None suffered more than the
English, ill suited as they were to live on the small
ration which kept the frugal Venezuelan alive and
well." *

Pore, at the foot of the Eastern Cordilleras, was
reached on June 25, and then the climb began.

* Petre.

Avoiding the ordinary route, where the enemy might be expecting him, Bolivar turned to his right and struck a disused track, blocked by landslides, leading over a desolate height, the Paramo de Pisba, a stony wilderness just below the line of perpetual snow, wrapped in cold fogs or swept by piercing northeast winds. The Venezuelans, accustomed to the hot plains, found more misery here than they had left behind them in the swamps. Every horse had by this time perished, and the half-naked men had to be flogged—even prayed to be flogged—to restore circulation to their limbs, lest they should fall and be frozen to death. No order could be kept as the wretched crowd straggled up and still up through ravines where a hundred Spaniards could have entrapped and butchered them like so many sheep. But no Spaniard could be seen, for none dreamed it possible that the invaders could attempt this awful passage.

By July 6 they were across the Paramo de Pisba, and had descended to Socha, only 9,000 feet above sea-level. Here, as they felt the sunshine once more and saw the rocky gorges open at their feet into broad valleys, green and fertile, they rejoiced as men awaking from a hideous nightmare. The inhabitants of Socha poured out to welcome them, and vied in supplying food, beer, and tobacco to the heroes, who gratefully rested and basked their exhausted bodies in the sun, each soldier busy with his rusty musket, scouring it for the fighting to come.

Barreyro, the Spanish commander, had been waiting on the main route with some 1,600 men. Finding himself outwitted by Bolivar's marvellous march, he turned northward to catch the invaders before they could slip past him. The two forces met at Pantano de Vargas, July 25, and after a bloody but indecisive battle—in which the British Legion specially distinguished itself by recapturing some heights when the day seemed all but lost—each fell back on its former position. On the 3rd of August Bolivar again advanced, and encamped that night in face of the enemy, who had withdrawn to a chain of heights commanding the road which led through Tunja to Bogotá, the capital. Next afternoon the Republicans made a show of retiring once more to their position on the hills ; but darkness had no sooner fallen than they turned about and, marching all night by a more easterly road, swept clean around Barreyro's army and captured Tunja, thus planting themselves between him and his communications. Barreyro turned to pursue, and was boldly met at the bridge of Boyaca, where the main road to the capital crossed the river Sogamoso. In the battle that followed the Republicans were completely victorious, taking prisoner the whole of the Spanish main body, with Barreyro himself, and nearly all his artillery and stores. The campaign, in fact, was at an end. There remained nothing to be done but march on Bogotá, whence the Spanish viceroy promptly fled. Bolivar entered the city on August 10, and was hailed as the Liberator of New Granada, now finally released from Spanish dominion.

It was time for him to return to Venezuela, and his return through that country to Angostura was a triumphal procession from town to town. Fortune had indeed begun to smile on the Republicans ; for whereas they had been living in dread that a fresh expedition was on its way from Spain to suppress them, they now had news that dispelled this worst fear. Ferdinand had indeed taken steps to assemble such an expedition at Cadiz, to be embarked there—20,200 infantry, 2,800 cavalry, and 1,370 artillerymen, with cannon and supplies of all sorts—but at Cadiz these troops broke into mutiny, which seemed likelier to end in overthrowing the Spanish monarchy than in reconquering the lost dominions ; and Ferdinand, taking fright, allowed the expedition to be dispersed.

Bolivar, aware of this, entered into parley with Morillo, and on November 25, 1820, concluded an armistice for six months, in the hope that the Spaniards would come to terms without further bloodshed. But Morillo was recalled. Another commander, La Torre, took his place, and the armistice was allowed to expire. Bolivar saw his opportunity of freeing Venezuela, as he had freed New Granada, by one decisive blow. Collecting his troops, he marched against La Torre, and utterly routed him at Carabobo, where again the British volunteers fought so splendidly that after the battle the victor, as they passed him, saluted them with the words, *" Salvadores de mi patria ! "* (" saviours of my country "). The war was at an end. Once more the Liberator entered Carácas in triumph ; and by the close of 1823 the last lingering Spanish garrison had been cleared out of Venezuela.

The next step was to consolidate under one government the territories thus won for freedom, and on August 30, 1821, New Granada and Venezuela adopted, under the name of Colombia, a common constitution, with Bolivar for president and Santander vice-president.

But Bolivar's work in liberating South America was not yet ended. Though expelled from Colombia, the Spaniards still held enormous territories to the south and down the west coast of the great continent— Quito and Guayaquil (now together known as Ecuador), Lower and Upper Peru (now Peru and Bolivia), and Chile. It was Bolivar's dream to unite all these with Colombia in one great republic. A brief revolt of Quito against Spanish rule had been crushed out so far back as 1812. In 1820 rebellion again broke out, this time in Guayaquil, and he quickly seized his opportunity. He had already sent a trusted general, Sucre, to help the insurgents ; and now, at the head of an army of 3,000 men, he himself marched southward upon Quito. Disease and privation killed off one-third of his men, but he held on indomitably, and reached the " avenue of volcanoes "—Pichincha, Cotopaxi, Chimborazo, and others less famous—through which that city is approached. A murderous battle was fought and won by him at Bombona ; another, more decisive, by Sucre, on the slopes of the Pichincha volcano ; and Quito was entered by the victorious Republicans on June 16, 1822. At Bombona the fight in its early stages had almost miscarried through a blunder of Torres, one of Bolivar's bravest fighters. Bolivar in a fury ordered him to hand over his command. Torres dismounted and seized a musket, crying, " Liberator ! if I am not worthy to serve my country as general, at least I will serve her as grenadier." Bolivar embraced him, and Torres resumed his command, to be shot down in the next charge.

Before the month was out Quito and Guayaquil had joined the Colombian republic. The Liberator now made southward for Lima, which the Spaniards evacuated on his approach. Here, too, the inhabitants welcomed him with wreaths and banners, acclaiming him dictator. The Spaniards, however, returned in force ; and finding that they had cut his communications with Guayaquil, he was forced to withdraw for a while to Trujillo, leaving the capital to be reoccupied and looted by the foe. But the rebuff proved to be a passing one. By July 1824 he had collected and reviewed on the plateau of the Sacramento an army of 7,700 men, besides some 1,500 guerillas. With these troops he swept down upon the Spanish general Canterac, and in the cavalry battle of Junin drove him into a demoralized flight. Sucre, following, inflicted the decisive defeat of Ayacucho ; and La Serna, the last of the proud Spanish viceroys of Peru, capitulated to the republic. There remained Upper Peru, which on August 6, 1825, declared itself an independent state, called Bolivia in honour of the great Liberator.

His work of actual liberation was now at an end, and it would be a tedious and sorrowful business to follow him through the quarrels and intrigues which too late convinced him that some states may be free and yet a long way from being happy. The men he had raised up to rule turned against him, often, it must be admitted, under provocation, for he was both vain and fierce. Deprived of popularity, of power, reduced to a mere ordinary citizen, he felt his health failing, and moved to Santa Marta, where on December 17, 1830, he died, after dictating his will, and closing it with the words : " Colombians, my last wishes are for my country's welfare. If my death helps to end party strife and consolidate the union, I shall go down to my grave in peace." At the age of forty-seven he had worn himself out, body and mind, to serve that patriotism which, since the death of his young bride, had been his one consuming passion. He had spent nine-tenths of his own patrimony in that service, and he died unpossessed of a shilling of public money. The republics he founded are to this day independent, and among them the name of Bolivar will ever and rightly be held in honour.

# JOHN BROWN

" John Brown's body lies a-mouldering in the grave,
But his soul is marching on."

DURING the great American civil war (1861-5) whole armies of the North marched and chanted to the tune of " John Brown's Body." Before the struggle ended, the Potomac and Shenandoah rivers, that meet at Harper's Ferry, ran with the blood of many thousands fighting to expiate or to vindicate what had happened there between Sunday night and Tuesday night, the

16th and 18th of October 1859. What had happened was a wild and violent, if heroic, deed, followed by a stern and savage punishment. John Brown was a hero ; he gave his life for the cause of his life—the emancipation of the negro slave ; he gave it in obedience to the deliberate rule of his life—the Golden Rule, " Whatsoever ye would that men should do to you, do ye even so to them." (He used to say that the Golden Rule and the Declaration of Independence summed up all his principles.) He made a brave end, and he left an inspiration. His death tolled the knell of slavery throughout the American states.

All this we may admit, yet without going on to denounce his enemies as murderers, or denying that even on the question of Slave-holding they had something to urge. Let us, to clear our judgment, suppose that the case for and against " Abolition " is being disputed between two fair-minded gentlemen, a Northerner and a Southerner, and that we are listening to their arguments.

*Pro.* " I must start by telling you that, as I read my Bible, I am firmly convinced of the wickedness of slavery as an institution. I hold it to be opposed to the doctrine of Christ."

*Con.* " You might say that of many things—of war, for instance. But suppose that I grant it, you have still to remember that we of the South did not invent or introduce slavery. It was fastened upon our American colonies by the greed of British traders, and we Southerners of to-day were born under the system, and have inherited it."

*Pro.* " Why not do away with it ? "

*Con.* " Do you realize, in the first place, what you are asking ? Our wealth, such as it is, largely consists of slaves. They were left to us by our fathers— they and the land and the cotton crops that cannot be raised without their labour. We have wives and children ; their well-being and all the comforts of home have come to depend on the system. Here and there you might find a man ready to reduce his household to beggary for the sake of a lofty moral principle ; but can you expect a whole population to follow his example ? "

*Pro.* " I put it to you that you would all be better in the long run ; that slavery lies like a blight on the South, keeping your sons in idleness, repressing commercial industry and inventiveness. It paralyses the energy of the white man, while the negro scamps his work. Forests are unfelled, rich mines unopened, and the harvests slight in comparison with what they might be."

*Con.* " All that is true enough, though you leave our enervating climate out of account. I have often wished that we could get rid of the slaves. One or two owners have gone so far as emancipation on a small scale, and the last state of their negroes has been worse than the first."

*Pro.* " Because the experiment was tried on a small scale."

*Con.* " Possibly. To me the *crux* is, that when you have emancipated your negroes you are not rid of them. They are there, just the same ; only they have become masterless, lazy, insolent, numerous, and therefore dangerous. You remember what Henry Clay said in 1829 ? If we were to invoke the greatest blessing on earth which heaven in its mercy could bestow on this nation, it would be to separate white and black, and establish them in distinct and distant countries. You of the North may talk easily of a general letting loose of all negroes ; we in the South, who live with them, see the awful risk."

*Pro.* " Then what would you counsel ? "

*Con.* " Patience—patience under the present system. As a matter of fact, we are slowly uplifting the slave."

*Pro.* " By the aid of whips and fetters, as I hear ;
by putting up his body for auction ; by selling him
away from his wife and children, by committing
him to the power of one man who is his absolute
master——"

*Con.* (*interrupts*). " My friend, you are taking the
rare exception for the rule, and *Uncle Tom's Cabin*
for gospel. The great mass of the slaves live con-
tentedly, careless of the morrow as children, well fed,
devoted to their owners, all of whom have a commercial interest in treating them well, and many of
whom take a patriarchal and almost parental care
of them."

*Pro.* " Well, then, the exceptions—be they even as
few as you suggest—are too many for my conscience.
Such crimes are committed, and their purpose is to
hold men in bondage to their happier fellows. More
than half of our nation detests this bondage, and
therefore the nation as a whole will have to make up
its mind one way or another, since a house divided
against itself cannot stand."

If all or most of the Southerners had been as reason-
able as our imaginary disputant, a solution, or rather
a compromise, might have been found by the slave
states being allowed to retain slavery on condition
that they kept it within their own confines ; and
some such compromise was attempted more than
once. The trouble was that the United States kept
expanding and adding to their number as settlers
pushed farther and farther west in the wilderness, and
wrested it from uncultivated Nature and the Red
Man. With the admission of each new state to
the Union arose the question, " Should it be slave
or free ? " For, on the one hand, the North had a
rooted objection to the spread of slavery ; on the
other, since each state sent an equal number of
representatives to Washington, the South was afraid
of being outvoted and coerced into doing away with

slavery altogether. From 1787 to 1820 the admissions of slave and free states kept a neck-and-neck race. Vermont was admitted in 1791, Free; Kentucky in 1792, Slave; Tennessee in 1796, Slave; Ohio in 1802, Free; Louisiana in 1812, Slave; Indiana in 1816, Free; Mississippi in 1817, Slave; Illinois in 1818, Free; Alabama in 1819, Slave. This left the balance exactly even, with 22 states, of which 11 were Slave and 11 Free.

But the territory of Missouri was now clamouring for admission as a slave state; and behind Missouri stood Arkansas, where also the pro-slavery party predominated. The Northerners took alarm, and were strong enough to force the famous " Missouri Convention," which became law in March 1820. This drew a line between North and South at 36° 30′ N. latitude—the only exception being that so much of Missouri as lay north of that line was allowed to be slave. At about the same time, too, Maine was admitted a free state, thus preserving the balance.

For some time the compromise worked well enough. It rested openly on expedience, putting the moral " yes " or " no " aside; but it served. Arkansas came in as a slave state in 1836; Michigan, free, in 1837. Then the South took a panic. The possibilities of extending slave territory were being used up, whilst their opponents had vast tracts lying to the north-west, out of which new states could be carved. They managed to admit Texas and Florida; but the North countered them by letting in Iowa (1846) and Wisconsin (1848)—neck and neck again.

Now the line of the Missouri Compromise did not extend right across the continent, but was understood to end at about 95° W. longitude, where the territory of the United States touched that of Mexico; and a successful war against that country reopened the whole question. In 1848 Mexico ceded California and New Mexico to her conquerors, and by 1850 these were qualifying to become states. If the dividing line of 36° 30′ N. were extended right across the continent, the whole of New Mexico and the southern part of California would descend to slavery, whereas in New Mexico slavery was by Mexican law forbidden, and California at once voted itself free. Here a stiff quarrel arose, the North urging that these new conquests lay beyond the reach of the compromise line, and that no line could be extended to enforce slavery on men who would have none of it ; the South as strongly contending that the line should be lengthened to bring them within slave limits—a very pretty instance of the final impossibility of drawing any line between right and wrong with a yard measure.

Still politicians went on attempting it. In 1850 it was agreed that California should be admitted as a free state, and the territory of New Mexico retain its laws against slavery—so much on the one side. To placate the South, a Fugitive Slave Law was passed, which made the slave a mere chattel, and decreed that any slave who had fled for his liberty across the border-line should be handed back to his owner, with heavy penalties for any one who aided or abetted his escape.

This law, denounced by no less a man than Emerson as one " which no man can obey or abet the obeying without loss of self-respect and forfeiture of the name of a gentleman," roused the North to indignation, which was increased to a flame of wrath in 1854, when, on the admission of two new territories, Kansas and Nebraska—both north of the line— Senator Douglas carried a bill which virtually repealed the old Missouri Convention by leaving the question of slavery open, *to be settled by the voters of the region*, or, as we should say, by " local option." No measure could have been better calculated to destroy all hope of a peaceful settlement, for it transferred the quarrel from the legislature and put it into the hands of the local squatters. Fierce men from the North and South began a race to take up holdings in Kansas and occupy the soil for freedom or for slavery. Armed bands poured over the border from Missouri, and not only cast bogus votes by the thousand, but kept a reign of terror around the ballot boxes. Of 6,218 votes given at the election for the Territorial Legislature, no less than 4,808 were afterwards found to be illegal. By means of them, however, the pro-slavery men elected all their candidates but one. Nor were they content with this, but started raiding the new " free-soil " settlements all along the border. Outrages, burnings, shootings, even massacres, were frequent ; until this battleground of freedom had earned the name of " Bleeding Kansas." Such was the stage upon which there now stepped forth a very remarkable figure.

John Brown of Kansas was a man well above fifty. The date of his birth was May 9th, 1800 ; the place, Torrington in Connecticut ; but during his early childhood the family moved to Hudson, Ohio. " I heard him say," says Thoreau, " that his father was a contractor, who furnished beef to the army there in the war of 1812 (with Great Britain), that he accompanied him to the camp and assisted him in that employment, seeing a good deal of military life—more, perhaps, than if he had been a soldier ; for he was often present at the councils of the officers. Especially he learnt by experience how armies are supplied and maintained in the field—a work which, he observed, requires at least as much experience and skill as to lead them in battle. He said that few persons had any conception of the cost, even the pecuniary cost, of firing a bullet in war. He saw enough, at any rate, to disgust him with a military life—indeed, to excite in him a great abhorrence of it ; so much so that, though he was tempted by the offer of some petty office in the army when he was about eighteen, he not only declined that, but he also refused to train when warned, and was fined for it. He then resolved that he would never have anything to do with war unless it were a war for liberty."

He had received little schooling. Of arithmetic he barely knew the four ground rules, and of grammar (to use his own words) no more than a farm calf. But he early showed remarkable strength of character. At the age of twelve he took a drove of cattle a hundred miles, single-handed, and would have scorned help had it been offered. His powers of observation, too, were extraordinarily quick, as the following anecdote will show. At one time in his varied career he turned wool-merchant, and, with his usual enterprise, visited England in the hope of finding a foreign market. One evening, being in company with several English wool-merchants and growers, each of whom had brought samples in his pockets, Brown was giving his opinion on certain varieties and their uses, when one of the party, willing to play a trick on the Yankee, handed him a sample of black wool, and asked him what he would do with such as that. Brown's fingers were so sensitive that he had only to touch it to miss the minute hooks by which the fibres of wool are attached to each other. " Gentlemen," said he, " if you have any machinery that will work up dogs' hair, I advise you to put this into it." Whereupon the joker confessed amid laughter that he had sheared a poodle and brought along the hair in his pocket.

But we are running far ahead of our narrative. At the age of twenty, having abandoned his first intention of entering the Congregational ministry, and being now a land-surveyor, Brown married Dianthe Lusk, of a neighbouring household at Hudson. It appears that he did so " on his father's advice," for she was a " remarkably plain girl," but neat and practical withal, a good housekeeper, and full of com-

mon sense. She learnt how to manage his " haughty
and obstinate temper," and their married life, though
none too prosperous, was exceedingly happy. She
died in 1832, leaving him with five children. The
next year he married Mary A. Day, of Meadville,
Pennsylvania, he being thirty-three and she but
eighteen. By this marriage he had seven sons and
six daughters.

Again he was fortunate in his helpmeet, Mary, his
second wife. He can have been no easy man to live
with. In discipline he was stern even to the point
of keeping a sort of book account with his sons over
their punishments. For an instance given by John,
the eldest—

> JOHN, Dr.
>> For disobeying mother.....8 lashes.
>> For unfaithfulness at work..3 lashes.
>> For telling a lie............8 lashes.

But with this severity his *rightness* so impressed
itself upon his sons that in the end they gladly died
with him. The eldest, after quoting the strange
parental bill rendered, proceeds :—

" On a certain Sunday morning he invited me from
the house to the tannery [he had given up surveying
for the tanning trade], saying that he concluded it
was time for a settlement. We went into the upper
or finishing room, and after a long and tearful talk
over my faults he again showed me my account,
which exhibited a fearful footing-up of debits. I had
no credit or offsets, and paid about one-third of the
debt, reckoned in strokes from a nicely prepared blue-
beech switch, laid on ' masterly.' Then, to my utter
astonishment, father stripped off his shirt and, seating
himself on the block, gave me the whip and bade me
' lay it on ' to his bare back. I dared not refuse to
obey, but at first I did not strike hard. ' Harder,' he

4

said, ' harder ! harder ! ' until he received the balance of the account.  Small drops of blood showed on his back when the tip end of the tingling beech cut through.  Thus ended the account and the settlement, which was also my first practical illustration of the doctrine of the atonement."

" Whatsoever ye would that men should do to you, do ye even so to them."  John Brown took the Golden Rule literally, and by it he read, without a shade of a doubt, that slavery was detestable.  As a child he had learnt to detest it ; he tells how, writing of himself in the third person, " he was staying for a short time with a very gentlemanly landlord, once a United States marshal, who held a slave boy near John Brown's age, very active, intelligent, and of good feeling, to whom John was under obligation for numerous little acts of kindness.  The master made a great pet of John, brought him to table with his first company and friends, called their attention to every little smart thing he said or did, and to the fact of his being more than a hundred miles from home with a company of cattle, alone, while the negro boy, who was fully, if not more than, his equal, was badly clothed, poorly fed and lodged in cold weather, and beaten before his eyes with hot shovels or any other thing that came to hand.  This brought John to reflect on the wretched, hopeless condition of fatherless and motherless slave children.  He sometimes would raise the question, *Is God their Father ?* "

This detestation of slavery grew with his growth until it became the overmastering passion of his life.  Poverty or ill-success compelling him, he shifted from one trade to another—like the true Yankee of those times, only more so.  But whether as tanner, land-surveyor, post-master, wool-dealer, stock-raiser, horse-breeder, or lumberman, he kept to one steady, if unpaid, employment—that of helping slaves to escape northward by what was known as the Underground Railway—that is, a line of isolated dwellings reaching through the states, where the fugitive found hiding and shelter, and would be helped a stage farther towards Canada and liberty. Mere evasion of the Slave Law, however, did not satisfy Brown. He wanted to strike at it and kill it, and he foresaw clearly enough that the system could never be ended but by force. After his stay in England he crossed over to France and Germany, where he took great interest in studying military reviews and manœuvres, seeking to learn how companies of fighting men should be handled, and even sketching out plans of log fortifications, breastworks, abattis, behind which, when the day came for a general rising, the slaves might fight for their liberty in the forests of the South.

His belief in his mission being confirmed by every word he read in his Bible—for he was a deeply religious man—he so imposed it upon wife and children that they counted all hardship, poverty, peril, as naught if only they might advance the one sacred cause.

When the troubles in Kansas began, Brown sent his five eldest sons—John, Jason, Owen, Frederick, and Salmon—to strengthen the party of the free state men, promising to follow if they had need of him. They settled in South Kansas, near the Pottawatomie River ; and presently, having their farms raided and their lives threatened by the border gangs, wrote to their father begging him to collect what arms he could and bring them in person. This he did, and arrived in Kansas in the autumn of 1855, just as the free state men had been maddened by a fresh outrage.

In the town of Leavenworth, during an election for Congress, a citizen named John Forman, on refusing to vote for slavery, had been chased through the streets by a gang howling, " Lynch him ! Tar and feather the Yankee ! " A shot was fired after him, and the bullet, after riddling his hat, passed through the boards of a house and killed a little child at play beside its mother. At the same time another citizen was knocked down, and was stabbed to death. Flesh and blood could not stand this. A hundred free state men armed themselves and gave chase, overtaking and stabbing one of the gang. Upon the top of this a man called Dow, going to recover the body of a friend whom the pro-slavery ruffians had murdered near the town of Lawrence, was arrested by Sheriff Jones of Missouri, but was liberated by a rescue party and carried home to the town, which put itself into a state of siege to resist the " law." The Sheriff promptly declared Lawrence to be in armed rebellion, and 1,500 Missourians marched to attack it. On the other hand, free state men hurried to the defence, 500 strong, and among them John Brown with four of his sons, armed with swords and revolvers. In spite of the disparity of numbers, Brown was for war at once ; but now the governor, Shannon, arrived on the spot, and the Lawrence men, fearful of defying in his person the authority of the United States, were disposed to treat for terms. " General " Lane, as they called their commander, called a council of war, Brown being included in the summons. " Tell the general," said Brown, " when he wants me to fight to say so, but that is the only order I will obey." In the end the Lawrence men promised not to resist the law henceforth, and the governor consented to let bygones be bygones.

But the raidings and murders went on, and the pro-slavery rowdies soon had an opportunity to avenge their check at Lawrence. In the following April, Sheriff Jones visited the town to serve writs upon several prominent citizens. He was, for his conduct in the late affair, peculiarly odious to the inhabitants, and a foolish youth shot at him and wounded him as he sat in his tent. The Lawrence men promptly disavowed the crime ; but 800 Missouri men, rapidly organizing themselves as " Sheriff Jones's Posse," attacked and looted the town, leaving it a complete wreck.

Now in the interim John Brown had been daring, and cunning too. His reputation had reached Kansas, but few of his enemies as yet knew him by sight. Using his old trade for a pretext, he set out boldly on a surveying expedition, carrying his lines right through his enemies' country. They, supposing him to be a government surveyor, talked to him freely (for a pro-slavery government held office), and told him, among other things, that an old abolitionist, John Brown, down by the Pottawatomie, was about to have a " hot time." Some neighbours of his, the Doyles, Wilkinson, and Sherman, had been over the border and arranged for a force to come over and smoke out his nest.

Brown hurried home, summoned a council, and discussed the peril. It was agreed that if the Doyles, Wilkinson, or Sherman made a move to attack, they should be handled without mercy.

Four days after the sack of Lawrence a free state man was set upon by Doyle and company in Sherman's store, and cruelly maltreated. Flushed with their easy success, the company marched on Brown's farm, where, Brown being away, they put the grossest insults upon his daughter and a daughter-in-law, and left, threatening to come next day and murder the men. The Brown "boys" returned, and learned what had happened. Their counter-stroke was swift and terrible. Next night the Doyles, Wilkinson, and Sherman were taken out of their houses, tried by lynch law, allowed time to pray, and put to death on the spot. John Brown himself had no hand in the slaying—the evidence goes to prove that he was many miles away—but he never denied that five men were killed that night by his order. His words are : " I did not myself kill any of those men at Pottawatomie, but I do not pretend to say they were not killed by my order, and in ordering it I believe I was doing God's service." He was asked, " Do you think God uses you as an instrument in His hands to kill men ? " He answered, " I think so ; and if I live I think He will use me to kill a good many more."

There is no doubt of it. John Brown took the Golden Rule and used it always as a two-edged sword —its one edge merciful for all merciful men, its other merciless upon those who knew no mercy.

He and his sons were now outlaws, and took to the forests. A few of the bolder spirits joined them— bandits, as one may say, for the cause of liberty, but very unusual bandits, as will be seen from the following account written by a sympathizer who, having lost his way in the Kansas woods, stumbled by chance upon one of Brown's sons fetching water, and was by him led after many devious turnings to the heart of the camp :—

" As we approached it we were twice challenged by sentries who suddenly appeared before trees and as suddenly disappeared behind them. . . . I shall not soon forget the scene that here opened to my view. Near the edge of the creek a dozen horses were tied, all ready saddled for a ride for life, or a hunt after Southern invaders. A dozen rifles and sabres were stacked against the trees. In an open space, amid the shady and lofty woods, there was a great blazing fire with a pot on it ; a woman, bareheaded, with an honest, sunburnt face, was picking blackberries from the bushes ; three or four armed men were lying on red and blue blankets on the grass ; and two fine-looking youths were standing, leaning on their arms, on guard near by. . . .

" Old Brown himself stood near the fire, with his shirt sleeves rolled up and a large piece of pork in his hand. He was cooking a pig. He was poorly clad, and his toes protruded from his boots. The old man received me with great cordiality, and the little band gathered about me. But it was for a moment only, for the captain ordered them to renew their work.

" In this camp no manner of profane language was permitted ; no man of immoral character was allowed to stay, except as a prisoner of war. He made prayers, in which all the company united every morning and evening. Often, I was told, the old man would retire to the densest solitudes, to wrestle with God in his secret prayer. ' I would rather,' said he, ' have the smallpox, yellow fever, and cholera all together in my camp than a man without principle.'

" I remained in the camp about an hour. Never before had I met such a band of men. They were not earnest, but earnestness incarnate. Six of them were John Brown's sons."

On the 30th of May 1856 two of Brown's sons, John and Jason, were taken prisoners by a gang of Missourians under a man named Pate, charged with murder, put in irons, and handed over to a company of United States dragoons. The dragoons drove them on foot like captured bullocks for twenty-five miles under a burning sun, until John's mind gave way and he became a maniac. Another day they were marched thirty miles without food or drink. They were finally released without ever having been brought to trial. Brown, hunting for his lost sons, came up with Pate, who had separated from the dragoons and was continuing his raid. The Missourians numbered sixty. Brown, with nine of his own followers, had picked up nineteen men by the way. He attacked at once, and twenty-two Missourians fell into his hands. The rest fled, leaving behind them wagons, camp furniture, and large quantities of " loot " taken from free state farms. All this with the prisoners (including Pate himself) Brown handed over to the authorities, having carefully nursed the wounded and treated Pate with kindness from the moment of his surrender.

Still raid followed raid. On June 7th, 170 Missourians sacked Brown's headquarters at Ossawatomie, committing many dreadful murders ; and in August assembled no less than 2,000 strong, to wipe the little township from the face of the earth, as part of a general invasion of the Kansas borders.

On the 30th some 500 of them, armed with government muskets and revolvers, and having several pieces of cannon, advanced on Ossawatomie. About a mile and a half beyond the outskirts they happened on Brown's son Frederick, who was not attached to his father's force, and shot him dead on the road. Old Brown, who was even then marching upon Ossawatomie with some fifty men, at first hoped to defend the town, being ignorant of the enemy's numbers. As soon, however, as he saw their approach, he gave up all idea of doing more than annoy. Withdrawing his men into the woods and posting them behind a thick screen of undergrowth, he kept up a galling fire upon the line of battle as it approached, utterly demoralized its left wing, and having shot down some thirty-one or thirty-two, coolly slipped away to the woods on the farther bank of the river. The Missourians contented themselves with burning the empty town, but did not pursue, having no heart for another brush with the old hero, whom men henceforth called " Ossawatomie Brown." Truly a formidable man—one who, in his own phrase, feared God too much to fear anything human ! A month or two later, when he visited the eastern states to collect money for the bold enterprise that was already shaping itself in his head, men asked him in wonder how he could have lived in Kansas at all, with a price set upon his head and so many hundreds of men, including the authorities, exasperated against him. He accounted for this very simply by saying, " It was perfectly well understood that I would not be taken."

He left Kansas moderately tranquil—a new gover-

nor, Geary, having brought down troops and informed
both sides impartially that this guerilla warfare must
cease. After collecting money and promises from the
" abolitionists " in the New England States, Brown
started a small military training-school at Tabor, Iowa,
and paid a flying visit back to Kansas to collect
recruits for it. He brought back a few ; he might
have brought back many but for the extraordinarily
high standard he demanded of his volunteers. " He
was never able to find more than a score or so of
recruits whom he would accept, and only about a
dozen, among them his sons, in whom he had perfect
faith." The little band accompanied him to Tabor ;
thence to Peder, where they remained drilling during
the winter months ; and from Peder, in April 1858, to
Chatham in Canada, where Brown's object was to
enlist recruits from among the escaped slaves.

His ultimate purpose, gradually shaping itself in his
mind, was not to carry away slaves to the North, but
to march boldly into the Southern States, proclaim
a rising, and fight the quarrel out on the actual soil
of slavery. A slave rising, whenever occurring in
history, has always been attended with terrible consequences ; and must, in the nature of things, be
attended with terrible risks. If Brown (whom some
called mad) chose to ignore these risks, he found in
Canada some whole-hearted men to whom he could
confide his purpose—among them K. H. Kagi, a young
man of Swiss descent, and so devoted a hero-wor-
shipper and hater of slavery that he was ready to throw
in his lot with the band and go wherever they dared.

But Brown, before the last great act, was to perform
one brilliant exploit in " slave-running "—an exploit
to make the fame of a lesser man. Recalled to Kansas
by news that the border troubles had broken out
afresh, and taking Kagi with him, he reached Lawrence on June 25th, 1858, pushed on to Ossawatomie
and past the ruins of that township to Little Sugar

Creek, at the extreme south of Kansas. The Missourians were gathering again, and " Ossawatomie Brown" resolved to teach them a lesson of " the biter bit." On Sunday, December 19th, a negro named Jim came to Brown's cabin imploring succour, as he and his family were about to be sold South. Brown sifted his story. On the next night he and Kagi with two small parties crossed into Missouri and carried off Jim with ten other slaves, spreading such consternation that a crowd of other slaves took advantage of it and made a dash to the cabin for protection. John Brown welcomed them all, and in a few days, forming up his convoy, started off on a journey of over twenty-five hundred miles to carry them to Canada and liberty.

A price had been promptly set on his head. The Fugitive Slave Act was in operation, and all along the route—through Nebraska, Iowa, Illinois, Indiana, Michigan—he was open to attack and arrest. But his reputation as " a man who would not be taken " served him now as it had served him in the swamps and forests of Kansas, and at length, on the 12th of March, he crossed over from Detroit into Canada and landed his negroes, free men under the protection of the " Union Jack."

Southward again now, sick and worn in body, but still with his spirits rising as the time drew nearer for his great venture. In May we find him in Boston, where he is suspiciously busy with inquiries about the making of beef-meal and biscuits. In June he is at Chambersburg, Pennsylvania, hiring a depôt into which he collects his stores and a goodly quantity of arms, a supply of pikes for which, some time since, he made a contract, and some scores of rifles formerly belonging to the Massachusetts State Kansas Committee. Towards the end of the month, with his two sons Watson and Oliver, he crosses into Maryland and takes a drive over to Harper's Ferry, the United States arsenal.

Harper's Ferry is a town in Jefferson County, Virginia, about 60 miles from Washington and 170 from Richmond, standing on a bluff of land at the confluence of the Potomac and Shenandoah rivers, where their united streams flow through a gap of the Blue Ridge Mountains. Across the Potomac, which is spanned by a railway bridge, lies Maryland. Steep cliffs line either shore, and also both sides of the bluff, which runs out to an angle at the point where the waters meet. Towards the same apex, too, converged the two streets which originally made up the town —Potomac and Shenandoah streets—each running alongside its river on a narrow low-lying strip of shore under the cliffs ; and at the apex stood the government arsenal (which usually contained from one to two hundred thousand stand of arms), with a musket factory. There was also a rifle factory on a small island in the Shenandoah River, reached by a short bridge. A large bridge, some distance below, connected the town with the right bank of the Shenandoah.

Brown and his two sons spent two or three days carefully reconnoitring the town and the country on either shore. They gave their name as " Smith," pretending to hail from western New York, and to be prospecting for a farm for raising sheep. In the end they hired one—Kennedy's Farm—some five miles up the Potomac on the Maryland side, paying the rent in advance up to March 1860.

The farm contained three unoccupied houses very suitable for their purpose ; and their next business was to bring down their arms and stores from Chambersburg, fifty miles away, without awakening suspicion. Old Brown effected this, mainly by night, and his neighbours guessed nothing of his goings and comings, though they wondered a little when they counted no less than twelve strapping men at work on Kennedy's Farm.

On one of these visits to Chambersburg, in an old

stone quarry near that place, Brown confided his project to an old and staunch friend, Frederick Douglass. They had met there by appointment and secretly—Brown, who was accompanied by Kagi, seeming to happen on the spot as he fished the stream hard by; and Douglass by request bringing Shields Green, a negro on whose fidelity they could depend. Douglass himself has told the story of the interview :—

" Captain Brown, Kagi, Shields Green, and myself sat down among the rocks and talked over the enterprise about to be undertaken. The taking of Harper's Ferry, of which Brown had merely hinted before, was now declared his settled purpose, and he wanted to know what I thought of it. I at once opposed it with all the arguments at my command. To me, such a measure would be fatal to the running of slaves (the original plan), and fatal to all engaged. It would be an attack on the Federal Government, and would array the whole country against us. Captain Brown did most of the talking on the other side. He did not at all object to rousing the nation ; it seemed to him that something startling was needed. He had completely renounced his old plan, and thought that the capture of Harper's Ferry would serve as notice to the slaves that their friend had come, and as a trumpet to rally them to his standard. I was no match for him in such matters, but I told him that all his arguments and all his descriptions of the place convinced me that he was going into a perfect steel trap. . . . He was not to be shaken, but treated my views respectfully. . . . Our talk was long and earnest ; we spent the most of Saturday and a part of Sunday in this debate—Brown for Harper's Ferry, and I for the policy of gradually and unaccountably drawing off the slaves to the mountains, as at first suggested by him. When I found that he had fully made up his mind and could not be dissuaded, I turned to Green and told him ' he heard what Captain Brown had said : his old plan was changed, and I should go home ; if he wished to go with me he could do so.' Captain Brown urged us both to go with him. In parting, he put his arms around me in a manner more than friendly, and said, ' Come with me, Douglass! I will defend you with my life ; I want you for a special purpose. When I strike, the bees will begin to swarm, and I shall want you to help hive them.' When about to leave I asked Green what he had decided to do, and was surprised by his saying in his broken way, ' I believe I'll go wid de ole man.' "

On Sunday night, October 16th, 1859, twenty-two men—five of them negroes—set out in the darkness for Harper's Ferry, Owen Brown and two companions being left behind in charge of the farm. John Brown led, and with him went two sons, Watson and Oliver. Kagi was of the party, and Stevens, in whom Brown placed great trust ; Edwin Coppock Copeland, Taylor, Cook, Hazlett, Tidd, Leeman, Leary, two Thompsons, two Andersons. Shields Green, the faithful black, must also be mentioned. Their baggage-train was a one-horse wagon containing pikes and a few tools needed for the work ahead.

Coming to a schoolhouse—at that hour, of course, deserted—a mile outside the town, they halted for a while and sent on two men to cut the telegraph wires. This done, they started afresh, and reached the town shortly before eleven o'clock, having overpowered and captured the sentry on the Potomac bridge. Passing across, they turned out the lights, surprised and made prisoners of the three sentries guarding the armoury, and forced open the door with a crowbar. As yet the town slumbered ; and Brown, having posted two men at the bridge-head to capture the relief watchman due at midnight, passed on and took possession of the arsenal, the Shenandoah bridge, and the rifle factory on the island. Whilst he was thus occupied the relief watchman arrived at the Potomac bridge, but managed to escape back to the town and raise an alarm. Nothing came of it, however, for a while. In the darkness the aroused inhabitants could little guess the weakness of the attacking force, which by this time held every point of vantage.

The night express for Washington was due to cross the bridge soon after midnight, and Brown detailed four men to stop it. They did so, but the passengers made some resistance before surrendering, and in the scrimmage a negro porter was shot dead. Brown held up the train for several hours, and then allowed it to proceed—one of many fatal mistakes. As it sped on towards Washington the passengers scribbled accounts of the doings at Harper's Ferry on scraps of paper, which they flung out of the windows, thus raising the whole countryside eastwards. As soon as the express had passed the railway track was torn up—on the principle of locking a stable door after the horse has been stolen.

Brown's one hope—the hope on which alone his chance of success depended—lay in an immediate rising of the slaves in the neighbourhood; and he had no sooner seized the bridge over the Shenandoah than he dispatched Stevens with half a dozen men across to the Virginia shore to capture several slave-owners and release their slaves. In the few hours before daylight Stevens did wonders, and not only liberated some scores of slaves, but led their owners back with them as prisoners of war. John Brown welcomed the negroes as the beginning of his army, and furnished them with pikes. "Give a slave a pike," he had been used to say, "and you make him a free man." He was now to find two of his pet beliefs betrayed: to discover that a serf not only is not turned into a fighting man in a moment by having a pike thrust into his hands, but that, even though wishful for liberty, he cannot lift his cowed spirit to grasp a sudden occasion.

Meanwhile the very madness of the attempt—in

which no precautions had been taken for retreat—
must account for its brief success. Day dawned, and
the inhabitants of Harper's Ferry awoke with difficulty to the situation. It was impressed on them as
the day opened for business, and the citizens who
ventured abroad were, one by one, quickly arrested,
until the armoury held about fifty prisoners.

The position at breakfast-time, when Brown com-
mandeered food from the nearest hotel, seems to have
been this :—Brown, with his two sons, Stevens, and
two others, occupied the armoury as headquarters ;
Kagi, with his contingent, held the Shenandoah side,
with the bridge over that river and the rifle factory ;
Cook and Tidd, the school-house up the Maryland
road ; while Owen Brown with his companions still
waited for news at Kennedy Farm. The remainder of
the force, dispersed at street corners and at the bridge
ends, kept making arrests.

The success upon which the day opened was early
and sadly marred by some bolder townsmen, who,
occupying a room that overlooked the armoury gates,
fired down upon Brown's sentries, killing one and
mortally wounding his son Watson. Nevertheless
through that Monday forenoon he was master of the
town, and could have drawn off to the mountains
without serious hindrance. He dallied, expecting the
slaves to rise.

At noonday, instead of these expected slaves, there
arrived at the end of the Shenandoah bridge a hundred
militia from Charlestown. The officer in charge, supposing from reports that he had to deal with four or
five hundred men, posted detachments at all the exits,
and proceeded to carry the Shenandoah bridge, defended by two of Brown's men, of whom one, William
Thompson, was made prisoner and the other shot.
Passing on and collecting volunteers from among the
townsmen, he delivered his next assault upon the
rifle factory on the island, held by Kagi, Copeland,

Leary, Leeman, and one negro. The five, finding it impossible to defend the place, made a dash for the river. Leeman was shot down as he ran after the others, but scrambled to his feet and staggered into the shoal water, throwing away his gun and cutting off his accoutrements as he fled. A militiaman waded in after him, and Leeman, faint with loss of blood, threw up his hands, crying, " Don't shoot ! " But the Virginian pointed a pistol at close range and blew his face in. The others escaped for a time to a small rock in mid-stream, where they were fusilladed by marksmen from both shores. Kagi dropped first, and his body, pierced with many bullets, was swept down the river ; the negro died next, and Leary fell mortally wounded. Copeland surrendered, and was carried prisoner into the town with his dying comrade. As for William Thompson, taken at the bridge, his captors would have killed him in the inn parlour where he had been placed under guard ; but the landlord's daughter " didn't want her carpet spoilt," so they dragged him out and, flinging him over the bridge, " potted " at him as he rose from the water and attempted to crawl around the base of a pier into the bridge's shelter, until a last shot laid him dead.

Meanwhile Brown, attacked on all sides, fell back from the arsenal to the armoury, and finally into the engine-house, which he loopholed and barricaded. He had with him ten selected prisoners, including Colonel Washington, a descendant of the great first president's brother ; and, with these for hostages, he seems to have thought he could make terms. At all events, he sent out Stevens with a flag of truce, but only to discover how accurately his friend Douglass had prophesied the event : " My dear fellow, Virginia will blow you and your hostages sky-high rather than you should hold Harper's Ferry an hour." In spite of his white flag, Stevens was shot down and taken prisoner.

Colonel Washington afterwards described in court how humanely, throughout the fighting, Brown treated his " hostages," addressing them always with courtesy and giving them the safest positions. His position was quite desperate. The slaves had failed to rise ; Kagi and the pick of his band were slain or held prisoners ; of his two sons Oliver was dead, and Watson dying in slow agony ; and fresh troops were pouring into the town. When Oliver dropped by his side, the old man had gone on coolly firing from his porthole ; but when night fell and firing ceased, he went to the dead body, removed the lad's accoutrements and straightened out the cold limbs. To one of the prisoners he said quietly, " This is the third son I have lost in this cause." He took no sleep during the night, but called out again and again, "Are you awake, men ? Ready, hey ? "

The railway had been repaired, and by seven o'clock on Tuesday morning 1,500 troops were gathered at Harper's Ferry. The final assault was entrusted to eighty United States marines, who had arrived during the night with two cannon, under command of Colonel Robert Lee, afterwards commander-in-chief of the Confederate armies in the great war. Before assaulting they called on Brown to surrender, offering him present protection and a trial by law. Brown, however, stood out for his old terms, and without further parley the marines set about battering down the doorway. Using a heavy ladder as a ram, they forced an entrance, one of the prisoners helping from within ; and as they poured into the engine-house, other prisoners climbed upon the engines and pointed out Brown and his companions. One marine was killed, two were wounded, and Anderson and Dauphin Thompson received their death-blow. Coppock and Shields Green were overpowered and taken. The day before, during the fight, this good negro had carried a message from

Brown to Anderson's brother and Hazlett in the arsenal. These two, having made up their minds that the enterprise had fatally miscarried, were resolved upon flight, and urged Green to escape with them. He turned and looked back wistfully towards the engine-house. " You t'ink dere's no chance ? " he asked. " Not one." " And de ole captain can't get away ? " " No," said both. " Well," he said slowly, " I guess I'll go back to de ole man."

As for Brown, although he had thrown down his arms and surrendered, a too eager lieutenant cut him down with his sword, and a marine gave him two bayonet thrusts as he fell to the floor. He was un- conscious when they carried him out and laid him on the grass with the dead and wounded, but recovered speech when they carried him to the guard-house, to protect him from the mob that yelled for his blood. " I have failed," he said. " You may dispose of me very easily—I am nearly disposed of now. But this question is still to be settled—this negro question, I mean. The end of it is not yet."

Next day the prisoners were taken to Charlestown jail—Brown himself, Stevens, Hazlett, Coppock, Shields Green, and Copeland. Cook was afterwards captured, and joined them. Of the rest of the band of twenty-two, ten were already dead ; five escaped.

After a scamped mockery of a trial—which was none the more excusable because his legal guilt was manifest—on November 2nd Brown was sentenced to be hanged. The date of his execution was fixed for December 2nd. He spent the interval in perfect com- posure and serenity of mind, writing many letters to his wife, friends, and sympathizers, talking with courtesy to visitors, and imparting his cheerfulness to the comrades who were to follow him out of the world. " Brown's conversation," said one who visited him in prison, " is singularly attractive. His manner attracts every one who approaches him, and while he talks he reigns. The other prisoners venerate him. Stevens sits in his bed, usually with his face away from the window, and listens all day to the captain's words, seldom offering a syllable except when called upon. Sometimes he gets a little excited, and springs forward to make some point about which the captain is in doubt; but his five bullets in head and breast weigh him down, and he is soon exhausted. As for the other men, they are always sending messages to the captain." In his letters from prison Brown steadily justified his deed and prophesied its consequences. "As I believe most firmly that God reigns, I cannot believe that anything I have done, suffered, or may yet suffer, will be lost to the cause of God or of humanity."

At 10.30 in the morning of Friday, December 2nd —a clear sunny day—the sheriff entered his cell. Brown was ready. After saying farewell to his comrades, and being informed that he would not be allowed to speak from the scaffold, he handed his jailers a slip of paper inscribed with these last words: " I, John Brown, am now quite certain that the crimes of this guilty land will never be purged away but with blood. I had, as I now think vainly, flattered myself that without much bloodshed it might be done." At eleven o'clock he stepped outside the prison gates. At sight of the bayonets lining the road he lifted his head proudly, and stepped like a conqueror into the cart which stood ready, containing his coffin. His bold gaze travelled across the landscape to the Blue Ridge Mountains in the distance, as though glad to escape from imprisonment.

" This is a beautiful country," he said. " I have not cast my eyes over it before." The scaffold stood on a knoll, surrounded by soldiery. He alighted and mounted with a firm tread. His last words after he had been pinioned were, " I am ready at any time; but do not keep me needlessly waiting." The trap fell, and John Brown was dead.

Many, even among the professed foes of slavery, blamed what he had done. Others accounted him a madman and monomaniac. Others, with longer vision, foresaw that this man in deliberately giving his life for the oppressed negro—" I pity the poor in bondage that have none to help them. That is why I am here," said he before his judges—had so raised the question of slavery that his fellow-countrymen could never again let it rest or palter with it.

" You may dispose of me very easily ; but this question is still to be settled."

How true this declaration was we shall see in our next chapter.

# ABRAHAM LINCOLN

ABRAHAM LINCOLN was born on February 12, 1809, in a one-roomed log cabin near Nolin Creek, Kentucky. His parents, Thomas and Nancy Lincoln, belonged to that race of poor and venturous settlers who, pushing their way farther and farther into the forest lands of North America, made clearings in the wilderness, and by small degrees brought it under cultivation ; and the cabin stood far from other habitations, in the midst of a wooded rolling country where the hills here and there rose to the dignity of mountains.

The settlers' life was a hard one as well as lonely— its sustenance wrung from Nature by one unremitting struggle. The mother could use the rifle ; and having shot the forest game, bear or deer, would cook the flesh for food and afterwards fashion the dried skins into garments and moccasins for the family wear. Like the virtuous woman in the Proverbs, she arose early to give meat to her household ; though it could not be said of her that " her candle goeth not out by night," for candles were a luxury, and when young

**ABRAHAM LINCOLN.**

*From a pen-drawing by*
*E. Heber Thompson.*

Abraham grew up and read every book he could buy, beg, or borrow, it was by the light of the pine knots which he kept stirring to a blaze on the poor hearth after his parents had gone to bed.

In this passion for reading he took after his mother, who devoured every book that came in her way. From her—their father being almost illiterate—he and his only sister, Sarah, received their first lessons in the alphabet ; and his earliest recollection was of their sitting together at the mother's feet, listening to the tales she wove for them by the firelight, while outside the forest wrapped the hut around with its silence or its mysterious noises. When the boy was in his seventh year, a teacher, Zachariah Riney, came and set up a log schoolhouse in the nearest settlement ; but soon departed, to be followed by an energetic young master, Caleb Hazel by name. These were Lincoln's first instructors. He was a full-grown lad before he saw a church, and the family, though God-fearing, depended for religious service on a wandering Baptist preacher whose way took him now and again through the region.

Next year his father, wearying of the Kentucky patch and having a purchaser for it, built a flatboat, launched it on the waters of the creek which runs down to the Ohio, and pushed off alone to prospect in Indiana for a new home. He reached the broad river in safety, but upset the flatboat there upon a snag, and lost much of her cargo of household furniture. Fortunately, help was at hand to right the boat and rescue some of the baggage. With these fragments he reached Thompson's Ferry, where he hired an ox-cart and drove eighteen miles into the forest. Here, in an oak clearing, he stacked his goods, and leaving them in charge of a neighbourly settler, returned to fetch his family.

Cheered by his reports of the richness of the land on the Indiana side, Mrs. Lincoln and the two children packed up what remained, loaded it upon two borrowed horses, and set forth with him. Trudging by day, sleeping at night in the open (luckily the weather was fine), they reached the Ohio, and looked across it to Indiana and the forest that was to be their home.

They crossed the ferry, recovered their goods and chattels, and, pushing their way through the wilderness, reached the grassy slope chosen by Thomas Lincoln for the site of the new camp. There was no time (the season being late) to erect anything better than a " half-faced " hut—that is, a three-sided shanty having its open front partially screened with skins and sacking. This screened portion served for the family bedroom ; in the other was the family hearth of clay, with a rude clay chimney. Thus they " tholed " the winter ; and, about the time of Abe's eighth birthday, set to work felling logs for a more solid house, cutting them afterwards to the proper lengths, notching the ends so that they would dovetail after a fashion, and for the time letting them lie. When all was ready the Lincolns, settler fashion, sent out invitations for a " house-raising." Helpers gathered — some from great distances — the more prosperous bringing their teams ; the logs were " snaked " or rolled up out of the woods, erected and clumped together—all with such energy that before nightfall the four walls of the cabin were in place, with the gables and roof-tree fixed. Thereupon all turned to merrymaking, and departed, leaving their good wishes. It remained for the family to lay the shingle roof, " chink " the cracks between the logs with clay and wood shavings, and pound the earthen floor to a suitable hardness.

Such was the home in which young Lincoln grew up. He wore the dress of the frontier—woollen shirt, homespun suit (dyed with colours obtained from the bark of trees), coonskin cap, and moccasins. (He never had a pair of stockings on his feet until he was

almost a man grown.) He disliked the shooting of
game, and only foraged for it when his father could
not spare the time ; but in woodcraft, as well as in
the hewing, splitting, and shaping of timber, he delighted. The boy was scarcely ten when he suffered
his first and for a child most dreadful loss. His
mother fell ill of the " milk sick "—a mysterious
disease resembling consumption—and died, without
medical succour, on October 5, 1818. The bereaved
husband buried her at the foot of a mighty sycamore,
little Abe helping to dig the grave ; nor was it till
early summer that a kindly Baptist minister came
and read the funeral service over the already green
mound that covered Nancy Lincoln.

A dismal year followed—Thomas Lincoln, well-
meaning but shiftless, being left with his two small
children, and a third, younger than either, an orphan
boy, Dennis Hanks, whose relatives had died of the
" milk sick " and left him without protector in the
world. Twelve-year-old Sarah did her best—a distracted little housewife. As for Abraham, his day's
work done he would turn to reading, to forget in his
books the muddle and discomfort around him. He
possessed a Bible, *Æsop's Fables*, *The Pilgrim's Progress*, Euclid's Geometry, a *Life of Henry Clay*, and
Ramsay's *Life of Washington*. Hearing of another
*Life of Washington*, written by one Weems, the boy
borrowed it of a neighbouring settler, took it home,
and at night kept it under his pillow, that he might
start reading as soon as he awoke. A storm came on
in the night; a driving rain blew in through the chinks
of the logs and soaked not only the pillow and the head
of the sleeping boy, but (a far more serious matter) the
precious book. Sadly he took it back to its owner,
and asked how he could make payment for the
damage. It was agreed that the boy should put in
three days' work " shucking " corn on the farm.
Young Abe was shrewd as well as honest. " Will that

pay for the book, or only for the damage? " he asked.
" Well," said the owner, slightly tickled, " I allow it's
not much account now to me or anybody else. You
pull the fodder three days, and the book is yours."

In the autumn Thomas Lincoln, widower, went off
on a visit to Kentucky, leaving (it sounds incredible
when we remember that by all accounts he was a
kind-hearted man) these three motherless children,
the eldest not fourteen, unfathered and alone in the
wilderness. He returned in December in a four-horse
wagon with a good-looking woman by his side, and
told little Sarah and Abe very jovially that he had
found a new mother for them. He had married, in
fact, in Elizabethtown, Kentucky, a young widow,
Mrs. Sally Johnston, having persuaded her to share
his lot in the forest. How the children took it is
not known. Very likely they had given up wonder-
ing at this unaccountable parent; very likely after
asking themselves, in those desolate weeks, if he ever
meant to return, they had no thought but of joy
in greeting him. Childhood is full of forgiveness.
And the wagon contained marvellous things brought
by the new Mrs. Lincoln—tables and chairs, chests
of drawers packed with clothes, bedding, crockery,
knives and forks. Forks were a luxury hitherto unknown to them. The new Mrs. Lincoln, too, proved
herself a cheerful, " adaptable " body. She " took
to " the children, and young Abe made friends with
her at once. The wagon, one must not forget to mention, contained also three children of hers by her first
marriage—John, Sarah, and Matilda Johnston. The
little cabin had to be enlarged; even so, it was full
and overfull. But Mrs. Lincoln cheerfully mothered
the whole brood; nor is it recorded that she " made
any difference " between her own children and poor
Nancy Lincoln's. " A noble woman," her stepson
said, summarizing in later life her character and her
kindness to him.

Civilization by this time was beginning to draw closer upon them. A new teacher had set up school in a log-house on Little Pigeon Creek, a mile and a half away, and thither the children trudged daily. A meeting-house arose, built of sawn lumber. Amid these encroaching improvements young Abraham shot up into a tall, leggy, raw-boned lad, known in the neighbourhood for his trustworthiness and his ability to throw anybody of his own age and weight in wrestling. He read every book on which he could lay his hands, and by-and-by, fired by a visit to an assize court at Boonville, where he heard " the famous Mr. Breckinridge " defend a prisoner on trial for his life, he began to practise public speaking, " spouting " to the tree trunks in the forest depth, as (we are told) Demosthenes tried his early orations upon the waves of the seashore.

By the time he was nineteen the neighbourhood of his home was no longer a wilderness. Settlers had crowded into Southern Indiana; hamlets and small townships were springing up, with churches and village stores; and these changes brought in their train a certain amount of social intercourse, with visitings, sports, harvest suppers, wrestling matches, and the like. Abraham Lincoln, who had grown into a strapping young giant of six feet four inches, excelled at wrestling, as at jumping and all feats of strength. There was no one, far or near, that could lay him on his back; just as among the younger men there was no one able to match him in book-learning, or to stand up against him in argument.

About this time a Mr. Gentry, a neighbouring storekeeper, enlisted him to take part in a trip down the Mississippi in a flatboat which carried produce down to New Orleans, there to be sold in exchange for sugar and rum. It was a voyage of 1,800 miles, and Lincoln had never even seen the lower Mississippi; but he and his companion, young Allen Gentry, started off undaunted—down Pigeon Creek into the Ohio, and down the Ohio until they floated on the broad current of the "father of waters." They met with plenty of adventures on the way, and once as they slept, having tethered their boat to the shore, were attacked by a gang of negroes intent on plunder. Snatching up hand-pikes, they knocked four of the invaders overboard, and drove the remaining three into the woods. But the most instructive lesson of the voyage awaited Lincoln at New Orleans, where the travellers disposed of their empty boat, having already sold the cargo to good advantage ; for there, while waiting for the steamer which was to convey them back up-stream, he saw for the first time, and had leisure to inspect, a great slave-market. Already, in the closing stages of the journey, he had passed gangs of slaves toiling in the plantations or on the riverside wharves ; and yet more melancholy gangs had met or had passed him, herded on steamboats—poor creatures torn from their homes and families and bound for distant servitude. But the slave-market itself sickened him to the soul, and left an impression that was never effaced. From this time forward he hated slavery, and yet—this is important—having mixed with slaveowners, he recognized that the mass of them were good men, quite sincere and honestly unable to see the iniquity of the system in which they had been reared. To the end Lincoln did not—as many thousands of men did in the Northern States—confuse his hatred of the institution with hatred of the men who fought against him in support of it.

The voyage occupied three months. He returned to find his father contemplating another move westward, this time to Illinois. In the spring of 1830 the family, having sold the crops and live stock, set off with a wagon across a prairie country, and after two weeks' travelling reached their new home near Decatur, Macon County. Here, after helping to build a log-house and splitting the rails to fence off the farm, Abraham picked up a living by hiring himself out for odd jobs in the neighbourhood. The winter that followed—the " winter of hard snow "—was a memorable one ; and, strange to say, its very severity kept the new settlers in plenty, for whole herds of deer could be taken and killed with ease, held prisoners as they were by the icy crust of snow through which their pointed hoofs had broken. So many were slaughtered that large game has never since been plentiful in Illinois, as it was before the " winter of hard snow."

In the following spring a trader named Offutt, having heard of Lincoln's previous voyage, engaged him and his friend Hanks to take a boatload of provisions down the Sangamon to the lower Mississippi ; and so our hero paid a second visit to New Orleans. On this trip he made a yet closer study of slavery, even to the flogging of female slaves, and the more he witnessed the more it nauseated him. Also, a short while after the start on the Sangamon, which was in raging flood, the small craft stuck on a mill-dam by the village of New Salem, and appeared likely to break up under the eyes of the chaffing riverside population. Amid their scornful comments the ungainly young giant who had been pulling the bow oar tucked up his trousers, waded into the stream, and began phlegmatically to unload the barge. When this was done, the party bored holes in her submerged stern ; lifted it, letting the water run out ; rigged up a contrivance to hoist her over the dam ; replugged the holes, floated and reloaded her ; and finally shot downstream, waving back acknowledgments to the onlookers, who had turned from criticism to cheers. Some time after, Lincoln, improving on his device, patented at Washington a small model of an invention for lifting boats over shoals—a contrivance by which, as he claimed, " a man might lift himself over a rail fence by the waistband of his breeches."

As it happened, New Salem was soon to make closer acquaintance with this young giant; for, on his return, Offutt engaged him to take up the management of a small store in that village. He had no sooner arrived than he was recognized as a young man out of the common run—a great reader of books, fearless in argument, and equally fearless (if necessary) with his fists; no seeker of company, yet eager to talk cheerfully with all who came to him; curiously tender-hearted with women and children, and chivalrous to protect them; above all, transparently honest. Hard by New Salem lay a group of farms known as Clary's Grove, and the Clary's Grove "boys," irritated by hearing praise of this newcomer, whom they agreed to consider a "prig," marched over to Lincoln's store and invited him to come out. He came to the door. Would he try a fall with Jack Armstrong, the bully of the band? He would, and he did. The two gripped, and Armstrong, getting the worst of it, attempted a foul clutch. Abe Lincoln loosed his clutch a moment, and gripping the bully by the throat with his enormous hands, held him aloft, shook him, and flung him to the ground. The gang were all breaking in upon Lincoln, who jumped back and set his back against the store to meet their onset, when Armstrong picked himself up and interfered. "Let be, boys. Abe Lincoln's the best man I've met in this settlement." The fight was stopped, all shook hands, and Armstrong thereafter was Lincoln's firm friend.

The young storekeeper, conscious of his ability, had now some thought of entering politics. In March 1832 he issued an election address as candidate for the Legislature. Before the election came on, however, trouble broke out with the frontier Indians. A famous chief, Black Hawk, had taken to the warpath, and volunteers were called for. Lincoln promptly offered his services. At the head of a band of Clary's Grove boys, now his sworn friends, he made his way north to General Atkinson, who commanded against the Indians, and was chosen captain of his company. The campaign was short and decisive. Lincoln saw no actual fighting; but one day, as the Clary's Grove boys were on frontier work, an old Indian came into camp under safe conduct. The "boys," not knowing the honourable protection he carried, and infuriated by some atrocities lately committed, were on the point of shooting the messenger, when Lincoln ran forward in front of their rifles. "Don't shoot!" he cried. "Boys, you must not shoot : this man is protected!" They lowered their rifles, and the Indian was saved.

Lincoln returned from this campaign in time to be defeated in his candidature for the election. But there was promise in the figures of his defeat. As an unknown man he had failed to carry the electorate; but in New Salem, where he was known, he had actually polled 208 out of 211 votes cast. Two years later he tried again, and was successful. This was financially the hardest time of his life. His employer had come to grief, and the village store was derelict. He raised money, and, in partnership with one Berry, started another. Berry, an idle and dissolute fellow, ate the profits and decamped, leaving Lincoln to wind up the business and accept all the burden of their joint debts. He did so manfully, though it took him seventeen years to win his way clear. Meanwhile, to keep himself going, he applied for and received the postmastership of New Salem, besides securing some work as a country surveyor; but in 1837 he threw up these occupations, and moving to Springfield, a small town recently made the "capital" of Illinois, set up in practice as a lawyer. It was a bold step. He rode into the town on a borrowed horse, with all his worldly possessions stowed in a pair of saddle-bags; he hired an office, and furnished it for seventeen dollars, on credit; and at night he shared a bedroom with a good-natured friend. But the experiment succeeded, and Springfield remained his home until he left it for Washington and the famous White House.

The country court-houses of Illinois were the merest log shanties, and the lawyers rode circuit on horseback in the wake of the presiding judge. On one of these journeys—the story is trivial but characteristic—after his comrades had stopped to water their steeds near a thicket of wild plum trees, Lincoln was missing. "Where's Abe Lincoln?" they asked of a straggler who overtook them. "Why, when I saw him last he had caught a couple of young birds that the wind had blown out of their nests, and was hunting for the nest to put them back. He'll find it too, if it costs him all day and he misses sessions to-morrow." He quickly became known for absolute fairness in presenting his own case and admitting a genuine point in an opponent's. He could do this the more safely, because it was known that he refused to take up any case in the justice of which he did not believe. He had a wonderful knack of conciliating and winning over opinion, whether in the courts or on a political platform; but he was shrewd to detect men whom no argument would convince, and on them throughout life he wasted no time. "One might as well," he said, "undertake to throw fleas across the barnyard with a shovel." By degrees, too, he came to be known as the man who would take up a case, however unpopular, if he believed in it—*even to defending the rights of a fugitive slave.*

Let us pause here to note that Lincoln was by this time deep in politics, and needed all the popularity he could honestly come by. In 1846 he was elected for Congress as a Whig, and in 1847 took his seat. He was very poor, and to defy public opinion is harder for a poor man than for a rich man. Lastly, he had found a devoted wife in Mary Todd, daughter of a Kentucky family that had migrated to Springfield. Already two sons had been born to him. Many a man ready

enough to take risks for himself will hesitate when
dear ones are dependent on him; and to stand up
for the slave was still, in 1846, a sure way to court
violent hatreds.

Nothing appeared more wonderful to Lincoln in
later years—there is indeed scarcely anything more
wonderful in history—than the march of events that,
as if under guidance of a Fate far above human forecast, led to the suppression of negro slavery in America.
In 1850 it looked as if slavery were fastened upon the
country, to endure for ever. Even the men whose
consciences it revolted despaired of breaking down
the system. Nor did they take the first steps. The
question was pushed to the forefront of politics by
men who desired to extend slavery, not to suppress it.
It was the question of *extending* slavery that, thrust
into prominence, swallowed up all other political
questions and brought about civil war. The war,
when it came, was not undertaken to liberate the
slaves; nor until it neared an end did their liberation
appear inevitable. The victors at length, laying aside
their arms, perceived that they had fought for an issue
unforeseen by them when they took up the struggle;
or, if foreseen by a small minority—and among them
by the great man who guided his country through—
still not the issue first in their thoughts or in his.

We have told, in the preceding chapter, the story of
the Missouri Compromise—how in 1820 Missouri was
admitted into the Union as a slave state, on the express understanding that henceforth, save within her
boundaries, slavery should be prohibited for ever
north of 36° 30′ latitude. This understanding, as
we have seen, lasted until 1854, when the new territories of Kansas and Nebraska desired to be admitted
as states. These lay north of the dividing line, and
came under the prohibition. But a bill was introduced into the Senate by Stephen Arnold Douglas of
Illinois, admitting them as states while *leaving the*

*question of slavery to be settled by themselves*. This was virtually a repudiation of the Missouri Compromise, and a great roar of indignation went up from the Northern States. Douglas, the cause of this hubbub, went back to Illinois (his own state just north of the border-line), and at Springfield, its capital, delivered a speech in defence of his action. There he met Lincoln; and there Lincoln, to whom men's eyes instinctively turned, stood up and exposed him. The speech not only discredited Douglas; it swept the audience along on a tide in which clear reasoning and strong emotion flowed irresistibly together. At the close men and women leapt up, waving hats and handkerchiefs. Every one felt that its whole argument was unanswerable; "every mind present did homage to the man who took captive the heart and broke like a sun over the understanding." Lincoln, in fact, as Douglas afterwards confessed, knew more about this question of prohibiting slavery than all the opposition in the Senate put together. The man was found, and the thousands of "free-staters" who were sworn not to permit slavery in Kansas looked to him to be their leader. They were men who, apart from this one question, differed widely and variously in politics. Lincoln's first thought was to unite them in one solid party; and "let us," he said, "in building our new party, make our corner-stone the Declaration of Independence. Let us build on this rock, and the gates of hell shall not prevail against us." They agreed with enthusiasm; a resolution was passed that the extension of slavery did not lie within the four corners of the Declaration of Independence; and the great Republican party was born.

For the elections that followed they had little time to organize, and their opponents, the Democrats, carried the day, electing James Buchanan of Pennsylvania President of the United States. The pro-slavery men, too, had been encouraged in their aggressiveness by a decision of the Supreme Court in what was known as the " Dred Scott case." A negro of that name, having been carried by his owner into a territory north of the line drawn by the Missouri Compromise, sued for his liberty and that of his wife and children on the ground that the change of abode made him legally a free man. The Court pronounced against him, saying in effect that a negro was not a person but a chattel ; and the Northern States now realized with growing indignation that, if the Court was right, slavery might be brought up from the South and planted anywhere in their midst. This decision swung thousands over to the Republican side, and Lincoln saw that the opportunity for a trial of strength was not far distant.

It came in 1858. The term for which his old adversary Douglas had been elected to the Senate was drawing to a close, and Douglas sought re-election. Lincoln, chosen by the Republicans of Illinois, boldly challenged the seat. A tremendous campaign followed, which drew the eyes of all America. After the custom of those days, the two men addressed their audience in turn from the same platform, so that their meetings were, in fact, public debates. Lincoln pressed Douglas with questions which, as the conflict went on, made that brilliant debater more and more uneasy. " Is the Dred Scott decision just and right ? " " If just and right, can it be put into force in the territories ? " Douglas, standing for votes in Illinois, dared not say " yes " to the latter question. He temporized, and answered that, while as an abstract principle the Dred Scott decision was just, it could not and would not be put into effect in the territories. " That has done for him," said Lincoln, rubbing his large hands. " He can never be president now." For he knew that Douglas meant to be president in 1860, and he meant that the arrogant South, flushed with its success in the Supreme Court, would never "run" a man for president who announced that the Court's decision would be merely a dead letter. "His chance two years hence is not your look-out," urged Lincoln's supporters: "you are after the secretaryship just now." "No, gentlemen," said Lincoln; "I am killing larger game. The battle of 1860 is worth a hundred of this."

When all the votes were in, 126,048 had been cast for Lincoln, 121,940 for Douglas; and though Douglas was subsequently chosen senator by the Legislature, there could be no doubt on which side the victory lay—even the immediate victory. The eastern states and their cities became curious to see and hear for themselves this strong man from the west; and in February 1860, Lincoln was invited by certain Republican leaders in New York to visit and address them, to make clear the purposes and principles of the new party. He accepted with trepidation. He feared this critical audience beforehand, and he feared it still more when he found himself in the vast hall of the Cooper Union, New York, surrounded on the platform by the greatest men of the republic—men whose very names he had been accustomed to worship; and, lo, they were gathered to listen to *him*!

Says one who was present:—

"When Lincoln rose to speak I was greatly disappointed. He was tall, tall—oh, how tall!—and so angular and awkward that I had for an instant a feeling of pity for so ungainly a man. His clothes were black and ill-fitting, badly wrinkled—as if they had been jammed carelessly into a large trunk. His bushy head, with the stiff black hair thrown back, was balanced on a long and lean head-stalk; and when he raised his hands in an opening gesture I noticed that they were very large. He began in a low tone of voice, as if he were used to speaking outdoors and was afraid of speaking too loud. . . . I said to myself, 'Old fellow, you won't do; it's all very well for the

wild west, but this will never go down in New York.'
But pretty soon he began to get into his subject; he
straightened up, made regular and graceful gestures;
his face lighted as with an inward fire—the whole man
was transfigured. I forgot his clothes, his personal
appearance. . . . Presently, forgetting myself, I was
on my feet with the rest, yelling like a wild Indian,
cheering this wonderful man. In the close parts of
his argument you could hear the gentle sizzling of the
gas-burners. When he reached a climax the thunders
of applause were terrific. . . . When I came out of the
hall, my face glowing with excitement and my frame
all a-quiver, a friend, with his eyes aglow, asked me
what I thought of Abe Lincoln, the rail-splitter. I
said, 'He's the greatest man since St. Paul!' And
I think so still.''

This famous speech not only gave the bugle-call for
the coming campaign; it settled the question of select-
ing a leader for the Republicans in the coming fight.
At the great Republican national convention which
assembled in Chicago on June 17, 1860, the new and
solid party nominated Abraham Lincoln, the back-
woodsman's son, as its candidate for the presidency.

On the other hand, the friends of slavery were hopelessly divided, as Lincoln had foreseen that they would
be. The Southern States, still arrogant, and in no
frame of mind to accept any half-measures, would
have nothing to do with Douglas, remembering the
temporizing answers Lincoln had forced him to make
two years before. The Northern Democrats would
have Douglas, and Douglas only. The Democratic
Convention, after fifty-seven fruitless ballotings, broke
up, unable to find a candidate for whom all sections
could unite. Separate conventions, meeting subsequently at Baltimore and at Richmond, nominated
Douglas, John Bell of Tennessee (a colourless Whig),
and John C. Breckenridge (a " whole-hogger " for
slavery, on whom the South pinned its hopes). When

the tidings of his nomination reached Lincoln in the newspaper office at Springfield, where he had been sitting among his friends awaiting the telegrams, he shook hands with his friends, and saying simply, " There is a little woman in Eighth Street who would like to hear about this," walked home to be congratulated by his wife and household. Even so quietly he waited at home through the rage of the actual voting for election. The papers were counted, and Lincoln was President by the largest popular vote ever recorded, up to that time, for a presidential candidate.

A howl of fury went up from the South and the pro-slavery party throughout the States. The South, foreseeing defeat, had been threatening in the event of it to " secede "—that is, to withdraw from the Union and set up as a separate nation. This could not be done without open war, and for war it accordingly prepared. It had much in its favour. A new administration had been elected, but for some months it could not take office ; and meanwhile the whole government at Washington remained in the hands of the Democrats and the discredited retiring President, Buchanan—all tools of the men who were planning rebellion. This interval they used with cruel effect. The Secretary for War, a Southerner, scattered the United States army all over the south, where it would be handy ; and, moreover, in his last weeks of office moved vast quantities of arms and munitions of war, emptying the Northern forts and cramming those of the slave states. Similarly, the Naval Secretary dispatched the nation's warships to all quarters of the globe, that they might be well out of the way when the moment was ripe for rebellion. The Secretary of the Treasury used his time to involve the national finances in every difficulty he could contrive, and left the treasury empty. To the last moment these men stuck to their posts in Washington, and then fled, each having done his best for treason. So bold were the enemies of the republic that, when Lincoln came to Washington, it was openly said that he would never be suffered to pass through Baltimore alive.

He passed through Baltimore, and he arrived. Before the day came on which he was to deliver his inaugural address, seven of the Southern States were already in open revolt, and a rival and hostile government had already been organized at Montgomery. Lincoln ignored this, though an inaugural address of the opposition government had contained the tempting phrase, " Slavery is the corner-stone of our new nation." He spoke in his own " inaugural " with careful and tender moderation. He closed his address with a noble, if vain, appeal :—

" We are not enemies, but friends. We must not be enemies. Though passion may have strained our relations, it must not break our bonds of affection."

He saw clearly enough that, if a struggle must come, it must end in the total triumph or the total abolition of slavery throughout the length and breadth of the land. But no one can begin to understand Lincoln who does not understand that from the first, and even to the very last, the suppression of slavery was not his prime object. He had entered politics not to suppress it, but to prevent its extension. He was now President of the Republic, and his single aim was to hold the republic together in one union. The words he wrote later to Horace Greely, the famous editor of the *New York Tribune*, indicate the policy from which he never swerved :—

" I would save the Union. . . . My paramount object is to save the Union, and not either to save or destroy slavery.

" If I could save the Union without freeing any slave, I would do it ; if I could save it by freeing all the slaves, I would do it ; and if I could do it by freeing some and leaving others alone, I would also do that.

" What I do about slavery and the coloured race, I do because I believe it helps to save this Union; and what I forbear, I forbear because I do not believe it would help to save the Union.

" I shall do less whenever I shall believe what I am doing hurts the cause, and I shall do more whenever I believe doing more will help the cause."

" Save the Union." " The Union before all else." As Lincoln, on the great open-air platform in front of the Capitol, concluded his first address as President, amid the cheering he looked quaintly around for his hat, of which some friendly hand had relieved him when he stood forward to speak. The man who had held it, and who now restored it with a smile, was Douglas. " Mr. President, may I have the honour of shaking hands with you?" said Douglas; " and will you accept an old opponent's word that we are all at one in supporting you to uphold the Constitution?"

Lincoln had now to form his Cabinet and organize the men of the North to meet that war for which the South had long been preparing. His invocation of affection, of friendship, moved the slave-owning states not at all. They intended war, and war they would have. Already South Carolina, Mississippi, Florida, Alabama, Georgia, Louisiana, and Texas formally declared themselves out of the Union. Lincoln, to whom it was the fundamental law of the republic that "no state could leave the Union without the assent of the other states," merely ignored their secession, and treated it as of no effect. The rebel states assembled in Congress at Montgomery, and on March 9th, 1861, passed a bill organizing an army. Lincoln made no move; he was determined not to be provoked into striking the first blow. Next, two commissioners were sent to Washington to negotiate a treaty, for all the world as though they represented a foreign government. Lincoln declined to see them, but with a touch of humour directed that each should be supplied with a copy of his " inaugural," lest they might be ignorant of his views.

He showed the same patience with his Cabinet, for which he had chosen a band of men, admittedly able, but of such extremely divergent views on all subjects but one that his friends declared he could never drive such a team. Seward, Secretary of State, had been Lincoln's only serious rival for the Republican nomination to the presidency, and Seward—a scholar, of good ancestry and fine presence—had a pardonable notion that he could manage this President from the backwoods and keep him straight. Within a month he wrote Lincoln a letter suggesting that the government had as yet no clearly defined policy. " Who is to control the national policy ? " the letter asked, and went on to hint that William H. Seward was willing to take the responsibility, leaving the credit to his nominal chief. Lincoln quickly answered, " There must, of course, be control, and the responsibility for this control must rest with me." His first War Secretary, Cameron, he promptly removed on discovering that the man was trafficking in appointments and contracts, and Edwin M. Stanton succeeded—a man of strong brain and will, and so conscious of these gifts that his truculency passed into a proverb. He would as lief insult and trample on friend as on foe, and he started on Lincoln—somewhat to the amusement of his colleagues, who had already, and within one calendar month, discovered that " there is in the Cabinet but one vote, and that is cast by the President." Having gently put Master Stanton on his back, so to speak, Lincoln as gently picked him up and wiped him down, and the pair became fast friends. To Senator Chase, a violent anti-slavery man, fell the task of raising money for the empty treasury ; and Chase did his work splendidly as soon as the President had made him see what he himself so clearly saw— that the Union must first be saved, and the downfall of slavery would inevitably follow. But Chase and Stanton detested one another, and their quarrels in the Cabinet were many and bitter. Lincoln, ignoring all personal issues, held on to Chase until the last year of the war ; and then, convinced at length that the Cabinet would work more smoothly without him, accepted his resignation and appointed him Chief Justice. As a set-off against Chase, the " Abolitionist " Montgomery Blair of Missouri, the Postmaster-General, came of a family " quite ready to fight for the Union, but very unwilling to do any fighting for the black man." Between him and Chase, again, it was not easy to keep the peace. The Secretary of the Navy, Gideon Waller of Connecticut, was a douce, steady-going man, constant to the work of his department, and devoted to his chief.

On April 12, 1861, the South, or Confederates as they were called, opened the war by firing upon Fort Sumter in Charleston Harbour, South Carolina, where a small government garrison in that hostile state was running short of supplies. Supplies were on their way, and the impatient Confederates chose to interpret the sending of them as an act of war. But to supply a needy garrison, and to fire shot into it, are to the plain mind poles asunder as acts of aggressiveness. By bombarding Fort Sumter into honourable surrender, by firing on what had been the flag of their common country and cutting it from its mast, the Confederates stood definitely before the world as the party seeking the quarrel. They had for the moment the stronger backing in foreign sympathy; but such an action in the end demoralizes its cause, as Lincoln foresaw. He had insisted on waiting until the rebels fired the first shot ; now that they had insulted the flag of the republic, he lost no time. In an instant, as the patriotism of the North caught flame, he issued a call for 75,000 men. The free states of the North responded nobly ; men fought for the privilege of enlisting. In response to the call for 75,000, more than 5,000,000 volunteered.

Had the Confederates had sense to perceive it, here was a most ominous threat of what the end would be in a protracted war. But there was much to blind them. To begin with, they had been making ready, and the North was caught unprepared. Further, they had the best military skill on their side, since for years the South, living as aristocrats on their slave-plantations, had sent their sons to officer the army of the Union ; while the sons of the North—the Yankees—had been crowding into commerce and the money-getting professions. In this story of Abraham Lincoln we cannot treat the long and intricate struggle of the Civil War. But at its opening the situation was this :—The South had the advantage of preparation and of munitions, with an immense advantage of military skill. For immediate success it commanded all the odds. But its chance was at best a fighting chance, dependent upon swift and stunning triumph. What these men of the South wholly failed to realize was that, unless they triumphed at once, the North held reserves of strength which must in the long run beat them to their knees. They utterly failed to realize that their population numbered nine millions, of which more than one-third were negro slaves, while the free states numbered twenty-two millions. On the issue of such a struggle a patient man could rely ; and Lincoln was that man.

He was more : he was the man to rally his countrymen in the early days of disaster ; to show a brave face when the hearts of men were sinking all around him ; to nurse back hope and method where all seemed chaos and despair. By the middle of July a Southern force of 18,000 men had pushed up close to Washington. The Union or Federal force in the capital, in numbers almost equal, marched out to oppose it. In the battle of Bull Run that followed, after a long struggle in which each side supposed it had won, at the last moment the Union troops, suddenly weakened, exploded in a panic, and fled back to Washington across the bridges of the Potomac, bedraggled, humiliated, spreading consternation with the wildest tales of catastrophe. The blow fell on the capital with a shock that passed into a kind of awful stupor. The talk was loud for surrender, even among men high in office. If the Southern officers, pressing on their victory, had marched straight upon Washington, nothing could have saved the seat of government.

"But the hour, the day, the night passed; and whatever returns, an hour, a day, a night like that can never again return. The President, recovering himself, begins that very night—sternly, rapidly, sets about the task of reorganizing his forces and placing himself in position for future and surer work. If there were nothing else of Abraham Lincoln for history to stamp him with, it is enough to send him with his wreath to the memory of all future time, that he endured that hour, that day, bitterer than gall—indeed a crucifixion day; that it did not conquer him; that he unflinchingly stemmed it, and resolved to lift himself and the Union out of it." *

Not only in 1861, but again and again in the dark days of 1862, there were crises "when human eyes appeared just as likely to see the last breath of the Union as to see it continue." But Lincoln met each crisis with the same unflinching courage, the same patience, the same gentleness, the same resolution. In November 1861 Jefferson Davis, the Confederate "President," sent two commissioners—Mr. Mason of Virginia and Judge Slidell of Louisiana—to visit London and Paris, present the case for the South, make a market for cotton bonds, and arrange for the

* Walt Whitman, *Specimen Days in America.*

purchase of arms and supplies to continue the war. Mason and Slidell made their way to Jamaica, and sailed from Jamaica for Liverpool in the British mail steamer *Trent*. A Captain Wilkes of the United States frigate *San Jacinto*, getting wind of these two envoys and their mission, lay in wait for the *Trent* a hundred miles or so out of Kingston, fired a shot across her bows to make her bring-to, sent a boat alongside, and took off Messrs. Mason and Slidell, with their secretaries, as prisoners. Immediately there arose in England a great outcry, and a demand for the release of these men, taken from under the protection of the British flag. Lord Palmerston, then Prime Minister, sympathized with the South, and saw an opportunity of flinging the weight of Great Britain on to the Confederate side. He drafted a demand in language so insolent that Queen Victoria very sensibly refused to sign the document, and another was substituted, although Palmerston threatened to resign. Even so, the Northern States, already furious with England's general attitude towards the war, clamoured against surrender. But Lincoln, though himself hurt and angry, and though he well knew that the submission would make him bitterly unpopular, insisted that this was no time to court a quarrel with a foreign power ; the Union must first be saved. He won over Seward, who, however, never forgave Great Britain for the indignity. A dispatch was most skilfully worded ; and although the envoys were surrendered, the form of surrender actually scored a diplomatic triumph, the United States Government politely expressing itself " well pleased that Her Majesty's Government should have finally accepted the old-time American contention that vessels of peace should not be searched on the high seas by vessels of war."

Equally patient was Lincoln with his generals, who gave him endless trouble. Of these perhaps the most exasperating was General M'Clellan, who, promoted on the strength of some early successes in Virginia to command the great Army of the Potomac, pride and hope of the North, wore away his own reputation and exhausted the country's patience by endless delays, marches, counter-marches, hesitations, demands for more men, more horses, more guns, more everything. Lincoln, always extremely modest in discussing military strategy, confined himself for long to the gentlest methods of suggesting that, after all, the secret of success in war could not possibly consist in doing nothing. M'Clellan answered that he proposed, with the President's permission, to write him a paper on "The Present State of Military Affairs throughout the whole Country." "If," replied Lincoln sweetly, "it would not divert your time and attention from the army under your command, I should be glad to hear your views on the present state of military affairs throughout the whole country." But M'Clellan became intolerable when, instead of doing something with his magnificent army, he held it at anchor while he lectured Lincoln on politics. "If," said the President quietly, "General M'Clellan has no use for the Army of the Potomac, I should like to borrow it for a little while." M'Clellan was removed, none too soon; and, after many "misfits," the North found its great soldier at length in General Grant. When asked how *he* proposed to win, Grant answered, "By pegging away and wearing them down." "I need this man," commented Lincoln; "he fights."

So in time the tide turned. Reports of successes began to reach Washington in a fairly constant stream. And now the Union and its armies discovered that they idolized their President—this once misprized man, so modest, so tender of heart, so full of quaint stories and homely Western phrases. He became "Father Abraham" to them—father of this new America reborn out of bloodshed. They marched to the war-song, "We're coming, Father Abraham, three hundred thousand strong." They quoted his sayings around the camp fires. They loved while they laughed at his eccentricities. But as in three years—so one tells who saw him daily in Washington—a deep sadness had passed into his humorous face, so by little and little his people discovered their President's greatness, and that it went deeper than they had ever dreamed. A poet * has told us how, as a youth, he saw Lincoln on a visit to the " front " ride along the ranks amid his full-uniformed generals; and how, at the contrast between them and this ungainly rider in an ill-fitting black suit and stove-pipe hat, the ranks rippled with laughter; and how—

" The President turned and gazed, and understood
    All in one moment, slightly shook his head,
    Not warningly, but with a cheerful glee,
    And sympathy and love, as if he spoke :
    ' You scalawags, you scamps !—but have your fun ! '
    Pushed up his stove-pipe hat, and all around
    Bestowed his warming, right paternal smile,
    As if his soul embraced us all at once.

" Then strangely fell all laughter : some men choked,
    And some grew inarticulate with tears ;
    A thousand veteran children thrilled as one,
    And not a man in all the throng knew why ;
    Some called his name, some blessed his holy heart,
    And then, inspired with pentecostal tongues,
    We cheered so wildly for Old Father Abe
    That all the braided generals flamed in joy ! "

But perhaps the words he spoke over the cemetery of the dead who had fallen in the bloody battle of Gettysburg did more than any other utterance of his to convey the depth of human love out of which he had served his people. He said :—

" Fourscore and seven years ago our fathers brought forth on this continent a new nation, conceived in

* Edward William Thomson, *When Lincoln Died.*

liberty, and dedicated to the proposition that all men are created equal. Now we are engaged in a great civil war, testing whether that nation, or any nation so conceived and so dedicated, can long endure. We are met on a great battlefield of that war. We have come to dedicate a portion of that field as a final resting-place for those who have given their lives that that nation might live. It is altogether fitting and proper that we should do this.

" But, in a larger sense, we cannot dedicate, we cannot consecrate, we cannot hallow this ground. The brave men, living and dead, who struggled here have consecrated it far above our poor power to add or detract. The world will little note, nor long remember, what we say here, but it can never forget what they did here. It is for us, the living, rather to be dedicated here to the unfinished work which they who fought here have thus far so nobly advanced. It is rather for us to be here dedicated to the great task remaining before us—that from these honoured dead we take increased devotion to that cause for which they gave the last full measure of devotion ; that we here highly resolve that these dead shall not have died in vain ; that this nation, under God, shall have a new birth of freedom ; and that government of the people, by the people, for the people, shall not perish from the earth."

" Dedicated to the great task remaining before us." Lincoln's own share of the task was almost complete. On September 22nd, 1862, he had issued a proclamation declaring freedom to all slaves in bondage throughout the United States. This great deed was accomplished ; and now the war was dragging to its inevitable end, which came on April 7th, 1865, with General Lee's surrender to General Grant of the great army of North Virginia, numbering over 28,000 men. Lincoln, however, looked beyond these events. The task he had in mind was that which he thus described

in his second "inaugural" on March 4th of that
year :—

"With malice toward none, with charity for all,
with firmness in the right as God gives us to see the
right, let us finish the work we are in, to bind up the
nation's wounds."

For Lincoln had been re-elected President. There
was, indeed, no other possible man while he lived.
For his past he had deserved too well of his people to
push any claim. Grant had been mentioned ; Chase
had been mentioned. "If people think," said Lincoln,
"that General Grant can end the rebellion sooner by
being in this place, I shall be very glad to get out
of it." And again, "If Chase becomes President,
all right. I hope we may never have a worse man."
The egregious M'Clellan did actually stand, and was
overwhelmed.

So Lincoln entered on his second term of office.
Late on the night of April 9th the news of Lee's surrender reached Washington, and for days the city was
given up to rejoicing. On the night of the 14th it
had been arranged that the President should visit
the theatre. An announcement to this effect had
appeared in the newspapers ; a large audience had
gathered ; and, punctually enough, Lincoln, with his
wife and some friends, entered the box reserved for
him. At half-past ten o'clock, while all in the audi-
torium were intent on the play, a half-crazed actor,
John Wilkes Booth by name, opened the door at the
rear of the box, thrust a pistol close to the back of
Lincoln's head, and fired. The ball entered the brain,
and Lincoln fell forward. As the audience arose in
consternation the assassin leapt over the front of the
box to the stage, strode across it shouting, "*Sic semper
tyrannis*" ("So may it ever be with tyrants"—the
motto of Virginia), and darted away in the confusion.
At the back of the theatre he had a swift horse ready,
and for a while escaped, to be hunted down in a Mary-

land barn and shot like a dog. The murder proved to be part of a crazy but all too successful plot. At about the same moment another man broke into the house where Seward lay confined to his bed by an accident, and inflicted several frightful dagger wounds upon the invalid before he could be beaten off. He too was caught, and suffered death.

Lincoln, carried from the theatre to a private house across the road, lingered unconscious amid the ministrations of the doctors. He was past help ; and between seven and eight o'clock in the morning he breathed his last.

This story has been very imperfectly told if the reader cannot imagine something of the grief to which Washington awoke next morning ; or of the sense of desolation carried north, south, east, and west by the news that " Father Abraham " was dead. Thus, for example, we have it recorded by one then serving with the victorious troops of the North :—

" I happened myself, on the day of those sad tidings, to be with my division in a little village just outside of Goldborough, North Carolina. We had no telegraphic communication with the North, but were accustomed to receive dispatches about noon each day. . . . In the course of the morning I had gone to the shanty of an old darkie, for the purpose of getting a shave. The old fellow took up his razor, put it down again, and then again lifted it up ; but his arm was shaking, and I saw that he was so agitated that he was not fitted for the task. ' Massa,' he said, ' I can't shave yer this mornin'.' ' What is the matter ? ' I inquired. ' Well,' he replied, ' somethin's happened to Massa Linkum.' ' Why ! ' said I, ' nothing has happened to Lincoln. I know what there is to be known. What are you talking about ? ' ' Well,' the old man replied, with a half sob, ' we coloured folks— we get news, or we get half news sooner than you uns. I don't know jes' what it is, but somethin' has gone wrong with Massa Linkum.' I could get nothing more out of the old man, but I was sufficiently anxious to make my way to division headquarters, to see if there was any news in advance of the arrival of the regular courier. The coloured folks were standing in little groups along the village street, murmuring to each other, or waiting with anxious faces for the bad news that they were sure was coming. I found the brigade adjutant and those with him were puzzled like myself at the troubled minds of the darkies. . . . At noon the courier made his appearance, riding by the wood lane across the fields ; and the instant he was seen we all realized that there was bad news. The man was hurrying his pony, and yet seemed to be very unwilling to reach the lines. The division adjutant stepped out on the porch of the headquarters with the paper in his hand, but he broke down before he could begin to read. The division commander took the word, and was able simply to announce, ' Lincoln is dead.' . . . I never before had found myself in a mass of men overcome by emotion. Ten thousand soldiers were sobbing together. No survivor of the group can recall that morning without again being touched by the wave of emotion which broke down the control of those war-worn veterans on learning that their great captain was dead." *

Looking over the few splendid names on this Roll Call of Honour, I see none likely to outlast Lincoln's, as no man of them all gave his mind more singly to a purpose, or more largely loved mankind and forgave his enemies. He is surely of the greatest, by whatever standard we measure him. To call his end tragic is surely to miscall a life which achieved the end of its voyage, came home to port and dropped a sure anchor in the affections of all whose hearts beat in answer to nobility, to whatsoever nation belonging.

* *Abraham Lincoln*, by George Haven Putnam.

" O Captain ! my Captain ! our fearful trip is done ;
The ship has weathered every rack, the prize we sought
    is won ;
The port is near, the bells I hear, the people all exulting,
While follow eyes the steady keel, the vessel grim and
    daring.
            But, O heart ! heart ! heart !
              Oh the bleeding drops of red,
            Where on the deck my Captain lies,
              Fallen cold and dead !

" O Captain ! my Captain ! rise up and hear the bells ;
Rise up—for you the flag is flung, for you the bugle
    trills,
For you bouquets and ribboned wreaths, for you the
    shores a-crowding,
For you they call, the swaying mass, the eager faces
    turning :
            Here, Captain ! dear father !
              The arm beneath your head ;
            It is some dream that on the deck
              You've fallen cold and dead.

" My Captain does not answer, his lips are pale and still ;
My father does not feel my arm, he has no pulse nor
    will ;
The ship is anchored safe and sound, its voyage closed
    and done ;
From fearful trip the victor ship comes in with object
    won.
            Exult, O shores, and ring, O bells !
              But I, with mournful tread,
            Walk the deck my Captain lies,
              Fallen cold and dead.''

# GARIBALDI

GIUSEPPE (Joseph) GARIBALDI was born on July 4th,
1807, at Nice, of Italian parents—his father, Domenico
Garibaldi, being a merchant-skipper and owner of the
little coasting-vessel in which he traded. Nice in

those days belonged (as it now again belongs) to France, which had annexed it in 1792; but in 1814, upon the downfall of Napoleon, it was restored to the kingdom of Sardinia, which included Piedmont and Savoy. This happened when Giuseppe was seven years old, and his parents—good pious Conservatives, glad enough to be Italian subjects again, though in a tiny kingdom—did not bother their heads with politics, or vex themselves that the great bulk of what we now call Italy had at the same time fallen back to be partitioned anew among the various alien rulers from whose misgovernment Napoleon had for a time delivered it. In the north the hated Austrians held Lombardy and Venetia; in the south the equally hated Spanish Bourbons were back in Naples, from which they had been twice expelled, and were ruling their kingdom of the Two Sicilies with all the vindictiveness of a family which, as the saying went, "had learnt nothing and forgotten nothing"; while across the centre of Italy, from one sea to the other, stretched a government more abominable than either —that of the Pope and his cardinals, who kept the people in darkest ignorance, and maintained a spy system to mark out for persecution any man who dared to talk of liberty or to hold an opinion distasteful to the priesthood.

But Garibaldi's parents, occupied with their own struggle for a livelihood, had no time to waste on listening to Liberal doctrines, or on dreams of a *risorgimento*, or resurrection of United Italy, or on sympathies with their oppressed fellow-Italians in Lombardy, Naples, and the Papal States. They had enough to do to make two ends meet in their small house by the seashore; and for the rest had their hands full with an unruly, affectionate boy, who played truant from school to roam the mountains with a borrowed gun and game-bag, or to loaf about the harbour and gossip with the sailors, from whose com-

**GARIBALDI.**

*From a pen-drawing by*
*E. Heber Thompson.*

pany he could not be weaned. Domenico Garibaldi
was set on bringing up his son as a landsman; but
Giuseppe, like most healthy boys, had a craving for
the sea, and with the sea a stone's throw from the door,
ever calling him to rebel, Giuseppe, at the age of
fifteen, brought the quarrel to an issue.

"Tired of school, and bored with the prospect of a
stay-at-home life, I suggested one day to some companions of my own age that we should run away to
Genoa to seek our fortunes. No sooner said than
done: we seized a boat, got some provisions and
fishing-tackle aboard, and sailed off eastward. We
were already off Monaco, when a craft sent by my good
father overhauled us, and back we were taken. It
was humiliating. A priest had revealed our flight."

Garibaldi (it may have been from this day) detested
priests all his life. After this escapade the father very
wisely gave over their hopes of training him to be one;
and in 1822 he was shipped as a cabin-boy. An old
playmate writes thus of him:—

"Though Peppino (Giuseppe) was a bright, brave
lad, who planned all sorts of adventures, played
truant when he could get the loan of a gun or coax one
of the fishermen to take him on board, went oyster-
trawling, never missed the tunny festival at Villafranca or the sardine hauls at Limpia, he was often
thoughtful and silent, and when he had a book that
interested him he would lie under the olive trees for
hours reading, and then it was no use trying to make
him join any of our schemes for mischief. He had a
beautiful voice, and knew all the songs of the sailors
and peasants, and a good many French ones besides.
Even as a boy we all looked up to him and chose him
our umpire, while the little ones regarded him as their
natural protector. He was the strongest and most
enduring swimmer I ever knew, and a very fish in
water."

While working his way up from cabin-boy to

master he visited many ports—Odessa, Gibraltar, the Canaries, Constantinople. On his second voyage his father's *tartana*, coasting along Italy, touched at the mouth of the Tiber, and he was taken up to see Rome. The " Eternal City " seized upon the boy's imagination at once. He wrote later :—

" The Rome I beheld with my youthful imagination was the Rome of the future—the Rome that I, though shipwrecked, dying, banished to the farthest depths of the American forest, have never despaired of ; the regenerating idea of a great nation, the dominant thought and inspiration of my whole life. It was then that she grew dearer to me than anything else on earth. . . . For me Rome was Italy—the symbol of one united Italy."

But he does not appear to have guessed that others were dreaming like dreams and seeing like visions, until, in 1833 (being by this time a certified merchant-captain), he fell in at Taganrog with a young Genoese named Cuneo, who spoke to him of " Young Italy," an association of ardent patriots sworn to rouse the spirit of Italian liberty, and invited him to be one of them. " Columbus," he says, " can hardly have been so happy at discovering the New World as was I on finding a man actually concerned in the redemption of our country."

The impetuous sea-captain had no sooner returned from his voyage than he hurried off to Marseilles, where Giuseppe Mazzini, purest-hearted and loftiest of purpose among all the brotherhood of Young Italy, was then living in exile. " When I was a youth and had only aspirations towards good," said Garibaldi, thirty years later, " I sought for one able to act as my guide and counsellor. I sought such a guide as one who is athirst seeks the water-spring. I found this man. He alone watched when all around slept. He alone guarded and fed the sacred flame—Joseph Mazzini, my friend and teacher."

He arrived at a critical moment. Fired by the spirit of liberty just then sweeping over Europe like a flame at which all the monarchies trembled, the Young Italians were on the point of invading Savoy. It may seem curious that they should have chosen to direct their first efforts against the one surviving Italian monarchy instead of against the Austrians, or the Papal government, or the Bourbons of Naples. But against Charles Albert of Savoy, King of Sardinia and of Piedmont, they bore for the moment the deeper grudge, because they had hoped much of him, and he had disappointed them. He hated the Austrians, but his mind was enslaved by the priests, under whose influence he had committed great cruelties in the attempt to suppress all Liberal doctrines. In Piedmont, scarcely less than in the Papal States, a man risked his life by daring to think for himself. Clerical spies were everywhere. It had been a crime in Mazzini that " he walked by himself at night, absorbed in thought." The governor of Genoa, his native town, had complained of it. " We don't like young persons thinking unless we know the subject of their thoughts." Moreover, if it be asked what prospect of success these young patriots could have held out to themselves, the answer is that they had hopes of drawing over to their cause the veterans of the Piedmontese soldiery, who, having fought under Napoleon and helped to overthrow great thrones, had not forgotten the experience. " If in youth one has trampled on kings and monks from Lisbon to Moscow, one does not crouch to them readily in later years. Besides, many to whom Napoleon had opened the career had been degraded in rank after the restoration." *

The part assigned to Garibaldi in the rising was to go to Genoa and attempt to win over the malcontents

* G. M. Trevelyan, *Garibaldi's Defence of the Roman Republic* (Longmans, Green, and Co.).

in the fleet. But the malcontents declined to rise. Mazzini's invasion proved the merest fiasco, and on its miscarriage Garibaldi found himself at the place of rendezvous not only without support but surrounded by hostile soldiers. With great coolness he walked through the streets to the house of a woman, a fruit-seller, on whom he could rely, borrowed a peasant's dress, and escaped from Genoa to Nice and from Nice into France. On reaching Marseilles he read in a newspaper that he had been outlawed and condemned to be shot: it was " the first time he had the pleasure of seeing his name in print!" A reward was out for his arrest. He shipped himself as a seaman under the name of Giuseppe Pane, and for almost two years was lost to sight.* But the spies of King Charles Albert were vigilant; and at length, tired of dodging from port to port and hiding, in 1836 he sailed from Nantes for Rio de Janeiro.

Shortly after his arrival in South America the province of Rio Grande do Sul rose in rebellion against the Portuguese rule of Brazil and proclaimed itself an independent republic. Garibaldi happened to be on the wharf when some Italians, who had joined the insurgents and been taken prisoners, were landed in chains. Indignant at the sight of his countrymen in fetters for the sake of liberty, he promptly threw in his lot with the Republicans, armed a fishing-boat, and with twelve companions made his first essay in war as a privateer. His little craft, which he called the *Mazzini*, was the first to fly the flag of freedom off the Brazilian coast; but he soon exchanged her for a larger one which he captured. During those buccaneering years his name became a terror to the Brazilians, while his adventures would fill an epic. He was once shot down on deck, and lay for days at the point of death, in the intervals

---

* A part of this time he spent in the service of the Bey of Tunis, as captain of a frigate.

of delirium setting the course of the ship, for his men, who had beaten the enemy off, knew nothing of navigation. He was once taken prisoner by the governor of Gualeguay and hung up by his wrists to the beam of the prison ceiling, in which indescribable torture he was left for two hours. (Later in the war the fiendish governor, Leonardo Millan by name, fell into Garibaldi's hands, to be treated with noble clemency and released without a word of reproach.) Again, being shipwrecked in a hurricane on the coast of Santa Caterina, he saved himself by his notable powers of swimming, after vain efforts to save many dear Italian comrades, who sank before his eyes. Reaching the shore with a few half-naked survivors, he at once marched and took part in the storming of the port of Laguna, where a Brazilian fleet, at anchor in the lagoon, surrendered with the town. Garibaldi was promptly appointed to command it, and was put on board his flagship, the top-sail schooner *Itaparica*, of seven guns. Fortune had been kind to him ; but he paced the *Itaparica's* deck in no jubilant mood, for his heart yet ached over his drowned friends.

" The loss of Luigi, Edoardo, and others of my countrymen left me utterly isolated : I felt quite alone in the world. I needed a human heart to love me, one that I could keep always near me. I felt that unless I found one immediately life would become intolerable. . . . By chance I cast my eyes towards the houses of the Barra, a tolerably high hill on the south side of the entrance to the lagoon, where a few single and picturesque dwellings were visible. Outside one of these, by means of a telescope I usually carried with me when on deck, I espied a young woman, and forthwith gave orders for the boat to be lowered, as I wished to go ashore.

" I landed, and making for the houses where I expected to find the object of my excursion, I had just given up hope of seeing her again, when I met an inhabitant of the place, an acquaintance, who invited me into his house to take coffee. We entered, and the first person who met my eyes was the damsel. . . . We both remained enraptured in silence, gazing on one another like two people who meet not for the first time, and seek in each other's face something which makes it easier to recall the forgotten past. At last I greeted her by saying, ' *Tu devi esser mia* ' ('Thou oughtest to be mine'). I could speak but little Portuguese, and uttered the bold words in Italian. Yet my insolence was magnetic. I had formed a tie, pronounced a decree which death alone could annul."

The damsel, Anita Riberas, had been promised by her father to a suitor she could not love. " She, a woman most direct and valiant—highly strung, too, by the prospect of the forced marriage that awaited her—suddenly saw face to face the hero of her time and country "—for already Garibaldi's deeds had won him so much fame—" with his lion-like head and flowing mane of gold, come as her deliverer, armed with the irresistible might of his will." * Under that spell she then and there gave him a love which endured until the day when, it may be truly said, she gave also her life for him. Her other suitor proving obstinate, Garibaldi boldly carried her off to his ship. They were married later at Monte Video, and the story of their ten years of married love is one " which none of the world's famous legends of love surpasses in romance and beauty." They sailed away to spend their long honeymoon in the wildest adventures by sea and land. In her first sea-fight Anita was struck down on deck by the wind of a cannon ball, across

* Trevelyan, who quotes Martinengo Cesaresco : " Probably a human face so leonine, and yet retaining the humanity nearest the image of its Maker, was never seen." Garibaldi had a superbly fine presence.

the bodies of three dead men ; but as her husband rushed to her she picked herself up and coolly reloaded her gun.   She was a brilliant horsewoman too, and when Garibaldi left the sea to command the insurgents' guerilla bands on the uplands of Southern Brazil and Uruguay, the married lovers rode side by side for days together on their stallions of the pampas, fierce and fond as mated eagles, feeding on flesh they roasted on green spits, sleeping on the hard earth under the stars.   Sometimes a few score of cavalry rode with them, sometimes a few thousand ; and the fame of Garibaldi the guerilla chief grew and eclipsed that of Garibaldi the buccaneer.   They fought on a losing side ; but what did that count ?   Once in battle Anita's horse was killed under her, and she was made prisoner.   At the close of the battle news came that her husband was slain.   With an escort they allowed her to search for him ; but she found only his mantle, for he was far away with the retreating army.   Slipping into the darkness from among her drunken guards, she found a high-spirited horse, and plunged in pursuit through jungle and forest, and alone, with no food but wild berries, sought after her husband for four days, crossing the most desolate plains, swimming through rivers in flood, stampeding in the hill passes the enemy's pickets—who took her for a ghost—and finally overtook her husband, who had given her up for dead.   Again, but twelve days after giving birth to her first-born son Menotti, she took to the wilderness with her husband, riding through the depths of the forest in the worst of the rainy season, feeding on what roots they could dig from the ground.   Usually she carried the infant at her saddle-bow ; but when the fords were deep Garibaldi carried him, as he writes, " slung from my neck in a handkerchief, trying to keep him warm against my breast and with my breath."

At length, despairing of a war in which he held

but a subordinate command, Garibaldi resigned his
service in the army of the Rio Grande and retired
to Monte Video, the capital of Uruguay; yet not to
enjoy peace, for Uruguay being threatened just then
by the rival republic of Argentina, he was induced
to accept the command of the small Uruguayan
squadron, and, on top of this, set about forming his
famous " Italian Legion." Monte Video contained
a large number of Italians, the most of them exiles
for the sake of liberty. Of these, with what additional material he could find among the flotsam and
jetsam of the port—needy adventurers, men broken
in fortune, shipwrecks of life—he formed his famous
corps. Its colours were " a black flag with a volcano
in the midst—symbol of Italy mourning, with the
sacred fire in her heart ; " and the one uniform part
of their dress was the " red shirt," afterwards made
historical on Italian battlefields. " I would not,"
said Garibaldi, after training and proving his men,
" exchange the title of Italian Legionary for all the
gold in the world." And he had cause to be proud,
for the Italian Legion saved Monte Video in battle
after battle, and crowned themselves with glory by
winning, against overwhelming odds, the battle of
Sant' Antonio, the fame of which spread to Europe
and to Italy, where the patriots now had need of
him.

For it was now 1848, and after twelve years of
disheartenment they saw the star of Liberty once
again in the ascendant over Europe. France had
proclaimed a republic ; Sicily had risen in revolt, and
for the while with success, against King Ferdinand ;
the Milanese had risen, and had driven the Austrians
from their city ; Venice had regained her liberties ;
and now the Austrian commander, Radetzky, stood
at bay in the famous " Quadrilateral "—the four
great fortresses of Mantua, Legnago, Peschiera, and
Verona—guarding the north of the Brenner Pass,

over which alone Austria could pour her troops south-ward across the Alps into Lombardy. But north of them the empire of Austria-Hungary seemed to be rent by internal dissensions, and on the point of falling to pieces; and King Charles Albert, remembering his patriotism, now saw a chance of driving the invaders from Italian soil. Best of all, a liberal Pope, Pio Nono, had mounted the throne of St. Peter, and was earning by his reforms the wildest gratitude of the people, who hailed him as the future deliverer of his country.

Garibaldi as yet knew nothing of these events, for they happened whilst he was on shipboard, crossing the Atlantic in the brigantine *Speranza*, with a few devoted comrades and some eighty men of his fight-ing legion. He only knew that Charles Albert, the king who had signed his death-warrant twelve years before, probably needed his help on the Lombard plain; and on this chance he sailed, having sent home Anita and the children by an earlier vessel. So these exiles returned across the ocean, and each eventide saw them gathered on the deck, bare-headed, chanting patriotic songs, as they drew nearer to the attainment of the passion and desire of their lives. The good news met them at sea from a passing ship, when they were already past the Strait of Gibraltar. They shaped their course for Santa Pola, where the tidings were confirmed. " Make all sail ! " cried the men. In a flash the anchor was weighed and the brigantine put under full canvas for Nice. Garibaldi hauled down the flag of Monte Video, and hoisted a tricolor, patched together out of a bed-sheet, a red scarf, and some green regimental facings. Under this flag he sailed into his native port on June 21st, 1848, and was rapturously welcomed by the populace. Anita, too, was there to meet him, with the little ones, having crossed the seas in safety. But Garibaldi could hardly stay to provide for them. Proceeding to the front, he arrived on July 3rd at Roverbella, the royal headquarters, and loyally offered his sword to Charles Albert. The king, however, received him coldly, and thinking perhaps that such a reception was good enough for an ex-traitor, referred him to Ricci, the Minister of War, who rejected his services for Piedmont, and advised him to go and make himself useful to the Venetians at his old trade of corsair. Insulted and hurt, Garibaldi went off to Milan, where the provisional government accepted his services, and sent him to Bergamo with a handful of badly-clothed, half-armed men. In a few days 3,000 volunteers had rallied to him. But his hour of victory was not yet ; for by July the 25th the bad generalship of Charles Albert had brought disaster on the main army at Custoza, and the unfortunate king, falling back upon Milan, was forced to surrender that city back to the Austrians. Little wonder that the citizens who five months before, unaided, by five days of heroic street fighting had driven these same enemies out, accused him of having betrayed the national cause ! The accusation was unjust, but as the Pope too had disappointed their hopes by publicly declaring that the idea of waging war against Austria was " far from his thoughts," the curses of the patriots upon Charles Albert and Pio Nono were deep and bitter. Most bitterly disgusted of all was Garibaldi, who had crossed the seas to fight for the cause, and had found so cruel a disillusionment. In his wrath he refused to acknowledge the armistice signed with the Austrians, and raising a banner inscribed with " *Dio e Popolo* " (God and the People), for three weeks waged a brilliant private campaign against Austria at the foot of the Alps. It was a protest rather than a serious war ; but before the heavy Austrian battalions drove him back he had planted in the hearts of his countrymen a conviction destined to bear fruit—that the cause of Italy was a " people's cause," not one of popes or of kings ; and, moreover, by his guerilla exploits had taught them where to look in due time for a soldier to champion that cause.

Struck down by fever, he disbanded his force, and returned to Nice.   But he had no intention of resting. The fever had scarcely left him when he set forth on the " People's War," making at first for Sicily, but altering his course and landing at Leghorn to march into the Romagna ; for the Austrians again were threatening.   On the frontier he was stopped by order of Rossi, the Papal minister, a capable man, who had no desire to admit such a firebrand as Garibaldi to inflame men's minds against the government. As a compromise, Garibaldi—though indignant at the check, for he had come as a friend—consented to turn aside through the Romagna to Ravenna and take ship for Venice, which was barely holding out against the Austrian troops.   But at Ravenna news reached him from Rome that the whole situation there had been changed by the stroke of a dagger.   The minister Rossi had been assassinated on November 15th ; and Pope Pio Nono, execrated by the populace and fearing for his own life, had fled away to Gaeta on the 24th, disguised as a peasant.

At once the Republican leaders flocked into Rome ; the Garibaldians, now 500 strong, crossed the Apennines in the teeth of snowstorms, and marched down through Umbria towards the imperial city, spreading the gospel of liberty among the towns and villages on their way.   Liberty, though but for a brief while, was at hand.   Since the Pope, with the obstinacy of a weak man, refused to treat with his rebellious subjects, and since some form of government was necessary, a Constituent Assembly met in Rome in the first week of February ;  and on February 8th a Roman republic was proclaimed, with Mazzini as chief of a triumvirate at its head.   The great patriot had never any illusions about the almost desperate chance of saving Rome from the foes which would soon and swiftly be gathering together against her. " We must act," said he, " like men who have the enemy at their gates, and at the same time like men who are working for eternity." His rule was firm, placable, liberal; he dispensed with bribery and espionage; he would have no revenge upon ancient enemies; he held the scales of justice level. But neither justice nor clemency could avert the fate he foresaw. It was hastened by the smashing defeat of Charles Albert at Novara, on March the 23rd, at the hands of Radetzky. The poor king, who had learnt his liberalism too late, vainly sought death in the battle. He had marched to it with his ears haunted by the cries he had heard in Milan, the cursings of a people he had been incompetent to deliver from slavery; he rode from the field a broken man, abdicated in favour of his son Victor Emmanuel, and, retiring to a Portuguese cloister, died within a short while of a broken heart. The young king managed to save Piedmont by persuading France to forbid the Austrian onrush; but his preservation was won at the expense of Rome, against which all the Catholic countries now united to restore the Pope—Austria marching from the north, Ferdinand of Napies from the south, while even Spain joined the crusade to extinguish the young republic. But it was France—France, the friend of liberty—which by the evil counsels of Louis Napoleon, and under the hypocritical excuse of delivering Rome from " foreigners "—such " foreigners " as Mazzini and Garibaldi—that struck a blow at her heart. Though France was afterwards to render invaluable help to the cause of Italian unity, it may be said that her crime in restoring the Papal States to the hateful rule of the clericals started her on that career of repressing liberty, abroad and at home, by which she was led straight downhill through the Second Empire to the final disaster of Sedan.

Scarcely less odious than her excuse for interference was the stratagem by which General Oudinot landed her 8,000 to 10,000 troops, as friends of the Roman people, at Civita Vecchia, some forty miles from the capital.   Rome soon proved what she thought of such friends by arming herself against them, and preparing to resist to the death.   Garibaldi, who had marched south to oppose King " Bomba," * was recalled to meet this nearer peril.   Mazzini, knowing that he must be crushed, resolved to be crushed heroically amid the ruins of the Eternal City, leaving the world an object-lesson that it would never forget.

But it was Garibaldi who, although not in chief command, put heart and soul into the defence, his red-shirted legion fighting emulously side by side with the gallant Lombard Bessaglieri, that famous regiment of which the dark uniform and broad-brimmed hat plumed with green cock feathers remain to this day a symbol in the eyes of all Europe of the army of the Italian king.   Since victory in the end was hopeless, it is idle to discuss whether the triumvirs would have done more wisely to appoint Garibaldi commander-in-chief instead of leaving him in a subordinate post.   He himself wrote to his old friend from whom a sharp quarrel or two had begun to estrange him :—

" MAZZINI,—Since you ask me what I wish, I will tell you.   Here I cannot avail anything for the good of the republic save in one of two ways—as dictator, with full and unlimited powers, or as a simple soldier.   Choose.
" Unchangingly yours,
" GIUSEPPE GARIBALDI."

Certain it is that when in their first assault on the city the French were repulsed with heavy losses,

---

* " Bomba " (shell) was the nickname given to Ferdinand II. of Naples, after a cruel bombardment of his subjects in Messina, where he impartially slaughtered men, women, and children.   It also alluded slyly to his figure, which was fat and round.

Garibaldi offered to pursue and drive them back "to their ships or into the sea," and could never quite forgive Mazzini that he was not allowed to follow up the victory. But he fought magnificently day after day, as the French gathered reinforcements and closed upon the doomed walls. Here let an eye-witness describe the man "whose name every one in Rome knew, and in whom many people had already placed their hopes."

"Of middle height, broad-shouldered—his square chest, which gives a sense of power to his structure, well marked under the uniform—he stood there before us ; his blue eyes, ranging to violet, surveyed in one glance the whole group. . . . Those eyes had something remarkable, as well by the colour as by the frankness—I know no better word for it—of their expression. His face was burnt red and covered with freckles. A heavy moustache and a light blonde beard ending in two points gave a martial expression to that open oval face. But most striking of all was the nose, with its exceedingly broad root, which has caused Garibaldi to be given the name of "Leone," and, indeed, made one think of a lion ; a resemblance which, according to his soldiers, was still more con-spicuous in the fight, when his eyes shot forth flames, and his fair hair waved as a mane above his temples.

"He was dressed in a red tunic with short flaps ; on his head he wore a little black felt sugar-loaf hat with two black ostrich feathers. In his left hand he had a light, plain horseman's sabre, and a cavalry cartridge-bag hung down by his left shoulder."

By his side in those days rode always a splendid negro, Aguyar, a giant of a man, who had followed his adored chief across the Atlantic. In the final desperate fight, when the French by sheer weight of numbers broke in through the suburbs, this faithful black was killed by a shell, while his master raged through the streets and gardens under a hail of bullets. In these last days of the siege Garibaldi ardently desired to die, for despair was in his heart, and bitterness that he should still be living when so many of his dearest comrades had fallen. On the terraces of the villa where his headquarters were he habitually and designedly exposed himself to the French marksmen. Yet he seemed to carry a charm against their bullets, while on three successive days officers whom he had invited to dine with him were killed where they sat. " God covered me with the shadow of His hand."

In the end he flung himself at the head of two companies and marched straight upon death, chanting an Italian hymn. " At that moment I confess I had but one desire—to get myself killed. I threw myself with my men upon the French. . . . What happened then ? I know nothing about it. For two hours I struck without intermission. When the day dawned I was all covered with blood. I had not a single scratch." Later in the morning, while he still fought on, word was brought to him that the Assembly had met in the Capitol and urgently desired his presence. He mounted, galloped across the Tiber in haste, and entered the Assembly just as he was, his face a-sweat, his shirt clotted with dust and blood, his sword so bent that he could not force it more than half-way into his scabbard. Three propositions divided the Assembly—to surrender, to die fighting in the streets, or to escape to the mountains, taking with them what was left of government and army. Garibaldi was all for this third course. Surrender he would not discuss ; to die like rats in a sewer was useless folly. " Wherever we go, there Rome will be," he said ; and so it proved, though for many a day Rome was but the Rome a few exiles carried in their hearts. Having made his speech, Garibaldi mounted again and galloped back to the Janiculum. The Assembly in his absence voted for surrender, Mazzini vehemently refusing to participate in it, and be " the executioner of Rome's honour." Declining any protection, this noble triumvir made his way out through the ruined city, escaped to Civita Vecchia, thence on shipboard to France, and so into Switzerland, to build up afresh from the broken foundations his dream of a united Italy, with Rome for its capital. As for Garibaldi, hastily calling his troops together, he proposed to them to quit Rome and march into the wilderness. " I offer you," he said, " new battles and fresh glory. I can give you no pay, no rest, and food will have to be eaten when it can be found. Whosoever shrinks from these conditions, let him remain and surrender." Five thousand men swore to follow him.

On the evening of July the 2nd, as the French were preparing to enter the city, this brave little army filed out through the Tivoli gate, not knowing whither. Beside Garibaldi rode Anita, his wife, dressed in the garb of a man ; with Ugo Bassi, ex-priest and dear friend, soon to be martyred by the Austrians. It was the " wildest and most romantic of all Garibaldi's marches," as also the most disastrous. They had scarcely passed out into the night before a flying column of French, Austrians, and Neapolitans was in pursuit. The patriots marched in silence, at the limit of their speed, across the Campagna. They reached Tivoli at seven in the morning, and after a brief bivouac took to the bypaths of the mountains, across which, with hostile armies on all sides, they made their incredible way, by tracks never trodden except by the goatherds, and by stratagems unknown save to that peculiar art of warfare which their leader had learnt in the South American wilds. " In Tuscany and in the Papal States alone there were some 30,000 French, 12,000 Neapolitans, 6,000 Austrians, and 2,000 Tuscans, who had no other enemy to contend with, and no other operation in hand but the chase of Garibaldi." " Hunger, thirst, forced marches, battle, and death "

—these and no better he had promised. Every night scores of men deserted to the enemy tracking him ; but still he eluded pursuit, and brought the remnant down through the eastward gates of the Apennines to the little " free " republic of San Marino. The Austrians, however, made no account of the freedom of any people that happened to be weak, and the Austrian general, Gorzkowski, surrounding the town, promised to sack it unless the Garibaldians were given up. To Garibaldi, on condition of surrender, he promised a free passage to America. The message was torn up. " I make no terms for my own life with him whose heel is on Italy," was the hero's comment ; but he released his followers from their vow, and 900 surrendered, most of them to learn in prison the worth of an Austrian promise.

Two hundred faithful ones followed their chief, on whose head a price was now set, with a threat of death against any who fed, helped, or harboured him. They reached the coast at Cesenatico, and seizing thirteen *bragozzi*, or fishing-boats, put out to sea, amid squalls of wind, shaping their course for Venice. The next night was fine, with a clear moon—fatally fine for them. They were sighted by an Austrian squadron which lay off the point of Goro, and pursued by pinnaces and longboats. Nine of the *bragozzi*, with 162 Garibaldians on board, had been captured or sunk ; with the remaining four Garibaldi reached land, and leaping out into the surf waded ashore with Anita in his arms. Throughout the march she had been fast breaking down in health, and at the embarkation had been carried on board on a litter. Her husband saw too plainly that she was dying. Bidding the rest of his boat's crew to disperse and hide as best they might, he with one devoted friend, Captain Culiolo, commonly called Leggiero, and his dear burden plunged off among the sandy dunes and reedy marshes that lined the desolate coast. The place of landing was a strip of land three miles wide by three long, extending between the sea and an inland lagoon; and very soon, as the Austrian longboats came to shore in pursuit, the whole line of coast swarmed with sailors and marines hunting down their prey. Nine of the Garibaldians—a father and two sons, one aged thirteen, a Genoese priest, and five other patriots— were captured together. "Dig nine graves," commanded the Austrian captain. The graves were easily dug in the sandy soil, and the nine shot and flung into them. Ugo Bassi, too, was taken and shot, after barbarous treatment. But Garibaldi, staggering along with Anita, and followed by the limping Leggiero—who had a gunshot in the leg—mercifully fell in with a friendly peasant, a beachcomber, who hid them, and ferried them by night over the still waters of the lagoon. Anita had ceased to moan for water where none but bitter marsh-water was to be had. She lay on her husband's breast, breathing painfully, conscious only of his presence. They landed, and carried her on a mattress to a small dairy farm—a lonely house, with the reeds of the marsh land growing almost to its door. She died as they bore her across the threshold. "I strove to detain her with me; I sought to catch her feeble breathing; but I pressed the hand and kissed the lips of the dead, and wept the tears of despair." A small crowd of peasants gathered outside the house whispered to one another that this man within was indeed the great Garibaldi; but he went out and passed through them, seeing nothing, and "there was not found among them one who would sell Italy for gold." He could not stay to bury Anita, lest his presence should endanger the good people of the house. When they bore out her body, to bury it in a sandy grave among the pine woods by the sea, he and Leggiero were already some distance on their way.

And on what a journey! It led them back, right

across the breadth of Italy, from the mouths of the Po to a little bay on the Tuscan Maremma.    For almost forty days they wandered in various disguises among the Apennines, descending at length to the Maremma for a last rush to the coast.    Secret word had reached the Tuscan patriots, and in the Cala Martina, a small bay opposite Elba, a fishing-boat lay ready.    At ten o'clock in the morning of September the 2nd, Garibaldi and Leggiero stepped on board, and as the little craft made sail, the chief, standing erect in the stern sheets, called back to the group on the shore the indomitable cry, " Viva l'Italia ! "

Truly a wonderful man, to lift this cry in Italy's darkest hour and his own !  Never had the hope of Italy as a nation sunk nearer to extinction ; while for himself the light of his life had gone out with Anita's last breath.    All his political hopes, ideals, dreams, were a shattered heap, and the great nations so hated his name that when he arrived at Nice, to visit his motherless children, the government of Victor Emmanuel, in fear of the wrath of Europe, hurriedly bundled him out of the country.   He sailed for Tunis. Tunis, at the dictation of France, refused him asylum. He sailed for Gibraltar :  the English governor ordered him to move on.   He sailed for America, and cheerfully earned his living there for a while as a candlemaker.    " Date tempo al tempo " (" Give time to time "), he said.

In 1851 he left New York for Nicaragua, and from Nicaragua made his way to Lima, where he obtained the command of an old sailing-ship, the Carmen, bound with a cargo for China, and made a prosperous year's voyage, returning by way of South Australasia.    In 1853 he sailed the Carmen around Cape Horn to New York.    In 1854 he returned to Europe as master of the Commonwealth (1,200 tons), bound for Newcastle, whence he sailed with a cargo of coal for Genoa.    From Genoa he hastened to Nice, to embrace

his children after five years of separation ; and at
Nice for a while he settled down to live with them,
having saved a little money from his voyages. By-
and-by, however, he purchased a small property,
the northern half of the island of Caprera, off the
Sardinian coast ; and there he dwelt in extreme sim-
plicity, tending his goats, tilling the soil, teaching his
orphaned children to read. He had a great love of
the rocky coast, and desired, as he told his friends, to
live out his days in this solitude until the call should
come for him, or—should it never come—until the
end.

"Give time to time." The call came in 1859. A
great statesman, Cavour, had arisen in Turin to advise King Victor Emmanuel ; a subtle-minded man,
who saw that if ever Italy was to win her independence it must be stolen, so to speak, out of the conflict of nations stronger than herself. This conflict,
always with an eye to Italy's ultimate gain, he set
himself to provoke. To this end, even against the
wishes of Victor Emmanuel and the Piedmontese, he
deliberately courted the friendship of France ; and
having obtained from Louis Napoleon, now Emperor
of the French, a promise of help, goaded Austria
by open insults into an unwise declaration of war.
Garibaldi, summoned to Turin, at once promised his
help. He had no love for Cavour, whose tortuous
methods he detested, in so far as his own simple mind
could follow them. But Italy needed his sword, and
he used it gloriously at the head of his own little army
of 5,000 volunteers, called the " Hunters of the Alps."
" This time we shall do it," he said. " I have been
satisfied in high places." The forces of Piedmont
numbered but 75,000, all told ; whereas Austria put
200,000 in the field. But the French army of 160,000
coming to the rescue decided the campaign in the two
great battles of Magenta and Solferino. Then in the
midst of the patriot's triumphant rejoicings came an

announcement from Napoleon, that "the idea of uniting Italy into one state is not to be entertained!" The emperor, in fact, had no mind to plant a new and strong nation on his borders. He proposed a truce with the defeated Austrians, and he and the Austrian emperor, meeting at Villafranca, concluded a peace in which Piedmont was largely ignored. Cavour and Garibaldi were alike mad with indignation. Victor Emmanuel alone kept his head, and counselling patience so won over his minister that, when Napoleon demanded Nice—Garibaldi's own Nice—in payment for his friendly services, the cession was not resisted. To the end of his days Garibaldi never forgave Cavour for this betrayal.

But the time was now come for him to strike the great blow, and in defiance of all kings and intriguers. In the madness following Villafranca the patriots of Sicily had risen desperately against Ferdinand's rule. "Come and help us!" they sent word. Garibaldi resolved to go. Cavour, getting wind of his intention, would have stopped him; but Victor Emmanuel was wiser. "Let him go. We will not help: openly we will know nothing about this wild folly; but so long as we keep clear of complicity he will do our cause no harm, and it is possible that some advantage may come of it." So Garibaldi went with just 1,000 men —the "Thousand" who live in history now with the men of Marathon and of Thermopylæ.

On the night of May 5th, 1860, having packed arms, ammunition, and stores in a small flotilla of boats, Garibaldi embarked from the shores below the Villa Spinola, at Genoa. Two boats had already pushed off, and quietly seized two merchant steamers in the harbour, the *Piemonte* and the *Lombardo*, easily overpowering the sleepy crews and persuading them to join the expedition. On the shore a large crowd was gathered in the darkness, and whispered as the garden gate of the Villa Spinola opened and the hero stepped down to the spit of rock, garbed in the dress he never afterwards abandoned, even for functions of state— loose grey trousers, the red shirt, a bright silk hand-kerchief knotted at his throat, on his head a black felt hat, in his hand a heavy cavalry sword. He was rowed off to the *Piemonte* under a night brilliant with stars.

" O night of the 5th of May, lit up with the fire of a thousand lamps wherewith the Omnipotent has adorned the Infinite ! Beautiful, tranquil, solemn with that solemnity which swells the hearts of gener-ous men when they go forth to free the slave ! Such were the Thousand ; and I, proud of their trust in me, felt myself capable of attempting anything."

Cases of arms and of stores were tumbled on board pell-mell. The engineers hastened to get up steam ; but with all their haste it was almost morning, and the peasant-girls had long been passing along the high-road to market, before the two steamers passed out of the harbour, and headed southward. Their chief, before starting, had left this letter for King Victor Emmanuel :—

" I embark on a perilous enterprise ; but I put confidence in God and in the courage and devotion of my companions. If I fail, I trust Italy and liberal Europe will not forget that it was undertaken from motives free from all egoism and entirely patriotic. If we achieve it, I shall be proud to add to your Majesty's crown a new and brilliant jewel—always on condition that your Majesty will stand opposed to counsellors who would cede their province to the foreigner, as has been done with my native city."

The two steamers arrived at Marsala, in Sicily, after dodging a Neapolitan squadron which lay in waiting off the coast. The presence of two English men-of-war in the harbour (England being known to sympa-thize with Italy's hopes for freedom) prevented the Bourbon governor from opening an artillery fire on the boats, and the landing was easily effected. The inhabitants welcomed Garibaldi as their saviour, and the municipal council proclaimed him dictator of the island, a title he accepted in the name of Victor Emmanuel. At dawn his little army, which grew to 12,000 as it went, started on its march to Palermo, and on the 15th fought its first set battle, storming the terraced hillside of Catalafimi, and driving the Neapolitan troops from the heights. At midnight on the 26th, after feinting and deceiving the enemy in Palermo by an exceedingly clever counter-march, the Garibaldians poured down on that city over the Pass of Gibilrossa, crept through the dark suburbs, and storming a barrier at the Terminus Gate, poured into the heart of the town. After three days of street fighting Palermo was theirs, and the Neapolitan general Lanza capitulated, with more than 20,000 regulars! After Palermo, town after town surrendered—not without hard fighting—until the island was Garibaldi's from west to east; and he halted his weary troops before crossing the Strait of Messina and attacking the enemy on the mainland of Italy.

Cavour would have hindered his pushing farther, and Victor Emmanuel, too, attempted to forbid his crossing over to Calabria. But Garibaldi had had enough of kings and their counsellors, and refused to listen. Landing at Melito, he forced fortress after fortress, capturing stores and ammunition in vast quantities. As he drew near to the capital, shepherding Ferdinand's troops before him, almost without firing a shot, the king and court took fright and fled to Capua; and on September the 7th, scarcely four months after his landing in Sicily, Garibaldi rode in triumph into Naples. On that day fell the detestable dynasty which Gladstone, after visiting its dreadful prisons, had not hesitated to denounce to Europe as " the curse of God." At three o'clock in the afternoon Garibaldi, true to his word, handed over

Naples, with its fleet and arsenal, to Admiral Persano, as the representative of King Victor Emmanuel, now in promise " King of Italy," as he was soon to become in fact, and the delivered populace met its deliverer in the cathedral to chant together the *Te Deum*.

It is painful to have to tell in what spirit Victor Emmanuel received Garibaldi's royal gift. Still influenced by the unfriendly Cavour, he issued a proclamation that he was coming " to restore order "—that, and that only, without a word of thanks. When he arrived, after Garibaldi had almost completed the campaign, and when the hero crossed the Volturno to meet him, leading his volunteers in the shout, " Hail, King of Italy ! ", Victor Emmanuel received him coldly, and would not invite his company. " Your troops must be weary ; mine are fresh," he said, and presently parted and rode off. The war-worn Garibaldians, who had witnessed the slight put upon their adored leader, were furious, and ready in their passion to revolt. " No, no," said Garibaldi. " Trust me. I shall do what is best." In the end the king's better nature prevailed, and he invited Garibaldi to ride by his side as he entered Naples with trumpets blowing and banners waving.

These rejoicings over, Garibaldi proudly retired to his farm at Caprera, having declined all honours and rewards—the title of Prince of Catalafimi, the rank of marshal, the Grand Cross of the Annunciata, a pension of 500,000 francs, etc. His one request to Victor Emmanuel was that his Thousand should not be forgotten and left to poverty. As he said good-bye to these men, who by courage and simple trust in him had shaken thrones, as they crowded around him, weeping and sobbing, his voice shook. " Thanks, my old brothers-in-arms ! You have done much with scant means in scant time. But more is yet to do. Farewell ! "

The war, with its struggle for the final deliverance

of the Papal States, had now passed over into the hands of Victor Emmanuel and Cavour, and in the end they harvested where Garibaldi had sown. In that war he was, after all, summoned to bear his part. But of the campaign which ended at Aspromonte and his subsequent fighting—always on the side of liberty—these pages have no room to tell. He lived to see the desire of his life accomplished when, in 1871, Victor Emmanuel rode into Rome, the King of United Italy into his capital. So the kingdom our great soldier had founded with his poor thousand followers was finally set erect in the city he had desperately defended in 1849.

He died, at the age of seventy-five, in his chamber at Caprera, with his window open and his eyes fixed on the sea. No man ever devoted a life more nobly to a single cause ; no knight-errant of modern times has more superbly proved that these are still the days of chivalry.

# DAVID LIVINGSTONE

DAVID LIVINGSTONE was born on March 19th, 1813, at Blantyre on the Clyde, above Glasgow. His father, Neil Livingstone, had migrated as a boy from the home of the family, a small farmstead on the island of Ulva, and crossing to Lanarkshire, became apprentice to a cloth-maker, Hunter by name, whose daughter Agnes he married in 1810, after the way of good apprentices. David was their second son. His grandfather Hunter was a great reader, with a never-ending stock of Scottish stories and legends, "many of which were wonderfully like those I have since heard while sitting by the African evening fires. The grandmother, too, used to sing Gaelic songs, some of which, as she believed, had been composed by captive Highlanders languishing among the Turks." The child quickly learned to read, and fastened eagerly, among his grandfather's books, upon the missionary Campbell's *Travels among the Hottentots*. These set him wandering along the banks of Clyde, playing at explorers with boys of his age, and it is recorded that on one of these expeditions David not only climbed higher up the ruins of Bothwell Castle than any of his companions, but carved his name aloft there. He was a strong and a willing youngster, and would scrub the floor for his mother, always on condition that she kept the door shut, lest the youth of Blantyre should spy him at the unmanly work.

The household was very poor, and at ten David went into the cotton-mills as a " piecer," working from six in the morning till eight at night. At eight o'clock he turned to his Latin—he had bought a small Latin grammar out of his first week's wages—and would read until midnight or until his mother took away the candle. Latin led him on to science (botany and some geology), and on the Saturday half-holidays, or when a flood stopped the mills, he and his brothers would scour the countryside for fossils, or for medicinal plants mentioned in Culpeper's *Herbal*. On these half-holidays, too, he learned to become an expert swimmer, and once at least poached a salmon. Brother Charles that day happened to be wearing an extra baggy pair of the family trousers, in a leg of which the fish was smuggled home. Their father read them a lecture on the sinfulness of taking salmon ; after which their mother broiled this one for supper.

Even while at work in the factory David managed to get through no small amount of study by fixing his book open upon the spinning-jenny so that his eye could catch the sentences as he passed to and fro. At nineteen he was promoted to be a spinner, and the better wage allowed him to attend the medical and other classes at Glasgow University, walking to and from his father's house, a distance of about nine miles. The lad, though willing enough to go to chapel, had conceived a dislike of " pious " literature, and resolutely preferred books of science and travel—a taste of which his father sternly endeavoured to cure him. " My difference of opinion reached the point of open rebellion, and his last application of the rod was when I refused to read Wilberforce's *Practical Christianity*." Being thereafter more wisely let alone, this dislike of religious reading conquered itself in time. The boy, in fact, was essentially religious all the while. At sixteen he had been so deeply moved by the story of Charles Gutzlaff, the medical missionary to China, that he resolved at first to give all his pocket-money to the missions. He was resolved to qualify himself and devote his life to this work. He consulted with friends, and they advised him to join the London Missionary Society, which, avoiding all differences of sect, sought only to carry the gospel of Christ to the heathen. He applied, and was summoned to London, where he arrived on September 1st, 1838, to be examined by the Mission Board. At the office he met Joseph Moore, a youth who had come from the west of England fired with a similar noble ambition, and afterwards became a missionary in Tahiti. The two lads made friends at once. Neither had been in London before, and they began their sight-seeing together with a visit to Westminster Abbey. So far as is known, Livingstone never again entered the Abbey alive ; yet he was to enter it once again—how, this story will tell.

Being accepted on trial, Livingstone and Moore were sent to Chipping Ongar in Essex for their " probation," a part of which consisted in preparing sermons and preaching them without manuscript to the village congregation—which thus, in its own way, suffered for the cause of the heathen. At his first trial Livingstone gave out his text—and paused.

The sermon had vanished. " Friends," he stammered, " I have forgotten all I had to say," and fled from the pulpit. This breakdown very nearly cut short his career ; but the probation was extended, and next time he preached with credit, and was fully accepted. He went back to London to walk the hospitals, and continued his medical studies until November 1840, when Glasgow admitted him a Licentiate of the Faculty of Physicians and Surgeons. On the evening after taking his diploma he travelled out to Blantyre, to be congratulated by his parents. He wished to sit up all night, having to leave for London early next morning ; but this his mother would not allow. The family sat talking till midnight, and were up to break-fast at 5 a.m. The mother made coffee ; David read the 121st and 135th Psalms—" I will lift up mine eyes unto the hills, from whence cometh my help. . . . Be-hold, he that keepeth Israel shall neither slumber nor sleep. . . . The Lord is thy shade upon thy right hand. . . . The Lord shall preserve thy going out and thy coming in from this time forth, and even for ever-more. . . . The idols of the heathen are silver and gold, the work of men's hands. . . . But ye that fear the Lord, bless ye the Lord." After prayer and tender farewells, father and son walked to Glasgow to catch the Liverpool steamer. On the Broomielaw they parted, never to meet again in life.

David Livingstone was ordained a missionary in London, on November 20th. Up to the last moment he held his intention of going to China ; but meet-ing with Dr. Moffat, the pioneer of mission work in Africa, he became so fired by the good veteran's experiences and example that on an impulse he said, " Sir, should I do for Africa ? " " Yes," answered Moffat, " if you won't waste time in an old station, but push on to the vast unattempted district to the north, where on a clear morning I have counted the smoke of a hundred villages, and no missionary has ever been." David's mind was instantly made up. On December 8th, 1840, he sailed for Algoa Bay on board the *George* packet.

The *George* reached the Cape, to be detained there for a month. Livingstone found the missionaries at Cape Town occupied with their own squabbles rather than with the great cause ; and having incurred their suspicions by a somewhat free-spoken sermon, he left them and resumed his voyage, resolved to go his own way and work on his own lines. Having landed at Port Natal, he started at once in an ox-wagon for Moffat's station at Kuruman, seven hundred miles up-country, and arrived on May 31st, 1841. No instructions had arrived from home, and he was thus left with what he most wanted—a free hand. While starting at once to heal the sick, he kept his mind fixed on two aims—to learn the language, and to find out all he could concerning the vast region northward of which Moffat had spoken. A short trial tour in the autumn among the Bakwains (the nearest tribe) convinced him that he must lose no time in pushing forward if he meant to found a mission station in the north ; for the district was rapidly becoming hostile owing to reports spread by slave-hunters and others against the missionaries, who were putting down slavery, polygamy, drunkenness, and cattle-raiding. His skill in healing the sick, however, did much to make the Bakwains his friends, and they made him promise on leaving to return to them before long. For this, after a short rest at Kuruman, he prepared himself by living for six months apart from all Europeans in a native village called Lepeloh, and assiduously studying the language and customs of the Bakwains. Fortified by knowledge, he started again, and was welcomed back by his friends as a great wizard. The sick crowded about his wagon, yet, strange to say, nothing was stolen. The doctor and the rainmaker are one and the same person among these tribes, and, writes

Livingstone, " as I did not like to be behind my professional brethren, I declared I could make rain too;" which he did, not by incantations, but by persuading the people to dig trenches from the river and so spread it over their country. " The idea took mightily, and to work we went instanter," even the local rainmaker joining in and laughing at the clever new method. North of the Bakwains he came to the Bamangwato, whose chief, Sekomi, had heard of his fame and made him welcome. " I want you," said Sekomi, " to change my heart. Give me medicine to change it, for it is proud, proud and angry, angry always." He would not hear of the gospel as a cure for a proud heart. " No; I wish medicine to drink and have it changed at once, for it is always very proud and uneasy, always angry with some one." From the Bamangwato Livingstone turned back, for his oxen were falling sick, and much of the return to Kuruman was done on foot; but on his way he fetched a circuit to the south-east and visited the Bakaa, a tribe that had recently massacred a trader with all his party. Seeing that Livingstone ate and laid himself down fearlessly to sleep, they asked him respectfully what news he had to tell; and he preached to these murderers in the Bechuana language of Christ's blood which cleanses from sin.

Still no instructions came from home, nor the permission without which he could not found a permanent station beyond Kuruman. In fact, the directors in London had been frightened by reports of the natives' hostility in the interior, and were averse to risking the missionaries' lives. Livingstone wrote reassuring them, and at length the welcome leave arrived. In June 1843 he wrote home of the " inexpressible delight with which I hail the decision of the directors that we go forward into the dark interior. May the Lord enable me to consecrate my whole being to the glorious work."

Early in August, then, he set off with another missionary, having chosen for the site of his station the beautiful valley of the Mabotsa, some two hundred miles to the north-east, where lived a tribe called the Bakatla. Here he built a house with his own hands, and abode for three years; and here occurred his famous adventure with the lion. The villagers had for some time been troubled with lions, which not only raided their cattle-pens by night, but, growing bolder, attacked their herds in open day. The Bakatla sallied forth once to attack the marauders, but without success.

" It is well known that if one in a troop of lions is killed the remainder leave that part of the country. The next time, therefore, the herds were attacked, I went with the people to encourage them to rid themselves of the annoyance by destroying one. We found the animals on a small hill covered with trees. The men formed round it in a circle, and gradually closed up as they advanced. Being below on the plain with a native schoolmaster named Mabalwe, I saw one of the lions sitting on a piece of rock within the ring. Mabalwe fired at him, and the ball hit the rock on which the animal was sitting. He bit at the spot struck, as a dog does at a stick or stone thrown at him; and then, leaping away, broke through the circle, and escaped unhurt. If the Bakatla had acted according to the custom of the country, they would have speared him in his attempt to get out, but they were afraid to attack him. When the circle was re-formed, we saw two other lions in it, but dared not fire lest we should shoot some of the people. The beasts burst through the line, and as it was evident the men could not be prevailed on to face their foes, we bent our footsteps towards the village. In going round the end of the hill I saw a lion sitting on a piece of rock about thirty yards off, with a little bush in front of him. I took a good aim at him through the bush, and fired both barrels into it. The men called out, ' He is shot, he is shot ! ' Others cried, ' He has been shot by another man too ; let us go to him ! ' I saw the lion's tail erected in anger, and, turning to the people, said, ' Stop a little till I load again.' When in the act of ramming down the bullets I heard a shout, and looking half round, I saw the lion in the act of springing upon me. He caught me by the shoulder, and we both came to the ground together. Growling horribly, he shook me as a terrier dog does a rat.

" The shock produced a stupor similar to that which seems to be felt by a mouse after the first grip of the cat. It caused a sort of dreaminess, in which there was no sense of pain nor feeling of terror, though I was quite conscious of all that was happening. It was like what patients partially under the influence of chloroform describe—they see the operation, but do not feel the knife. This placidity is probably produced in all animals killed by the Carnivora ; and if so, is a merciful provision of the Creator for lessening the pain of death. As he had one paw on the back of my head, I turned round to relieve myself of the weight, and saw his eyes directed to Mabalwe, who was aiming at him from a distance of ten or fifteen yards. His gun, which was a flint one, missed fire in both barrels. The animal immediately left me to attack him, and bit his thigh. Another man, whose life I had saved after he had been tossed by a buffalo, attempted to spear the lion, upon which he turned from Mabalwe and seized this fresh foe by the shoulder. At that moment the bullets the beast had received took effect, and he fell down dead. The whole was the work of a few moments, and must have been his paroxysm of dying rage. In order to take out the charm from him, the Bakatla on the following day made a huge bonfire over the carcass, which was declared to be the largest ever seen. Besides crunching the bone into splinters, eleven of his teeth had penetrated the upper part of my arm. The bite of a lion resembles a gunshot wound. It is generally followed by a great deal of sloughing and discharge, and ever afterwards pains are felt periodically in the part. I had on a tartan jacket, which I believe wiped off the virus from the teeth that pierced the flesh; for my two companions in the affray have both suffered from the usual pains, while I have escaped with only the inconvenience of a false joint in my limb. The wound of the man who was bit in the shoulder actually burst forth afresh on the same month of the following year. This curious point deserves the attention of inquirers."

While recovering, Livingstone paid a visit to Kuruman, to which Dr. Moffat had returned; and at Kuruman, under one of the fruit-trees, Mary Moffat, the eldest daughter, promised to be his wife. They were married, and spent their first year at Mabotsa. From Mabotsa they moved, still northward, to Chonuans, a village of the Bakwains, where lived a chief Sechele, whose daughter Livingstone had cured of a severe illness. Sechele became his first convert, and was in some haste to Christianize all the tribe. " I can make them do anything for me by thrashing them. If you like I will call my head man, and with our whips of rhinoceros hide we will soon make them all believe together." When Livingstone declined this summary method Sechele fell sad. " I know not how it is," said he. " In former times, if a chief was fond of hunting, all his people got dogs and became fond of hunting too. If he loved beer, they all rejoiced in strong drink. But now it is different. I love the Word of God, but not one of them will join me."

A drought fell on the land, and lasted for four years. The tribe suffered so that by Livingstone's advice they migrated, still northward and for forty miles, to Kolobeng, on the banks of a small river; whither he accompanied them, and where for the third time he built a house for himself. But the drought continued, and the small river shrivelled up. The Bakwains believed that Livingstone had bewitched them. "We like you," they said pathetically, "but we wish you to give up that everlasting praying and preaching." It was now, too, that he began to incur the enmity of the Boers, by whom the tribes to the east of Kolobeng were kept in a condition little short of slavery. The Boers resented his teaching the blacks. "You might as well try to teach the baboons," said they; and this resentment was to cost Livingstone dear.

The drought continued, and he began to fear that the stream at Kolobeng had perished for ever. Yet whither could the tribe move? The Boers blocked the way on the east; on the north and west stretched the vast, inhospitable desert of Kalahari. Rumours had reached him of a great lake away in the north beyond this desert, and of a chief who lived there, Sebituane, head of the Makololo, and an old friend of Sechele's. This Sebituane had gathered up the remnants of his people, broken in warfare with the Boers, and "trekking" across the desert had won out to a fertile country on the other side. Could his example be followed?

Livingstone, with two English sportsmen who had wandered to Kolobeng in search of big game, resolved to go and see. They started for the desert on June 1, 1849, with eighty oxen, twenty horses, and twenty men. The journey was arduous, and once the oxen went four days without water. The travellers were almost at the last extremity when one of the Englishmen spied something skulking in the bush, and rode after it, taking it in the distance for a lion. It proved to be a Bushwoman, one of the stunted folk that can live in the Kalahari. For a few beads she led them to Neckockotsa, where one of the party threw his hat in the air and huzzaed, proclaiming that he saw the lake just ahead. It was a mirage : the lake lay yet three hundred miles north. But the worst of their trouble was over, for they had cleared the desert, and by-and-by they came to a fine river, the Zouga. It led them to Lake Ngami, on the shore of which they stood on August 1st—the first white men who had ever looked on its waters. Defying alligators, they worked hard to build and launch a raft ; but all the wood to be found was worm-eaten, and the raft would carry nothing. There was nothing to be done but to turn back. They had, at any rate, gained a sight of the promised land ; and one of the Englishmen, named Oswell, undertook that on reaching Kolobeng he would journey to Cape Town and bring up a boat for next year.

They won back to Kolobeng. The village was deserted, the natives dispersed by the drought, and at the mission station Mrs. Livingstone and her three children were making a hard fight with hunger. Affairs were so bad that Livingstone made another attempt, without waiting for Oswell and the boat, but only to be driven back. The family retired upon Kuruman to recruit, and here news came that the Royal Geographical Society had heard of his discovery of Lake Ngami, and voted him the sum of twenty-five guineas. " It is from the Queen," he wrote. " Long live Victoria ! " The great northern chief Sebituane, too, had heard of his attempt and the reason of it, and sent presents of cattle down to the starving Bakwains. Encouraged by this, in April 1851 Livingstone started on a third attempt, this time taking his wife and children. All went well while they followed the old track. Then they unhappily listened to a Bushman guide, who promised them to find a short cut, lost his way, and deserted them. For five days they wandered over a waterless desert. The supply of water in the wagons was almost exhausted, and the children began to cry for water.

" The idea of their perishing before our eyes was terrible. It would almost have been a relief to me to have been reproached ; . . . but not one syllable of upbraiding was uttered by their mother, though the tearful eyes told the agony within." On the afternoon of the fifth day one of the men returned with water. He had found a river, and Sebituane himself had come down to an island to meet the party. Livingstone and Oswell rode forward to greet him—a mighty figure of a man, the greatest warrior in Central Africa. He gave them food and soft skins to sleep upon. Early next morning they awoke to find him sitting by their fire. He led them to his home, and on the way they heard many tales of his wisdom and prowess. But, alas ! he had scarcely reached his village before he sickened of inflammation of the lungs, and died under the hands of the native doctors, large-heartedly refusing Livingstone's help lest—his death being imputed to the white man's interference—the whole party should be massacred. Still seeking a site for a settlement, Livingstone and Oswell rode a hundred and thirty miles to the north-east, and so came to the flood of the great Zambesi River, pouring through the plain, three hundred yards wide from shore to shore.

Here was a discovery indeed, and it changed all his plans. He and Oswell had found no healthy site for a mission station. It is doubtful if at the moment he thought much of the site of which he had come in quest. Here, flowing through the centre of Africa, was a mighty river, and all rivers lead, soon or late, to the sea. Here was a great pathway, hitherto unguessed by Europeans. It led to the sea ; but it led also through unknown dangers, to which, having in mind their sufferings from thirst in the Kalahari, he could not commit his devoted wife and his children.

He turned back, for a better assault on these unknown regions. He travelled all the way back to Cape Town, revisited by him after eleven years, and shipped his wife and family home to England on April 23rd, 1852. The strong man would go alone. He wrote home to the Board of Directors : " Nothing but a strong conviction that the step will lead to the glory of Christ would make me orphanize my children. Should you not feel yourself justified in incurring the expense of their support in England, I shall feel called upon to renounce the hope. But stay, I am not sure. So powerfully am I convinced it is the will of the Lord I should, I will go, no matter who opposes."

And he went. His old detractors, the Cape Town missionaries, helped him not at all. He was denied ammunition, but obtained it. He could not afford good oxen, and his wagon was a ramshackle one that constantly broke down and had to be mended. But even the delays were used by him to attend the Cape Observatory, and learn how to take astronomical observations, so that in all the subsequent journey he never missed his bearings. He left Cape Town on June 8th, 1852, and his ten poor oxen dragged the wagon so painfully that it was September before he reached Kuruman. He reached it to hear that the Boers had broken into his station at Kolobeng in an attack on the Bakwains, burned it, and looted it of all the gear he possessed (outside of this ox-wagon) in the world. " Friend of my heart's love," wrote Sechele, " I am undone by the Boers, who have attacked me though I have no guilt with them. . . . They killed sixty of my people, and captured women and children and men. They took all the cattle of the Bakwains ; and the house of Livingstone they plundered, taking away all his goods. I am Sechele, the son of Mochoasele." Livingstone hardened his heart and pressed on for the Kalahari desert, giving the Boers a wide berth to the westward. He travelled light now in the matter of worldly possessions, having lost his household gods, besides having exiled his wife and children. Even so, his oxen dragged wearily enough what remained to him over the arid waste to what had been Sebituane's country. Day after day the party had to halt and dig wells and wait until enough water flowed in for the poor beasts to drink. He reached the tribe of the Makololo at the end of May. Sekeletu, son of Sebituane, received him effusively, and kept him for some time at Linyanti, the head village. It was an unhealthy spot. He convinced himself that neither here nor anywhere near was a site for a mission station. That must lie yet farther inland or westward on the long road, which was no road, to the coast. But slave-traders had already visited the Makololo from out of those unknown regions ; and, wrote Livingstone to his father-in-law, " cannot the love of Christ carry the missionary where the slave trade carries the trader ? I shall open up a path to the interior or perish. . . . Be a father to the fatherless, and a husband to the widow, for Jesus' sake. The Boers, by taking possession of all my goods, have saved me the trouble of making a will."

On November 11th, 1853, he left Linyanti, embarking on a river, the Chobe, deep and full of hippopotami. This led his small flotilla into the Zambesi, which they followed up-stream with few hindrances save three of the rapids, where more than once the canoes were in danger ; and Livingstone's men worked well, which was fortunate, for he himself was weak with fever. By the New Year (1854) he was out of the Makololo country and in a region of dense forest, in the clearings of which dwelt the Balonda, a tribe concerning whom he had some fears, for the Balonda and the Makololo were at variance. He had brought with him, however, to restore to their parents several children whom the Makololo had raided, and this won him a welcome. The chief, Shinte, lent him a guide, who proved a great nuisance, but led them (for they had left the river) across the flooded plains of Lebala

to another great chief, Katema, a good-natured vain
fellow, who received them in audience wearing a snuff-
coloured coat laced with tinsel and a helmet of beads
and feathers. "I am the great Katema," he kept
repeating. "I am the great Katema, of whom you
have doubtless heard." He provided three guides,
and begged Livingstone to buy a new coat for him
at Loanda on the coast, for the one he was wearing
showed signs of age.

From this point they were involved in troubles.
Game was scarce; rivers difficult to ford intersected
the forest swamps; and, as they drew nearer to the
coast, the chiefs of various small tribes—corrupted
by Portuguese civilization—demanded heavy tolls,
and made them pay dearly for supplies. On March 4th
they reached a tribe called the Chiboque, who gathered
round them with intent to plunder, but were restored
to reason by the sight of Livingstone's double-barrelled
gun. They struck north to avoid further dealings
with the troublesome tribe; but the guides missed
their way, and brought them back to the Chiboque
again. From here to the first Portuguese outpost in
the valley of the Quango they had to stockade their
camp at night, and make their way by day through
forests in which resentful enemies dogged their heels,
for their stock of presents was spent. At every ford
they met with opposition, and some of the fainter-
hearted were even now turning back; but on April 1st
they gained the ridge overlooking the Quango, and
reached the river on the 4th. At the ford there was
a final altercation with the tribesmen; but a young
half-caste Portuguese sergeant of militia opportunely
happened on the scene and restored order. They
crossed, and their difficulties were at an end.

From the Portuguese outpost of Cassange, where
they were hospitably entertained, there lay yet three
hundred miles to be traversed to reach Loanda and
the sea; and Livingstone, after no less than twenty-

seven attacks of intermittent fever, could scarcely remain on oxback. His men, when they caught their first sight of the sea, were completely nonplussed. "We were marching along with our father," said they, "believing what the ancients told us was true, that the world had no end. But all at once the world said to us, ' I am finished ; there is no more of me.' "

So this truly heroic band staggered down into Loanda. Mr. Gabriel, Commissioner for the Suppression of the Slave Trade—the one English gentleman in the port—welcomed Livingstone heartily, and seeing how ill he was, gave up his own bed to him. It was delicious to lie between sheets and blankets after six months' sleeping on the ground, and the traveller had fallen asleep almost before he could thank his host.

There were English vessels in the port, and it was taken for granted that Livingstone, in his wretched state of health, would sail for home in one of them. He had no such thought. To be sure, he had opened up the way ; but his faithful Makololo could never return without him, and moreover he had pledged his word to Sekeletu to bring them back. As it turned out, his decision saved his life. The *Forerunner* mail-packet, in which he was urged to return, and in which he dispatched for home all his letters, journals, maps, and observations, was lost off Madeira, with all her passengers but one.

His men had become the pets of Loanda. They visited and marvelled at the ships ; they strutted the streets in uniforms of red calico, with red caps, and imitated the gait of the Portuguese soldiers. The people loaded them with presents when, on September 20th, 1854, they started on the return journey, turning their faces southward for a coastwise circuit through Angola before they struck back into their old route. The country was rich and fertile, but they moved slowly, suffering from footsoreness and frequent fevers, through which Livingstone nursed them. At

Pungo Ndongo he called a halt, and spent several weeks over the infinitely wearisome task of reproducing his journals and maps to supply the place of those lost in the *Forerunner*.

Setting forth again in February 1855, he re-entered the territory of his old adversaries, the Chiboque; but this time, having presents to distribute, he received less annoyance, and only once had to force a passage by showing his six-chambered revolver. After a deviation northward among the Luba, a cheerful tribe " spending their time in gossip, funeral assemblies, and marriages," the travellers struck their old path again, and reached Katema's town, where Katema's heart was made glad by a cloak of red baize ornamented with gold, purchased at Loanda. Onward they went, repassing through Shinte's country, distributing seeds and cuttings brought from Angola, and so came to Libonta, the first Makololo town, where they were welcomed back as men risen from the dead. After a day of thanksgiving, and a service at which Livingstone's " braves " cut a great dash, wearing their white suits and red caps and swaggering like Portuguese soldiers, they set off down the Barotse valley, progressing in triumph from village to village, and reached Linyanti and the embraces of Sekeletu on September 11th, 1855. The return journey had taken a year, less nine days.

At Linyanti Livingstone spent eight weeks writing letters and dispatches; and on November 3rd started afresh. " But whither? " you may ask. " Back to Cape Town? " Not a bit of it—no more Cape Town for Livingstone! This amazing man, having come half-way across Africa, was resolved to push right across it, trusting to reach the east coast at the mouth of the Zambesi, and committing to God his path through the unknown country, where no white man had travelled before. Sekeletu accompanied the party to Shesheke, on the river bank, and thence, having bidden him farewell, they set their faces eastward, and followed down the broad stream until they came in sight of the marvel of which Livingstone and Oswell had heard rumours years before—the " smoke that sounds," as the natives called five tall columns of spray perpetually tossed and held in air above five gigantic cataracts. In a canoe manned by natives who knew the river he went down the rapids to an island in mid-stream, close by the verge of the falls.

" Though within a few yards of the falls, no one could see where the vast body of water went ; it seemed to lose itself in a transverse fissure only eighty yards wide. Creeping with awe to the end of the island, I peered down, and saw that a stream eighteen hundred yards wide leapt down some three hundred and twenty feet, and then became compressed into a space of fifteen or twenty yards. The falls are simply caused by a crack in a hard basaltic rock from the right to the left bank, and then prolonged from the left bank away through thirty or forty miles of hills."

Most children have now seen pictures or photographs of the Victoria Falls ; but Livingstone in 1855 was the first European who had ever looked on this beautiful and awful scene, and he called the falls by the name of his sovereign—" the first and only English name I have affixed to any part of the country."

They now quitted the Zambesi and marched northeast. Their way at first lay through friendly tribes, subjects of the Makololo, but beyond these they met with serious trouble. They came to the Zambesi again where it is joined by the Loangwe River, and hundreds of armed natives gathered around them waiting only an excuse to attack as Livingstone made preparations for crossing in the one canoe he had secured. He had to send his men across in detachments, and as his company thinned the strain grew almost unbearable. Still he kept a brave face, amusing the savages with his watch, his burning-glass, and other toys. He was the last man to step into the canoe, and he wished them peace as he pushed off. By night he and his men were safely encamped on the farther bank. A dreaded chief, Mpende, at war with the Portuguese, allowed the party to pass on hearing that Livingstone was too fair of skin to be of the race of his enemies. He also helped them to recross the river; after which, among unwarlike tribes and through a delicious country, they came to the Portuguese outpost of Tete. Here the Portuguese commandant received Livingstone most hospitably, and took a great weight off the explorer's mind by offering grants of land to the faithful Makololo, with licences to hunt and trade. The men accepted, and Livingstone—his sense of honour thus relieved towards them—stayed only to see them comfortably settled before taking his departure for the coast in the commandant's boat. He reached Quilimane on May 20th, 1856, whence the British brig-of-war *Frolic* gave him a passage across to Mauritius. At Mauritius he took his passage home in the P. & O. steamer *Candia*, landed at Marseilles, travelled home by Paris and Dover, and at once hastened down to Southampton, where his wife was awaiting the ship.

He found England ringing with his name and his exploits. Medals and testimonials and honorary degrees; public meetings, receptions, gold caskets, with the freedom of London, Glasgow, and other cities —from the beginnings of this lionizing he broke away in January to visit his mother and his kin. (His father had died while he was on his homeward way.) Then returning to London, he sat down to write a book of his travels. It was published, and brought him a small fortune (as he conceived riches). He had already begun to make preparations for returning to East Africa, to his faithful Makololo, when the Prime Minister, Lord Palmerston, offered him the appointment of British Consul in those parts. This would give him an opportunity for the work which had gradually become dearest to his heart—the suppression of the slave trade. He accepted, and reluctantly severed his connection with the London Missionary Society. The parting was deeply regretted on both sides.

The Admiralty fitted out his expedition. To his joy, Mrs. Livingstone was allowed to accompany him. He made his will, ending with the bequest of his left arm (the one the lion had crushed) to Professor Owen, the great anatomist. On March 10th, 1859, he and his party embarked at Liverpool in H.M. colonial steamship *Pearl*, and reached the east coast in May, after touching at Sierra Leone and the Cape. His first work was to fit together a steam launch, the *Ma Robert* (which he had brought out, packed in sections), and examine the four channels by which the Zambesi reaches the sea. After much prospecting in the *Ma Robert*—which wheezed and snorted so evilly that they rechristened her the *Asthmatic*—Livingstone ascended the Shiré, the largest northern affluent of the Zambesi, and discovered Murchison Falls and Lake Shirwa, a magnificent sheet of water some 1,800 feet above sea-level. Here he heard of a far larger lake—Nyassa—lying some way to the north, and in August 1861, after refitting, started in quest of it. Again his men toiled past Murchison Falls—these cataracts extend for thirty-five miles, and cost them three weeks of portage—launched their boat on the upper waters of the Shiré, and on September 16th floated into the great Nyassa. This splendid lake Livingstone declared to be the key of East Central Africa. It was swept by storms so violent that his party could not venture far from shore. They coasted the south-western side for many miles, passing a continuous chain of villages, all devastated by the slave traffic. They could not complete their discovery or learn how far off lay the northern shore of the lake, which is really an inland sea, long and narrow (if a width of fifty or sixty miles can be called narrow).

They had to return for another task which lay

heavy on Livingstone's mind—that of restoring his faithful Makololo to their homes. This he did in the summer of 1860, revisiting the Victoria Falls on his way, and arrived to find the good Sekeletu friendly as ever, but in a sad way, having been attacked by leprosy. Livingstone treated him, and left him in better health ; though, by reason of his sickness, the Makololo supremacy in those parts was fast crumbling away. On November 21st our traveller reached Tete again. He was expecting a new steamer from England to replace the *Asthmatic*, and with the steamer the Universities Mission, with Bishop Mackenzie and his staff, of whom he hoped great things. These hopes were fated to be vain. The new steamer, the *Pioneer*, arrived indeed, and the mission was taken up the Shiré and established at Magomero. Livingstone left it, as he hoped, cheerfully planted. His last advice to the bishop was to avoid interfering in native quarrels. This counsel was not observed. Some time later Bishop Mackenzie reported cheerily that the Manganja, the tribe around the mission, had, with the mission's help, defeated the Ajawa, with whom they were at war. Livingstone heard this with misgiving. Next came the fatal news that Mackenzie, in rescuing two Manganja carriers, taken captive by the Ajawa, had died of exposure, that his second in command was also dead, and, in short, that the Universities Mission was a wrecked scheme. Livingstone rescued the survivors, and took them down to the coast. " But this will hurt us all," was his thought. Worse, far worse, for him was to come. Mrs. Livingstone sickened of a fever, and died after a week's illness. Since the old days at Kolobeng she had been a perfect wife, brave and helpful in all hardships, bravest of all when called upon to abide afar and without news.

" They also serve who only stand and wait."

" For the first time in my life," writes Livingstone in his journal a fortnight later, " I feel willing to die." To understand the rest of his life one must understand what this dearest loss meant to him.

He was engaged in preparing a road between the lower and upper waters of the Shiré, still with his eyes on a full exploration of Nyassa, when a letter came from the government, recalling him to England. He had been expecting it. Following the collapse of the Universities Mission, he knew that Portugal was making polite remonstrances with our Foreign Office over his interference with " commerce "—in plain words, with the slave traffic. In April 1864—mark the pluck of the man—he sailed for Bombay in a tiny steamer, constructed under his orders for exploring Lake Nyassa. He had fourteen tons of coal on board ; he was captain and sole pilot, with three English sailors and nine natives who had never seen the sea. He steamed into Bombay on June 13th, 1864. The vessel was so small that no one noticed her arrival. At Bombay he paid off his crew, and, taking ship for England, arrived at Charing Cross Station on July 21st. His second expedition had proved a mournful one, unsuccessful on the whole. But he had discovered Lake Nyassa !

The days of wild public applause, of presentations and awards and general triumph, were over ; but some use had to be found for this wonderful, indomitable man. Yet for the government to employ him was by no means easy, owing to his sworn feud with the slave traffic, whereby he had made himself obnoxious not only to the Arab slavers but to the Portuguese, who accused him of spoiling their commerce in the interior. At length Sir Roderick Murchison hit on the idea of sending him out on the Royal Geographical Society's behalf, as an explorer pure and simple, to explore the watersheds of the country around Lakes Nyassa and Tanganyika, and, if possible, to solve what mystery remained concerning the sources of the Nile. A poor £2,000 was subscribed. Government continued him in his consulship, and to the end he wore the gold-braided cap, sadly tarnished, which, with old blue coat and " shepherd's plaid " trousers, made up the costume now as familiar in the picture books as it was singular in the African wilderness. The appointment carried no pay ; and so the old lion-heart fared forth once more, trusting that the Lord would provide. He left Marseilles on August 19th, 1865, and in September for Bombay, where he sold his old Nyassa steamboat for £2,600—and afterwards lost the whole through depositing the money in an Indian bank which came to grief. From Bombay he sailed to Zanzibar ; and from Zanzibar, on the 19th of March 1866, for Mikindani Bay, on the East African coast, near the mouth of the river Rovuma. The expedition consisted of thirty-seven souls—Livingstone himself, ten natives of Johanna, thirteen natives of the Zambesi, and thirteen sepoys of the Bombay Marine, whom he soon sent back for their laziness and their cruelty to the animals. They started in a south-westerly direction, intending to cross the Rovuma and make for the north end of Lake Nyassa, and for years the wastes of Africa swallowed them. A few letters reached the coast for friends at home. Then came a long pause. It was broken in December by news that the doctor and most of his party had been set upon and massacred by the Mazitu, a tribe inhabiting the unexplored lands among the western tributaries of the Rovuma. The bearer of this grievous tale was a Johanna man named Musa.

The tale reached home, and was credited. But some Englishmen who had met Musa on the Shiré knew him to be a liar, and Murchison inclined to the

same view. At his instance the Geographical
Society induced government to send up a boat expedition under Mr. E. D. Young, a warrant officer of
the Royal Navy, to discover the truth or falsity of
the report. Young made his way to Lake Nyassa,
and in eight months returned with tidings that
Livingstone had passed on towards the north-west.
No more could be discovered. Still Musa's tale—he
and the Johanna men had, in fact, deserted—was
largely believed, until, in 1868, letters came from
Livingstone himself, dated at Bemba, February 1867.
He had been unable to send dispatches before, there
being no carriers or caravans in the country he was
traversing.

It may be doubted whether Livingstone realized
the anxiety at home concerning his fate. A passion
for Africa would seem to have taken possession of him,
to the exclusion of all other thoughts. He had lost
his wife ; he felt old age approaching ; often enough
he wished for death as he forced his way past the
southern end of Nyassa and painfully up to the north-
west to Lake Tanganyika. The slave trade had
depopulated the villages everywhere, and the people
were starving. He reached the southern end of
Tanganyika in April 1867 ; but hearing of war in
front, turned back southward, and discovered Lakes
Moero (November 8th) and Bangweolo (July 18th,
1868). On his way between them, coming to a
solitary grave in the forest, he writes in his journal,
" I have nothing to do but wait till He who is over
all decides where I have to lay me down and die.
Poor Mary lies on Shapanga brae." In the autumn
he turns northward again with five faithful followers
to reach Ujiji, on the northern end of Lake Tanganyika, where he is expecting supplies and letters. He
reaches it to find his stores plundered. Still northward he goes to Bambarre, to Nyangwe, tracking the
Lualaba River, if perchance he may find whether it

may be a western arm of the Nile or an eastern head-water of the Congo. In this district he wanders long, having engaged reinforcements. On February 25, 1871, he is fairly confident that the river flows into the Congo—as in fact it does, though he did not live to know it. At Nyangwe a horrible mutiny and massacre broke out among the men of Dugumbe, an Arab trader on whose help he was relying. There was nothing to be done but go back to Ujiji and engage other men from among the riff-raff of that place. So back he toiled. He reached Ujiji on October 23, 1871, to find that a second time his stores had been broken up and scattered. Until fresh supplies arrived he must live in beggary. On the 28th, when his spirits were at their lowest ebb, a faithful servant, Susi, came running at the top of his speed and gasped out, " An Englishman ! I see him ! "

" The American flag at the head of a caravan told of the nationality of the stranger. Bales of goods, baths of tin, huge kettles, cooking-pots, tents, etc., made me think this must be a luxurious traveller, and not one at his wits' end like me. It was Henry Morton Stanley, the travelling correspondent of the *New York Herald*, sent by James Gordon Bennett, at an expense of more than £4,000, to obtain accurate information about Dr. Livingstone if living, and if dead to bring home my bones."

Livingstone stood outside his door and lifted his tarnished cap as Susi brought the newcomer gleefully towards him. " Doctor Livingstone, I presume ? " said Stanley ; and they shook hands.

They went into the hut and seated themselves. A letter-bag brought by Stanley lay across the doctor's knees. " Tell me all the news you can," he begged. " No, doctor ; read your letters first." " I have waited years for letters ; I can wait a few hours longer. Tell me how the world is getting on."

So Stanley told the news while they sat at their first meal together; told of the terrible Franco-Prussian war, of Atlantic cables, Cabinet changes, the election of General Grant, the reforming zeal of Mr. Gladstone's ministry. They pledged one another in champagne Stanley had brought for the occasion. That night Livingstone sat up late reading his letters. They brought good news and bad. Many old friends were dead, but his family were doing well.

Stanley describes the great traveller as "reduced to a skeleton by illness and fatigue. He was sick, destitute, and forlorn. All his men except four had either deserted or had died, and there seemed to be no hope for him. His piteous appeals for help to his friends at Zanzibar were neglected, or his letters were lost. There was no prospect but that of lingering illness and death before him." Under the influence of good cheer he speedily revived. But there was one point on which Stanley's persuasions were vain. He would not return to England. The spell of Africa lay on the old man; its wizardry had claimed him, and would claim him to the end. He had no sooner recovered a little strength than he was impatient to be up again and doing. Stanley proposed that they should visit together the extreme north end of Lake Tanganyika, a part Livingstone had never explored. They did so, and found a river—the Lusizi—flowing into the lake through a broad gorge in the otherwise impenetrable mountain walls. No outlet could be found. After a journey of seven hundred and fifty miles together, the two friends parted at Unyanyembe on March 14th, 1872, and parted for ever. Livingstone hardened his heart and sat down to await the escort which Stanley sent up from Zanzibar. It did not arrive until the middle of August. Five weary months he had waited, eating his heart—that brave heart, dauntless to the end. He knew that he had come to the dregs of life, yet hoped against hope that in the little time left it might be granted to him to realize his dream, and discover to the world the true source of the Nile. On August 25th he marched out of Unyanyembe, at the head of fifty-six men. He believed that the Nile rose somewhere between 10° and 12° south latitude, and he died in that belief. There was an unexplored lake to the southward, at the head of which he hoped to find the key of the secret. He set his face southward and westward again. He never arrived, and even on his way his doubts grew as his weakness increased upon him ; but to the end, when he felt himself a beaten man, he still practised towards his fellows that fatherly kindness and forbearance which had moved Stanley to write, " Religion has tamed him and made him a Christian gentleman, the most companionable of men and indulgent of masters."

The end came at Ilala, beside Lake Bangweolo, in mid-Africa. For days he had been sinking, and for a time his " boys " had carried him on a litter. Finally they laid him in a hut. For themselves they lit a camp fire just outside ; a lad, Majwara by name, slept inside, to be ready at the patient's slightest call. At four in the morning of May 1st, 1873, Majwara awoke them. " Come," he said, " I am afraid. I don't know if he is alive." The lad's evident alarm made them hurry. They looked inside. Livingstone was kneeling by the bed with his head on his hands, and for a moment they drew back, supposing that he was praying. Majwara said, " He was like that when I lay down to sleep." They drew nearer and watched, holding a candle aloft. He did not stir. They touched him. He was cold—dead. He had died on his knees.

Attend now to what these brave fellows did. It is a deed to live among the great ones of history. They gathered outside the hut.  It was raining a drizzle, and dark, an hour or two before cock-crow.

They were fifty-six in number, and all had followed Livingstone for nine months; two—Susi and Chumah—for far longer. The others said to Susi and Chumah, speaking low in the darkness: "You are old men in travelling. You must tell us, and we will obey."

Susi and Chumah consulted, and said, "We will take back his body to Zanzibar—his body and all that belonged to our master."

And they did it. They buried his heart at the foot of a great tree, and carved his name on it, with the date. Chitambo, the native chief at Ilala, promised that the grave should be respected. They then dried the body and packed it in bark after a process known to them. They made inventory of all the goods, and having catalogued them, started for the coast with their burden.

Through swamps they went, over desert plains, amid hostile tribes. Once they were attacked, and had to storm their path through a village. Thus for ten months they held their way, carrying Livingstone to the sea, and on February 15th, 1874, delivered all to the British consul at Zanzibar—not an article missing except some of the instruments. Was ever a nobler story of faithful loyalty?

From Zanzibar Livingstone's bones were carried by H.M.S. *Calcutta* to Aden, and thence by P. & O. steamer to Southampton, where they were landed with ceremony, and forwarded to London. Sir William Fergusson identified them by the false joint in the arm broken years ago by the lion. And so on April 18th, 1874, Livingstone returned to Westminster Abbey; for so the nation honoured all that was left of him. He lies buried in the centre of the nave. On his monument is written: "*Other sheep I have which are not of this fold; them also I must bring, and they shall hear My voice.*"

# FLORENCE NIGHTINGALE

THERE is a story, quoted in the life of our heroine by Mrs. Sarah Ann Tooley, that at a dinner given to the naval and military officers at the close of the Crimean War each guest was asked to write on a slip of paper the name of the person whose services during the late campaign would be longest remembered by posterity ; and that when the papers were examined all agreed on one name—" Florence Nightingale." And indeed, while the results of Crimean battles are to-day almost nothing, the great work which Miss Nightingale undertook and carried through in the hospital at Scutari outlasted the signing of peace, and has ever since been carrying on its impulse, extending its influence, bringing comfort to thousands of homes ; so that the honourable testimony of that dinner-table, accurate though its forecast was, might be extended to-day from the campaign in the Crimea to that which men and women have been carrying on ever since against alleviable human pain. If—looking around upon all the hospitals, infirmaries, dispensaries, nursing associations, boards and officers of health, district nurses, with which our country is blessed to-day—one were asked, " Who, under Almighty God, was the source of it all ? " the answer would still be—" Florence Nightingale." And it has all come about because one woman prepared herself for a call not anticipated, and because, when the call came and found her, she had the courage to obey it instantly.

On March 27, 1854, Queen Victoria's message to Parliament announced that negotiations were broken off with Russia, and that she felt bound to give aid to the Sultan. Next day her Majesty's formal declara-

**FLORENCE NIGHTINGALE.**

*From a pen-drawing by
E. Heber Thompson.*

tion of war was read from the steps of the Royal
Exchange amid wild enthusiasm.  The people, urged
on by the press, were spoiling for a fight ; they had
known no serious battle since Waterloo, and were
confident, even hilarious, over the prospect.  Tenny-
son hailed the day when—

" No more shall commerce be all in all, and Peace
    Pipe on her pastoral hillock a languid note
    And watch her harvest ripen, her herd increase,
    Nor the cannon-bullet rust on a slothful shore,
    And the cobweb woven across the cannon's throat
    Shall shake its threaded tears in the wind no more."

" The British nation," wrote Lord Palmerston, " is
unanimous in this matter.  I say unanimous, for I
cannot reckon Cobden, Bright, and Co. for anything."
So war it was ;  and the Guards marched off to the
cheers of London, and " Cobden, Bright, and Co.,"
who maintained that war was, if avoidable, a wickedness, could gain no hearing.

But a nation which elects to be bellicose should
first take care that it is military—which means, to
be thoughtfully prepared for war, from its strategy
down to the last details of commissariat and hospital.  British people in 1854 vainly supposed that all
could be done by bayonet-thrusting (on which, as it
turned out, they could depend, so far as it went) ;
but the troops were scarcely landed before dismal
stories reached home of our unpreparedness in all
these details.  Mr. (afterwards Sir) William Howard
Russell, the famous war correspondent for the *Times*,
reached our first encampment, at Gallipoli on the
Dardanelles, to note with shame the completeness
of the French arrangements—" hospitals for the sick,
bread and biscuit bakeries, wagon trains for carrying stores and baggage, every necessary and every
comfort "—as compared with ours.

" In every respect the French can teach us a lesson

in these matters. While our sick men have not a mattress to lie down upon, and are literally without blankets, the French are well provided for. We have no medical comforts—none were forwarded from Malta."

From Gallipoli to Scutari on the Bosphorus, and from Scutari to Varna, these complaints, as we follow Russell's letters, grow steadily more serious. The French have admirably organized their postal service; ours has broken down.

"I regret very much to have to state that for several days last week there was neither rice nor sugar, no preserved potatoes, nor tea, nor any substitute for these articles, issued to the men; they had, therefore, to make their breakfast simply on ration brown bread and water. After breakfast they were paraded and exercised for an hour or two in the hot sun (on one occasion for more than four hours), and the result has been that sickness increased rapidly. The dinners of the men consisted of lean ration beef boiled in water and eaten with brown bread, without any seasoning to flavour it. The supplies ran out, and it was no fault of the commissariat that they did so. Who was to blame? I don't pretend to say."

Thus fed, and herded in insanitary camps, the men were soon attacked by dysentery, then by cholera, and began to drop off like flies: this, be it observed, long before they had so much as caught sight of the enemy. On September the 14th and 15th they were disembarked from ships upon the shore of the Crimea, and, still before a blow has been struck, we read,—

"It is clear that neither afloat nor on shore is the medical staff nearly sufficient. I myself saw men dying on the beach, on the line of march, and in bivouac, without any medical assistance; * and this within hail of a fleet of 500 sail, and within sight of headquarters."

* *Sic!* One of those truths which might be better expressed differently. War correspondents have to write in a hurry.

The battle of the Alma was fought on the 21st. After the victory—

" When I was looking at the wounded men going off to-day, I could not see an English ambulance.  Our men were sent to the sea, three miles distant, on jolting *arabas* or tedious litters.  The French—I am tired of this disgraceful antithesis—had well-appointed covered hospital vans, to hold ten or twelve men, drawn by fine mules, and their wounded were sent in much greater comfort than our poor fellows, so far as I saw."

Above all, the French had nurses—Sisters of Mercy, women trained at home in convents for the work— who in camp and hospital moved from stretcher to stretcher, from bed to bed, administering food and medicines, allaying the tortures of the wounded.  Our men had no such help.\*  Russell's descriptions culminated in this appeal in the *Times* :—

" Are there no devoted women amongst us able and willing to go forth to minister to the sick and suffering soldiers of the East in the hospitals of Scutari ?  Are none of the daughters in England, at this extreme hour of need, ready for such a work of mercy ? . . . France has sent forth her Sisters of Mercy unsparingly, and they are even now by the bedsides of the wounded and the dying, giving what woman's hand alone can give of comfort and relief. . . . Must we fall so far below the French in self-sacrifice and devotedness, in a work which Christ so signally blesses as done unto Himself ? *'I was sick, and ye visited Me.'* "

Russell's appeal did not fall on deaf ears.  In a few

---

\* See the Duke of Newcastle's evidence before the Roebuck Commission, 1855.  The employment of nurses in the hospital at Scutari was mooted in this country at an early stage, before the army left our shores, but it was not liked by the military authorities.  It had been tried on former occasions.  The class of women employed as nurses had been very much addicted to drinking, and they were found even more callous to the sufferings of soldiers in hospitals than men would have been.

days hundreds of Englishwomen of all ranks were flooding the War Office with letters, beseeching leave to go out to Scutari as nurses.   But to all such might be applied the words in which he had argued—of our deficiencies in baggage, pontoon trains, etc.—that these things can only be ready on the call of war through slow preparation in times of peace.  " All the gold in the treasury cannot produce at command these great qualities in administrative and executive departments which are the fruits of experience alone. A soldier, an artilleryman, a commissariat officer, cannot be created suddenly, no matter how profuse may be your expenditure in the attempt."

So it was with the nurses.   These patriotic Englishwomen lacked one thing only—a capacity, even the smallest, to fulfil the services they were burning to undertake.   They had received no training ;  they knew nothing of hospital duty, less than nothing of hospital organization.   In 1854 there was, strange as it sounds, in England scarcely a nurse whom to-day we should entrust with the care of the meanest " district" or "cottage hospital."  Ladies could not be said to shun—it never crossed their minds to consider—a calling left in the hands of women of the lowest class, proverbially coarse in feeling and addicted to drink— " Sarah Gamps," in short, with the not infrequent addendum of gross immorality.   In 1854, one may fairly say a gently nurtured lady would sooner have offered herself to be a charwoman than to be a nurse.   In our Protestant land the vocation of a Sister of Mercy, or of anything like it, did not fall within the dreams even of women devoted to religion.

These shoals of letters, all penned on impulses pathetically good, in the midst of the excitement and general futility of things, reached the War Office in due course, and were submitted to her Majesty's Secretary of State for War, who happened to be a remarkable man.

The Hon. Sidney Herbert (afterwards, for a brief while before his death, Lord Herbert of Lea), second son of the eleventh Earl of Pembroke, was born in 1810 and derived his Christian name from the famous Sir Philip Sidney, the hero of Zutphen and most perfect knight of Queen Elizabeth's reign, whose sister—

> " The gentlest shepherdess that lives this day,
>    And most resembling both in shape and spright
>    Her brother dear—"

had married Henry, second Earl of Pembroke, in 1577. Men said that Philip Sidney, " the president of nobleness and chivalry," lived again in his nineteenth-century namesake ; for beyond all doubt Sidney Herbert was one of the most fascinating men in Europe.

" He was strikingly handsome, with a commanding figure and courtly manners. He appeared to possess every social advantage—high birth, a great estate, a beautiful wife and children, one of the happiest homes in England, many accomplishments, a ready address, a silvery voice, irresistible manners, and a rare power for making friends. It was said that men would give up to Sidney Herbert what they would grant to no one else."

From Harrow and Oxford he had proceeded to public life, entering the first reformed Parliament of 1832 as member for South Wilts. In 1834 Sir Robert Peel offered him a Lordship of the Treasury, which he declined on the ground that it involved no hard work. In 1841 he became Secretary to the Admiralty, and in 1845 Secretary of State for War, with a seat in the Cabinet. He introduced many reforms, especially in the management of regimental schools, and as head of a department spared himself no labour—indeed, his industry was proverbial ; though, as Gladstone afterwards said, great as was his work, " there was something if possible still greater, and that was the character of Lord Herbert. . . . His gentleness combined with a modesty such as I, for one, never knew equalled in any station of life." Sir Robert Peel, just before his death (in 1850), prophesied that either Sidney Herbert or Gladstone would one day be Prime Minister. With the resignation of Peel's ministry Herbert had left office, and remained out of it for six years, devoting himself mainly to private benevolence in and around his home at Wilton House, near Salisbury. In 1852 he was recalled to his old post of Secretary for War, and was prosecuting reforms with all the old spirit when the outbreak of hostilities with Russia suspended all his plans, throwing upon him work which broke down his health and brought him to a premature grave. He died (to conclude this account) in 1861. " It is difficult," said Gladstone, who had no dearer friend, " to speak of Herbert ; because, with that singular harmony and singular variety of gifts— every gift of person, every gift of position, every gift of character—with which it pleased Providence to bless him, he was one of whom we may well recite words that the great poet of this country has applied to a prince of an early history, cut off by death earlier than his countrymen would have desired—

> " A sweeter and a lovelier gentleman,
>     Framed in the prodigality of nature,
>     The spacious world cannot again afford."

Such in 1854 was the Minister for War, who of a sudden found himself bombarded by hundreds of letters from Englishwomen begging to be sent out to the Crimea, all burning to devote themselves, but all alike ignorant of the terrible duty they sought. Herbert's trained mind too surely perceived their incompetence as he read and rejected appeal after appeal. Where, in all this well-meaning hysteria, was any sign of capacity, of grasp, of power to lead and to organize? He could find none. Was there in England, then, no one woman endowed with strength of character for the task, and prepared by training with the skill for it? Yes, there was one—a gently nurtured lady and (as it happened) an honoured friend of his; one who for some years had studied nursing and knew more of its realities than did all those frenzied petitioners put together. His thoughts turned to her. Amid the hubbub of patriotism she had kept silence and made no sign, simply, as he could understand, because she knew, while others did not, the magnitude of the difficulty. He felt that, unless she volunteered, he could not ask her to take her life in her hands, to brave the cholera, the hardships, the exposure, the breaking toil, and, worse than these, the certainty of slanderous criticism from folk who, as public opinion then was, would cry aloud at the bare idea of a "lady" going out to nurse common soldiers.

But who was this lady?

A Mr. William Edward Shore of Tapton, Derbyshire, had in 1815 succeeded to the estate of his mother's uncle, old Peter Nightingale, a roistering squire of that county; and to the ownership of Lea Hall, high above the valley of the Derwent. As a condition of his inheritance he took at the same time the name of Nightingale. Three years later he married Frances, daughter of William Smith, Esq. of Parndon, Essex, for fifty years member of Parliament for Norwich, a constant and notable opponent of the slave trade. Mr. Nightingale was a cultured gentleman, whose mind had been broadened by travel, and for a few years he and his beautiful wife spent much of their time abroad, chiefly in Italy. Their first child, a daughter, was born at Naples and christened with the classical name of that city, Parthenope. About a year later, on May 12, 1820, a second daughter was born to them at the Villa Columbaia, near Florence. She too was named after her birthplace, and thus one of the best beloved of English heroines came by her melodious name—Florence Nightingale.

Returning to England, the parents at first took up their residence at Lea Hall; but removed some five years later to Lea Hurst, a house which Mr. Nightingale had erected on a site of extreme beauty, about a mile distant from his old family seat. Here the two girls, Parthenope (who afterwards became Lady Verney) and Florence, spent the greater part of their childhood, but a part too at Embley Park, Hampshire, an Elizabethan mansion which their father had purchased and restored. The custom was for the family to pass the summer months at Lea Hurst and migrate to Embley for the winter and early spring. These journeys between north and south were sometimes made by stage-coach, but more often in the family carriage, the servants travelling ahead with the luggage, that the inns on the road might be prepared to receive these " persons of quality," and Embley made ready for their arrival. Mr. Nightingale being, in homely phrase, a stickler for education, lessons were not neglected. Parthenope and Florence did them together under a governess, their father supervising. Parthenope's accomplishments were the more artistic —she excelled her sister in music and drawing; Florence's the more severely intellectual. From her father she learned some Latin and Greek, with elementary science and mathematics. She read the standard authors, and showed great aptitude for foreign languages. There was plenty of out-of-door health with all this—scampers on ponies and rambles over park and dale; a certain relaxation, too, of routine in the summer months at Lea Hurst. But at Embley throughout the winter the routine of the schoolroom would be resumed, and went forward on very strict lines. Mr. Nightingale detested careless work. Mrs. Nightingale saw that her daughters became capable needlewomen, and that they learned to dance and carry themselves gracefully.

So in due course Florence Nightingale reached the

age of seventeen, " came out " in the country society of Derbyshire and Hampshire, and " began to take her place as the squire's daughter," visiting the sick, organizing Bible classes, interesting herself in the village schools. " At Christmas-time her work-basket was full of warm comforts for the poor. She was invaluable at bazaars," etc. In short, she was a very charming and fortunate young lady of the early Victorian period, and, like many another fortunate young lady, was taken to London for " the season," with its dances and other gaieties, and to Buckingham Palace to make her curtsy to the Queen.

Nevertheless there was something—her friends could not define it, and she herself was hardly conscious of it yet awhile—which marked her out as different from those other young ladies ; and if we define it now as a certain high seriousness, which so often appears, they know not how, in the youth of those destined to be great, the reader must not infer that Florence Nightingale was at this time, or ever in her life, a dull, solemn person. On the contrary, she had a shrewd wit and a very mirthful laugh ; only there began to arise in her mind some obstinate questionings. Was this comfortable life of hers a really useful one ? Or, if useful in its way, was it really effective ? This district-visiting and distributing of goodies—did it go beyond " coddling," playing around the edge of a problem which was in truth both deep and terrible for those who had eyes to see ? While so much relievable suffering went unrelieved in the world, was it right that women should be cramped, tied down to these petty, if pretty, ministrations ? Was there no nobler work—work to be done thoroughly—work demanding stern, practical preparation ? She had pondered these questions, and her mind was still demanding the answer, when at this critical period in her life she met with a woman who could put her in the way of finding it. This was

Elizabeth Fry, the Quakeress, whose courageous work in visiting the outcasts in our prisons had done so much to get those prisons reformed. The two women —the one old and stately and very wise, the other young and ardent—met as kindred spirits ; yet it was understood from the first that Florence Nightingale had no desire to become Elizabeth Fry's pupil and assume the mantle when that aged prophetess laid it down. She had already decided on her own sphere of work. It was to be hospital nursing.

In this, as it happened, Mrs. Fry could help her. She was a friend of Pastor Fliedner, the founder of a nursing institution at Kaiserswerth, near Düsseldorf, on the Rhine, where Protestant " deaconesses " were trained to attend on the sick as " knowledgeably " as any Roman Catholic Sister of Mercy. From a crazy old summer-house in which Fliedner had lodged one or two women—discharged prisoners—and taught them to lead useful lives, the institution had grown to an ample hospital, with branch hospitals scattered all over Germany, and from Jerusalem to Pittsburg in America.

It was in 1849 that Florence Nightingale entered the Deaconess Hospital at Kaiserswerth and donned its uniform—a plain blue cotton dress, white apron, and muslin cap. Her coming created a flutter among the deaconesses—all women of peasant birth—who found it hard to understand why an English lady of wealth and position should want to come and study among them. But the newcomer soon showed that she meant strict business. Years afterwards she wrote, " Three-fourths of the whole mischief in women's lives arises from their excepting themselves from the rules of training considered needful for men ; " and again, " I would say to all young ladies who are called to any vocation, Qualify yourselves for it as a man does for his work." This was strange doctrine in 1849, but Florence Nightingale acted upon it, having persuaded

herself of its truth. She underwent two rigorous
courses of training at Kaiserswerth, where the deaconesses came to adore her. When she said good-bye,
Pastor Fliedner rested his hands on her bowed head
and blessed her. " May God the Father, the Son, and
the Holy Ghost, three Persons in one God, bless you ;
may He establish you in the truth until death, and
give you hereafter the crown of life. Amen." After
her return home Miss Nightingale published a little
book on the institution, and prefaced it with some
words on the principle her own career was soon to
illustrate so splendidly, that women longing for a
vocation should prepare themselves for it by business-
like training. " Woman," she wrote, " stands askew.
Her education for action has not kept pace with
her education for acquirement. The woman of the
eighteenth century was perhaps happier than her
more cultivated sister of the nineteenth century.
The latter wishes, but does not know how to do
many things ; the former, what she wished at least
*that* she could do."

From Kaiserswerth she visited Paris, spent some
time with the Roman Catholic Sisters of St. Paul,
studied surgery, and compared French hospital
systems and methods of organizing charity with those
methods and systems she had already studied in
London, Edinburgh, Dublin, and one or two foreign
capitals. In the midst of this work her health broke
down, and she returned to Embley. On her recovery
she went up to London to take charge of the Harley
Street Home for Sick Governesses, which had been
brought low by mismanagement. In a few months she
had brought order out of chaos ; but again the strain
proved too much for her bodily powers, and again she
was forced to seek recovery in a restful life at Embley
and Lea Hurst.

Here, then, was the woman to whom the War
Minister's thoughts kept turning. He knew her inti-

mately, and Embley Park lay within visiting distance of his own country home over the Wiltshire border ; and, indeed, he and his wife had few dearer friends than Miss Nightingale, as she had none who took a warmer interest in her schemes than did the Herberts. He spoke to his colleagues in the Cabinet, and received their promise that if Miss Nightingale would undertake this work she should be given undisputed control, and be supported by the government. They promised, indeed, readily enough, but still he hesitated to write to her. For hers was the capable brain, as he knew, but it had already twice overtaxed her frail body. If she went to Scutari, she would take her life in her hands. Could he ask this sacrifice ? He decided that a heart so noble as Florence Nightingale's would perhaps never forgive him if he denied this noble opportunity. On the 15th of October he sat down and wrote the fateful letter. After telling her of the lack of nurses at Scutari, and the number of offers he received daily from volunteers "who have no conception of what a hospital is," he went on :—

" There is but one person in England that I know of who would be capable of organizing and superintending such a scheme. And I have been several times on the point of asking you if, supposing the attempt was made, you would undertake to direct it. . . My question simply is, Would you listen to the request to go out and supervise the whole thing ? You would, of course, have plenary authority over all the nurses, and I think I could secure you the fullest assistance and co-operation from the medical staff, and you would also have an unlimited power of drawing on the government for the success of your mission.

" I do not say one word to press you," he continued ; " yet I must not conceal from you that upon your decision will depend the ultimate success or failure of the plan.

" There is one point which I have hardly a right to touch upon, but I trust you will pardon me. If you were inclined to undertake the great work, would Mr. and Mrs. Nightingale consent? The work would be so national, and the request made to you proceeding from the government, your position would ensure the respect and consideration of every one. . . . This would secure you any attention or comfort on your way out there, together with a complete submission to your orders. I know these things are a matter of indifference to you, except so far as they may further the great object you may have in view; but they are of importance in themselves, and of every importance to those who have a right to take an interest in your personal position and comfort. I know you will come to a right and wise decision. God grant it may be one in accordance with my hopes.—Believe me, dear Miss Nightingale, ever yours,    SIDNEY HERBERT."

It so happened that, while Herbert was writing this letter, Florence Nightingale was seated in her garden pondering Russell's appeal: "*Are there no devoted women amongst us, willing and able to go forth and minister to the sick and suffering soldiers of the East?*" Hundreds were willing enough, she knew. But what of the ability she had been preaching—preaching for years? Was *she* able? Yes, if God would lend her strength.

She walked back to the house, and wrote to Sidney Herbert offering her services. Their letters crossed.

In just one week from that 15th of October, and while the public were still asking, "Who is Miss Nightingale?" she had her first batch of thirty-eight nurses marshalled and ready to start with her, and this, although the first advertisement in the newspapers had brought in applications which almost reduced her to despair with their hysterical foolishness. This first contingent was made up of fourteen Church of England Sisters, ten Roman Catholic Sisters of Mercy, three chosen by Lady Maria Forrester (who had been forming an independent plan for sending nurses to Scutari), and eleven selected from the miscellaneous volunteers who had answered the advertisement. A Mr. and Mrs. Bracebridge, two particular friends, accompanied the expedition; a clergyman and a courier completed it. The "Angel Band" left London on the evening of October 21st. A few friends and kinsfolk had gathered at the railway station to see them off. She had wished for a quiet departure. Quietly dressed, she said her farewells with a calm smile of confidence meant to hearten those she left behind. Her own heart foreboded only too well the task that lay before her.

They reached Boulogne early next morning, to meet with a surprising reception. France was our ally in this war. Word of these good women and their mission had preceded them across the Channel, and they were met on the quay by a crowd of Boulogne fishwives who seized their trunks, and jostled and almost came to blows over the privilege of carrying their luggage on board the train. Tears ran down the faces of these honest women as they shouldered the boxes and staggered with them across the rails. Some gabbled messages to be conveyed to sons and husbands afar at the seat of war. Not one sou would any one accept, but hand-shakes again and again, and the train steamed out of the station amid cries of "*Vivent les sœurs!*"

After a short halt at Paris with the Sisters of St. Vincent de Paul, the party took train again for Marseilles, their port of embarkation, and here again the porters declined any fee for their services. The *Vectis*, a steamship of the Peninsular Line, awaited them, and through terrible weather she drove her way eastward to Malta, which was reached on October 31st. Here the nurses transhipped, and reached Scutari on November 4th, the day before the battle of Inkerman.

The barrack hospital at Scutari stood on a hill overlooking the waterway of the Bosphorus, which by common consent is one of the loveliest scenes in the world. The building itself was palatial—an enormous quadrangle, each side of it close upon a quarter of a mile in length. Its galleries and corridors made up a total extent of four miles, and in the vast central court no less than twelve thousand men could be deployed. No hospital could appear more desirable—until one entered it and found a scene of filth and confusion not to be described. To right and left of the interminable corridors the wounded lay in closely packed rows, the majority of them with wounds undressed and fractured limbs still unset, although days had elapsed since they left the battlefield. Many were starving ; all lacked the barest decencies of life.

" There were no vessels for water or utensils of any kind ; no soap, towels or cloths, no hospital clothes ; the men lying in their uniforms, stiff with gore and covered with filth to a degree and of a kind no one could write about ; their persons covered with vermin, which crawled about the floors and walls of the dreadful den of dirt, pestilence, and death."

After landing at the ferry below, the sufferers crawled or were dragged up the hill to reach the hospital and lie amid these horrors upon polluted beds, between sheets of canvas so coarse that many begged to be left in their blankets. At night, when the wards were lit only by the glimmer of candles stuck in empty beer-bottles, rats would venture out and bite the weakest of the sufferers, drawing blood ; for the rats too were starving. One of Miss Nightingale's first actions, on entering the place, was to dislodge a Scutari rat from above a bed with the point of her practical British umbrella. Another was to order the removal of six dead and decomposing dogs she had counted close beneath the windows.

She arrived on November 4th. Next day was fought the hand-to-hand " soldiers' battle " of Inkerman—" the bloodiest struggle ever witnessed since war cursed the earth," wrote Russell—and before she could begin to cope with the miseries already about her, more were steadily accumulated, day after day and all day long, by the streams of wounded men pouring up from the ferry as the warships disembarked them, many bringing fever and cholera besides their wounds. They packed every inch of space in the vast hospital; many had to lie on the muddy ground outside, waiting until comrades died within and so made room. Medical stores had been sent out by the ton weight, never to reach Scutari. They lay rotting on the shore at Varna, or (an old trick of officialdom) had been packed in the holds of vessels *beneath* heavy guns and ammunition. These disasters culminated on November 14th, when the *Prince* transport, laden with stores, went ashore and was broken up in a furious hurricane.

These were the days—days when all seemed hopeless—that really proved Florence Nightingale ; days when she was known to stand for twenty hours at a time, dealing with fresh detachments of sick as they arrived, apportioning quarters, directing the nurses to their duties. She and her staff had taken up their quarters in a tower at a corner of the great quadrangle, and from her room by little and little the presence of an organizing brain began to make itself felt along the miles of galleries. Fortunately government had given her full authority to back up her own power of command. The orderlies found that they could not scamp their work of inspecting the wards. Woe to one who brought a false report that all was right when Miss Nightingale, who had a knack of finding things out, cross-questioned him and discovered that all was wrong ! The orderlies indeed soon became her devoted knights, and endured for her sake toils and vigils that far outwent their " official " duties. " Never," she said afterwards, " came from any one of them one word or one look which a gentleman would not have used. . . . The tears come into my eyes as I think how amidst loathsome scenes of disease and death there arose above it all the innate dignity, gentleness, and chivalry of the men, shining in the midst of what must be considered as the lowest sinks of human misery, and preventing instinctively the use of one expression which could distress a gentlewoman."

Even in those terrible early days she personally attended to scores of the worst operations. But for a time her work was done in the turret chamber, whence, as from the " conning-tower " of a modern battleship, the brain in command sent out its orders, bringing system out of confusion. A helpless kitchen, in which the vats seethed with offal that would have disgraced a soap factory, was reduced to cleanliness, to order, finally to such efficiency that in one day it would turn out thirteen gallons of chicken broth and forty gallons of arrowroot for the sick, with plenty of well-cooked food for the convalescent. Distributers of government stores had to mend their ways and be punctual. A Levantine who had the washing contract, and broke it so repeatedly that two or three thousand sick lay without a change of linen, found himself superseded. In the course of the first three months Miss Nightingale, from her own resources and her friends', provided the ten thousand shirts. Next she set up a laundry in a house hard by the hospital, and—with the help of a fund started by the *Times* —had it fitted with ample coppers in which five hundred shirts, to name no other articles, were washed each week. Her nurses were never idle. What time could be spared from the bedsides of the sufferers was employed in tearing up bandages—miles of bandages —making lint, fashioning splints, sewing mattresses and pillows. Possibly more distressful than the condition of the wounded and dying was that of the soldiers' wives, who had been allowed to accompany their husbands to Scutari, and who, left behind there, herded in the squalidest corners of the hospital. For

these, too, Florence Nightingale cared. Some were
widows, poor souls, and these were by degrees sent
home. For the others she did her best, supplying
them with food and clothes from her watch-chamber
in the tower, organizing work for them—decently paid
work—in her new laundry. They had been lodged,
after official delays, in three or four dark rooms in the
hospital basement; and in these cellars, from November to December, twenty-two children were born.
Then fever broke out, through the bursting of a drain.
Finally a Turkish house was procured and furnished
out of private funds, and the poor women were lodged
there. A school even was opened for the children.
By Christmas Day of that bitter Crimean winter the
barrack hospital had been swept of its filth; its in-
mates lay between clean sheets, and had invalids' food
in plenty; and they drank—some of them out of
medicine glasses—to the Queen of England, who had
sent a Christmas message to her " beloved troops,"
and to their lady-in-chief.

Fifty additional nurses arrived with the New Year,
and were drafted out on various services; for Scutari
had a " general " as well as a " barrack " hospital,
and there was the Kullali Hospital, across the Bosphorus, and temporary ones at the front. The war
had by this time settled down to a sullen siege of
Sebastopol, and men were dying now, not of wounds,
but from exposure in the icy trenches where sometimes they spent thirty-six hours at a stretch, starved
of rations, sleeping—when sleep overtook them—on
the frozen mud. Cholera devastated them.

" The cholera was of the very worst type, and the
attacked men lasted only four or five hours. Oh,
those dreadful cramps! You might as well try to
bend a piece of iron as to move those joints."

Against these cramps, as the sufferers were landed
after tossing for a day or two on the Black Sea, nurses
and orderlies worked heroically, wrapping the patients

in blankets steeped in boiling water and sprinkled with chloroform. A very small proportion survived. Streams of stretchers bringing in the stricken men passed streams of stretchers carrying out the dead. There were the frost-bitten too, from whose feet the boots had to be cut off bit by bit, flesh coming away with the leather. For two months the death-rate stood at 60 per cent. Still fighting through the worst, Florence Nightingale, after the orderlies had retired to snatch some rest, would go her round, lamp in hand, along the endless galleries, moving from bed to bed, here pausing to soothe the delirium of a poor fellow who fancied himself still storming Sebastopol, there taking (and never forgetting) the last message of the dying. As she passed, still holding her lamp, sick men raised themselves to kiss her shadow on their pillows.

As spring came in devoted helpers began to fall—Miss Smythe at Scutari, Sister Winifred at Balaklava, where the cholera had broken out afresh. But at Scutari the back of the work had by this time been broken, as they say. It had endured six months, when on May 2, 1855, Miss Nightingale felt free to take a journey to inspect the hospitals at the actual seat of war. In lovely weather she sailed up the Bosphorus, was welcomed at the harbour of Balaklava by the medical staff, paid a first visit to the hospitals, and then, with an escort, took a ride to view the siege operations around Sebastopol. Her holiday spirit made her reckless for once ; and although a sharp artillery fire was being exchanged, she insisted on entering the trenches and even proceeding to a battery (called the Three Mortar Battery) for a near view of the fortress. With the party rode M. Soyer, the famous chef, who had volunteered in February to come out and reorganize the hospital kitchens. He had done invaluable work, and to-day was in irrepressibly high spirits. "Before leaving the battery," he records,

"I begged Miss Nightingale as a favour to give me her hand, which she did. I then requested her to ascend the stone rampart next the wooden gun carriage, and lastly to sit upon the centre mortar; to which requests she very gracefully and kindly acceded." Having beguiled Miss Nightingale into this position, the gallant Frenchman cried, "Gentlemen! behold this amiable lady sitting fearlessly upon that terrible instrument of war! Behold the heroic daughter of England—the soldiers' friend!" All present shouted "Bravo! hurrah! hurrah! Long live the daughter of England!" The sentry of the Three Mortar Battery had been aghast at her incurring this peril. "My good young man," said Miss Nightingale, "more dead and wounded have passed through my hands than I hope you will ever see during the whole of your military career. Believe me, I have no fear of death." Yet the sentry was right, and her life too valuable to be lightly risked.

How valuable it was just then could be seen in the consternation that swept through the whole army a few days later, upon a report that Miss Nightingale had taken the Crimean fever. It was true. She had overtaxed her strength in visiting and reorganizing the Balaklava hospitals, and the fever had seized upon her weakness. For twelve days she lay dangerously ill, and on her recovery the doctors advised her returning at once to England. But she would not hear of this, and demanded to be taken back to Scutari, intending, as soon as her convalescence was assured, to return to Balaklava, and take up again the task of reforming the hospitals.

Her health, however, was barely re-established when, on September 8, the allies delivered their final assault upon Sebastopol, and in the following night the Russians evacuated the city, leaving it in flames. Peace was in sight, and amid the general rejoicings at home people were asking how best the nation could show its gratitude to the heroine of the war. Already Queen Victoria, anticipating the wish of her people, had put this question to Sidney Herbert. This was his answer :—

"49 BELGRAVE SQUARE, *July* 1855.

"MADAM,—There is but one testimonial which would be accepted by Miss Nightingale. The one wish of her heart has long been to found a hospital in London, and to work it on her own system of unpaid nursing ; and I have suggested to all who have asked for my advice in this matter to pay any sums that they may feel disposed to give, or that they may be able to collect, into Messrs. Coutts' Bank, where a subscription list for the purpose is about to be opened, to be called the ' Nightingale Hospital Fund '—the sum subscribed to be presented to her on her return home, which will enable her to carry out her object regarding the reform of the nursing system in England."

The scheme was inaugurated at a public meeting held at Willis's Rooms on November 29, the Duke of Cambridge presiding. At the meeting Sidney Herbert told a story that had reached him from a simple soldier, saved from death in the Scutari hospital. "She would speak to one and another," he said, "and nod and smile to many more ; but she could not do it to all, you know, for we lay there by hundreds. But we could kiss her shadow as it fell, and lay our heads on the pillow again content."

In time the Nightingale Fund grew to £44,000, and would have reached £50,000 if she had not stopped the flow of subscriptions, declaring that she had enough. While the money flowed in, and while statesmen were discussing peace, she had gone back to the heights of the Crimea, and was nursing the wounded who remained, and the sick men of the army of occupation—constantly visiting the camp hospitals in a carriage specially built for service on the uneven Turkish roads. While thus occupied she received from Queen Victoria a beautiful jewel (for which the Prince

Consort had made the design) with the following letter :—

"WINDSOR CASTLE, *January* 1856.

"DEAR MISS NIGHTINGALE,—You are, I know, well aware of the high sense I entertain of the Christian devotion which you have displayed during this great and bloody war, and I need hardly repeat to you how warm my admiration is for your services, which are fully equal to those of my dear and brave soldiers, whose sufferings you have had the *privilege* of relieving in so merciful a manner. I am, however, anxious of marking my feelings in a manner which I trust will be agreeable to you, and therefore send you with this letter a brooch, the form and emblems of which commemorate your great and blessed work, and which I hope you will wear as a mark of the high approbation of your Sovereign!

"It will be a very great satisfaction to me, when you return at last to these shores, to make the acquaintance of one who has set so bright an example to our sex. And with every prayer for the preservation of your valuable health, believe me, always yours sincerely,

"VICTORIA R."

When at length Florence Nightingale's time had come to return, she took every precaution to avoid a public demonstration. She declined the government's offer of a British man-of-war to bring her home, and travelling privately under an assumed name reached England unrecognized, and proceeded to Lea Hurst, where she arrived on August 8. Local tradition even asserts that she entered her home by the back door. While the land rang with her praises, she remained quietly with her family, nursing her strength back, that she might next take charge of the great nursing movement on which her heart was set. But this was not to be. The malady from which she suffered increased its hold, and to her bitter disappointment she realized that her life's active work was done.

But the movement went forward, never lacking inspiration in the memory of her good deeds, or words of shrewd and kindly advice from the writing-room in which she lived as a recluse.  Books came from her pen—*Notes on Hospitals* in 1859, and in 1860 *Notes on Nursing*, of which over 100,000 copies have been sold ; with many pamphlets.

Towards the close of her long life, when (we may almost say) she had become too weak to resist, honours were showered on her.  She had received the Red Cross from Queen Victoria.  On May 12, 1904, as a compliment upon her eighty-fourth birthday, King Edward VII. conferred on her the dignity of a Lady of Grace of the Order of St. John of Jerusalem.  In November 1907 he advanced her to the Order of Merit, of all rewards to-day the rarest and the most highly prized.  Florence Nightingale was the first woman to earn it, and has been the only one.  Her true reward, however, lay in the abiding gratitude of a nation ; in that, and in the fidelity with which Englishmen who followed the path she had found and carried more and more light to the dark places of human misery—as the Roman vestals tended one fire, never suffering it to die out night or day—turned over to " the Lady of the Lamp " to bless and kindle their beneficent torches.  "*The people that walked in darkness have seen a great light : they that dwell in the land of the shadow of death, upon them hath the light shined.*"   If such a light shine to-day in our great cities and in thousands of villages, it has grown and spread from the tiny flame borne by Florence Nightingale from ward to ward along the awful galleries of Scutari.

> " So in that house of misery
>     A lady with a lamp I see
>         Pass through the glimmering gloom,
>         And flit from room to room.
>
> " And slowly, as in a dream of bliss.
> The speechless sufferer turns to kiss
>         Her shadow as it falls
>         Upon the darkening walls.

" On England's annals, through the long
        Hereafter of her speech and song,
            A light its ray shall cast
            From portals of the past.

" A lady with a lamp shall stand
        In the great history of the land—
            A noble type of good,
            Heroic womanhood."

# PASTEUR

THROUGHOUT the late autumn of 1870, while the Prussian troops were crushing upon the frontier of France, there dwelt in the little town of Arbois in the Jura, and in a cottage not far from the bridge which crosses the stream of the Cuisance, a middle-aged man, short of stature, plain of feature, noticeable only, when you met and passed him, for a pair of curiously deep grey-green eyes and the drag of a paralyzed left leg. This was Louis Pasteur, administrator of the École Normale * in distant Paris, beloved there until yesterday by colleagues and pupils for his single-hearted devotion to science.

At Paris to-day there were no pupils left to teach. In spite of the privilege which freed *normaliens* from military service in exchange for a ten years' engagement at the university, the lads had enlisted eagerly as *chasseurs à pied*, soldiers of the line, artillerymen, marines. Pasteur's own son, a youth of eighteen, had started for the front. He himself had sought to be enrolled in the National Guard, until reminded that such service was not for a half-paralyzed man.

* The École Normale, or Normal School, was founded by Napoleon in 1808 for the training of young professors. By "normal" is meant that its methods of teaching are intended to serve as the "norm," or standard model, for other schools.

The École Normale, deserted of young life and forlorn, had been turned into an ambulance hospital in readiness for the now inevitable siege. For some time the administrator haunted the empty laboratories and tried to continue his scientific researches. " Do not stay in Paris," his friends advised. " You have no right to stay ; you would only be a useless mouth during the siege." So on September 5th he had packed up and started for Arbois, his native place.

There in the cottage by the bridge he tried to return to his books, his plans for future work. "*Laboremus*" (" Let us work "), he would repeat as in brighter days, looking up to cheer his wife and daughter, whose thoughts were at the front. But just then the town-crier's trumpet would sound up the street ; the vast workings and inscrutable laws of Nature would be forgotten in a moment ; and with a heart wrung with anxiety for France the little man would rush out, mix with the townsmen on the bridge, listen breathlessly to the news—which grew worse and worse—and return to his room with tears in his eyes, despair in his heart.

His father had died in that room, a veteran sergeant-major of Napoleon's, decorated for his service in the Third Regiment of the line—the " regiment brave amongst the brave." On the wall hung a medallion portrait of Bonaparte as a young general, with a larger effigy in bronzed plaster of the great emperor. On the shelves were books of his great campaigns, read again and again by the old soldier in his last days. All these traditions, all the imperial glory on which, even in Arbois, humble lives had fed, were ended now in Sedan.

To understand the indignant wrath that burned in a good Frenchman's heart during those days of humiliation, it must be remembered that Bismarck had brought this war about by means of a forged telegram. The whole business was a crime ; and

**LOUIS PASTEUR.**

*From a pen-drawing by*
*E. Heber Thompson.*

men, taught to believe that such a crime must be abhorrent in the sight of God, saw that it was successful, and wrote, as Pasteur wrote, " Should we not cry, Happy are the dead ! "

He, well on in years and half paralyzed ; he, dismissed from Paris as a " useless mouth "—what could *he* do towards lifting the *patrie* from the dust and restore her to her proud place among the nations ? Nothing, as it seemed, or less than nothing. He was not even a politician.

But wait ! If he had learnt anything in his laboratory, it was to think clearly ; and it is wonderful what one clear perception in the brain of an honest man will sometimes do in this world. Pasteur had two such perceptions, both equally clear. He saw that the only true leadership among the nations— the only leadership worth regaining for France—was a leadership in well-doing, for which a nation, as a man, must have a trained intelligence. It does not suffice to mean well ; one must learn the skill to carry that meaning into practice. He saw further— all question of right and wrong apart—that Germany had for years been setting a value on learning, education, intelligence, while France had been neglecting these things. " The real cause of our misfortunes lies *there*," he wrote to one of his pupils.

" It is not with impunity that a great nation is allowed to lose its intellectual standard. We are paying the penalty of fifty years' forgetfulness of science, of its immense influence on the destiny of a great people, and of all that might have assisted the diffusion of light. . . . I cannot go on ; all this hurts me."

Again :—

" Whilst Germany was multiplying her universities, setting up healthy rivalries between them, honouring her masters and doctors, creating vast laboratories and stocking them with every instrument and appliance, France was giving but a careless attention to higher education. . . . *The cultivation of science in its highest expression is perhaps even more necessary to the moral condition than to the national prosperity of a nation.*"

This clear perception he never lost, though now and again passion might cloud it for a moment as he thought of his country's humiliation.

" How fortunate you are to be young and strong ! Why cannot *I* begin a new life of study and work ? Unhappy France ! beloved country ! if only I could help in lifting thee out of thy disasters ! "

" I wish that France may fight to her last man, to her last fortress. . . . Every one of my future works shall bear on its title-page the words, ' *Hatred to Prussia ! Revenge ! revenge !* ' "

But " the best kind of revenge," says an old philosopher, " is not to be like them ; " and Pasteur's revenge was to be of this nobler kind. " I know not what destinies Fate has in store for me," he wrote ; " but I do feel most deeply that if I had to choose between the present situation of France and that of Prussia, I should decide for the former." Let us see what this modest man of science did towards lifting France out of her disasters ; but first let us see how his life had been preparing him for the attempt.

With the fall of his master Napoleon in 1814 Sergeant-Major Jean Joseph Pasteur, of the Third Regiment of the line, sought for and received his discharge. He could not bear it when the white cockade replaced the tricolour his regiment had carried through so many battlefields. Sad at heart, he retired home to Salins in the Jura, to work in his father's tannery. The mayor of Salins, an ardent Royalist, issued an order that all the late soldiers of Napoleon must bring their sabres to the mayoralty. Pasteur reluctantly obeyed ; but when he heard that these glorious weapons were to be distributed among the police, he snatched his own sabre back and refused to give it up. A small riot followed. The town was still garrisoned by an Austrian regiment, and to its colonel the mayor appealed, requiring him to quell the disturbance. The Austrian refused, answering that as a soldier he both understood and condoned the ex-sergeant-major's action. Pasteur was allowed to keep his sword, and returned home at the head of a cheering crowd.

He was not a quarrelsome man, however ; he only asked to be let alone, to work in peace. He never spoke of his campaigns, never entered a café. His fellow-townsmen found him shy and reserved. The tanyard lay beside the little river Furieuse, and faced a garden in which day by day he watched a young girl at work. Her name was Jeanne Etiennette Roqui, and, as such things befall, she soon perceived that the " old soldier "—who by the way was but twenty-five, though a veteran in service—studied her movements with extraordinary attention across the stream. He heard good reports of her : she was modest, intelligent, good-natured, the child of respectable parents living in a quiet way. He asked for her hand in marriage. Consent was given, and it proved an entirely happy union.

The young couple migrated to Dôle, then to Marnoz, lastly to Arbois. All these places lie within close range, but Arbois had advantages for the tanning business. The Pasteurs by this time had four children—three daughters, and little Louis, born at Dôle on the 27th of December 1822.

Louis Pasteur grew and thrived, and was sent in due course to the primary or (as we should say) elementary school of Arbois. Neither here nor at the Arbois College, to which he proceeded, did the boy show any special cleverness, unless it were at drawing, a gift inherited from his father. The old soldier, walking out every Sunday along the Besançon road, in

military-looking frock-coat decorated with the ribbon
of the Legion of Honour, pondered much on the
future of his one boy, so tractable and studious,
but possessing, so far as could be seen, but this
one modest talent.    M. Romanet, headmaster of the
Arbois College, did something to reassure the father.
He had perceived that young Louis's mind, while
it worked slowly, was unusually conscientious : he
never supposed " this " or " guessed " that, but before
affirming, waited until he was absolutely sure.    M.
Romanet talked with the parents and hinted at the
École Normale.    They hesitated, demurred ; finally,
at the close of October 1838, in a shower of rain and
sleet, young Louis Pasteur and a school friend, Jules
Vercel, were hoisted with their luggage on board the
country coach in the courtyard of the Hôtel de la
Poste and driven off for Paris, hiding themselves
from the weather under a tarpaulin beside the
coachman.

They were received in Paris by a good fellow-
countryman, M. Barbet, who kept a small school in
the Latin Quarter.    But although Louis did his best
to work, his homesickness was acute, and soon became
intolerable.    It so preyed on his mind that at length
good M. Barbet wrote a letter to his parents.    One
day in November Louis had word that a friend
wished to speak with him in a café at the end of the
street.    He went, and found, at a small table behind
the shop, a man sitting with his face in his hands.
It was his father.    " I have come to fetch you," he
said.

So back Louis went.    He was ashamed of having
let his feelings master his will.    He turned again to
his pastel drawings and worked feverishly, restlessly ;
but all the while his conscience was accusing him.
He had run away from his duty, and honour bade
him return.    Since he could not trust himself for a
second assault on Paris, he sought and obtained his

father's leave to go to the college at Besançon, where he could pass his *baccalauréat* and prepare himself, still with an eye on the École Normale. Besançon is scarce fifty miles from Arbois, and his father visited it three or four times a year to sell hides from the tanyard.

To Besançon accordingly he went, and was entered at the Royal College, where in 1841 he began to earn a small salary as " preparation master." Elated by this he wrote home offering to pay for the schooling of his youngest sister, Josephine, at a girls' college. " I could easily do it," he wrote, " by giving private lessons. I have already refused to give some at twenty or twenty-five francs a month." But this his parents would not allow. In 1840 he took his degree of Bachelor of Letters, and in August 1842 that of Bachelor of Science, passing both examinations creditably, but without special distinction. He was eager by this time to make another attempt on Paris, whither Charles Chappuis, a beloved and intimate college friend, had preceded him. His father refused his consent for some time, fearing a repetition of the 1838 fiasco, but at length gave way ; and in October Louis made his second start, in company with Chappuis, who was returning to work after a vacation.

As before, he boarded with good M. Barbet. He was no longer a homesick boy, but a grown lad, able to take care of himself, eager to learn, regular in attendance at the Lycée St. Louis and the lectures at the famous Sorbonne ; and at the end of the school year was admitted fourth on the list to the École Normale. It was in keeping with his character that he at once wrote to M. Barbet, who had boarded him gratis in return for his teaching some of the younger pupils, offering to give some further lessons on his half-holidays as a small token of his gratitude for past kindnesses.

It is related that in his hurry to enter the École

Normale he presented himself some days before the other students, and was allowed to sleep in the empty dormitory. His parents soon began to worry about his health ; and not without excuse, for he spent so much time among the retorts and test-tubes that his comrades nicknamed him " the laboratory pillar." On half-holidays he taught M. Barbet's classes. All his recreation consisted in an occasional walk with Chappuis, when the two would dispute over the comparative claims of philosophy and science—for Chappuis was taking his course in philosophy.

One day—they were walking in the gardens of the Luxembourg—Pasteur began to talk excitedly of tartaric acid and an allied but highly curious substance called " paratartaric " or " racemic " acid. What bothered Pasteur, and did not bother Chappuis at all, was this—that while in combination with soda, or again with ammonia, these two acids produced crystals which in other respects could not be distinguished from one another, a beam of light passing through these crystals was quite differently refracted ; just as a ray falls differently through a prism and through a flat sheet of glass. Here were two crystals alike in shape and apparently in every other respect ; yet the tartaric slanted the light, and the racemic passed it straight through. Of course this is an extremely rough-and-ready way of stating a problem over which Pasteur had been brooding for months, and with which he wearied his friend during their walk, explaining that (nobody knew why) certain crystals reflected light to the right hand, others to the left, while others again remained inactive. " Why should this be ? " the young man eagerly demanded. Chappuis, of course, had not a notion, and wondered how his friend could be eager over such trifles of science while the problem of philosophy—the great riddle of the universe—remained unsolved. Pasteur's father, when the youth wrote home hinting at possible discoveries, was even more practical. "Before being a captain," he answered, "you must become a lieutenant."

But this crystallography had taken hold of Pasteur; and, having passed through the ordinary examination course at the École Normale with more than fair credit, he plunged into the study with a newcomer at the laboratory, one Auguste Laurent, a young professor full of bold ideas. These two worked together until their experiments were interrupted by Laurent's promotion as assistant to M. Dumas, the great chemist, at the Sorbonne. Pasteur worked on alone; the differences in crystals occupied his spare thoughts even during the Revolution of 1848, when young men in Paris threw up barricades in the holy cause of the republic and chased Louis Philippe from his throne. Like most generous youths of his time, he had visions of a France devoted to the ideas of liberty and fraternity—a state of free men and brethren. But the struggle over and apparently successful, he returned to his crystals.

If an object reflected in a mirror—say a table or a square flight of steps—has its two sides alike or "symmetrical," you can lay the image of the thing over the thing itself, and they fit. But if the staircase be spiral, you cannot lay its image exactly over it; the one turns to the right, the other to the left: and a right hand seen in a mirror is a left hand.

Now Pasteur, examining the crystals of tartaric acid, discovered—what had escaped all previous observers—that they had little facets on one side, and always on the same side, to the right. "Now," reasoned he, "if the paratartaric or racemic crystals have these facets on *both* sides, we shall know exactly why, with them, the ray is neutralized and falls straight." To his disappointment, these crystals, too, were faceted only upon one side, but not on the same side. It occurred to him to pick them out one by one and sort them, putting on one side those which turned to the right, and on the other those which turned to the left. Having done this, he mixed an equal number of each kind together, and threw the ray upon the mixture.

The equal and opposite facets exactly neutralized one another, and the light fell straight. " I have it ! " he cried, and rushing from the room embraced a casual curator who happened to be coming down the corridor.

In Paris the report of a scientific discovery spreads quickly. The report of this one reached the great chemist Biot, aged seventy-four, who had spent the best years of his life in studying crystals, and was inclined to be sceptical. Pasteur heard of his disbelief, and wrote very modestly asking him for an interview. An appointment was made.

Every detail of that interview remained for ever fixed in Pasteur's memory. Biot began by fetching some paratartaric acid. " I have most carefully studied it," he said to Pasteur : " it is absolutely neutral in the presence of polarized light." Some distrust was visible in his gestures and audible in his voice. " I shall bring you everything that is necessary," continued the old man, fetching doses of soda and ammonia. He wanted the salt prepared before his eyes.

After pouring the liquid into a crystallizer, Biot took it into a corner of his room, to be quite sure that no one would touch it. " I shall let you know when you are to come back," he said to Pasteur when taking leave of him. Forty-eight hours later some crystals, very small at first, began to form ; when there was a sufficient number of them Pasteur was recalled. Still in Biot's presence, Pasteur withdrew them, one by one, and divided them into two groups—left and right.

" So you affirm," said Biot, " that your right-hand crystals will deviate to the right, the plane of polarization, and your left-hand ones will deviate to the left ? "

" Yes," said Pasteur.

" Well, let me do the rest."

Biot himself prepared the solutions, and then sent again for Pasteur. Biot first placed in the apparatus the solution which should deviate to the left. Having satisfied himself that the deviation actually took place, he took Pasteur's arm and said in these words often deservedly quoted : " My dear boy, I have loved science so much during my life that this touches my very heart."

Thanks in great measure to Biot's enthusiasm, the young man's reputation spread among the scientific bigwigs, who were delighted to find him as modest personally as he was ambitious for the cause of learning. In the autumn of 1848 he was offered a professorship of physics at Dijon, a post which he exchanged in the following January for a professorship of chemistry at Strasburg. A new rector, M. Laurent, had recently been appointed to the Academy of Strasburg—a man of excellent heart and charming manners, blessed with a wife and three daughters, all—and it is saying a great deal—as good as he deserved. Together they made of the academy a home where professors and pupils alike found a cordial welcome, and witnessed a family affection which was none the less merry and cheerful for being trained upon the highest principles and ideals. Pasteur, made welcome with the rest, fell in love with the youngest daughter, Marie. The discovery of his passion dismayed him, for the family was of a higher social position than his own, and he had no wealth to compensate for this inferiority ; but with that simple directness which was a part of his nature he wrote to M. Laurent, professing his suit :—

" My family is in easy circumstances, but with no

fortune—I do not value what we possess at more than 50,000 francs ; and as for me, I have long ago decided to hand over to my sisters the whole of what should be my share. I have therefore absolutely no fortune. My only means are good health, some courage, and my position in the university."

The answer was delayed. Meanwhile Pasteur was sadly afraid that Mademoiselle Marie would have nothing to say to him. " There is nothing in me to attract a young girl's fancy. But my recollections tell me that those who have known me very well have loved me very much." The proposal was accepted, and he was married on May 29th, 1849. " I, who did so love my crystals ! " he wrote whimsically. But from the first Mme. Pasteur made up her mind that the laboratory must come before everything, and her husband become a great man of science.

The next few years were occupied with hard work and domestic happiness. He studied his crystals with infinite patience, and the supply of racemic acid having unaccountably ceased, we find him travelling in quest of it over Germany, Austria, Bohemia. " Never," said an enthusiastic journalist when the quest was over—" never was treasure sought, never adored beauty pursued over hill and vale with greater ardour ! " He discovered it here and there in tiny quantities. But he did more : *he discovered the key of the secret of making it.* At length, on June 1st, 1853, he was able from his laboratory at Strasburg to send the following telegram :—

*Monsieur Biot, Collège de France, Paris. I transform tartaric acid into racemic acid ; please inform M.M. Dumas and Senarmont.* " The discovery," he wrote, " will have incalculable consequences." As a by-product, one may mention, he obtained from it the red ribbon of the Legion of Honour.

In September 1854 he was made professor and dean of the new Faculty of Science at Lille, the greatest industrial town of Northern France. It is the centre of a country of distilleries, and Pasteur, besides organizing his classes and attracting pupils by the hundreds to his lectures, flung himself into the study of fermented liquors, especially the ferments of alcohol. This study led him to hope that one day he might even solve the question of "spontaneous generation." Can life start into being of itself, without deriving that existence from other life ? "You will never find your way out," Biot warned him. "I shall try," said Pasteur. "I would advise no one," said Dumas, "to dwell too long on such a subject." Pasteur set himself to work. He had just been elected administrator of his beloved École Normale. He said his farewells at Lille, returned to Paris, set up his scientific installation in two attics close under the roof, and so started on a campaign of research which lasted four years. It is, of course, impossible here to follow the paths by which he reached the answer to that all-important question. He sought it in his garret laboratory—he sought it on the summits of the High Alps ; for gradually he became convinced that the air we breathe, even the most rarefied, contains dust, which in its turn contains germs of animal life, and that therefore no discoverable thing on this planet comes, or can come, into life of itself. If from nothing else, it receives life from the germs of the all-surrounding air.

At length, on April 7th, 1864, Pasteur entered the lecture-room of the Sorbonne and explained to a crowded audience—for "all Paris" had gathered to hear him—his discovery. With the aid of a phial or two he showed that "there is now no circumstance known in which it can be affirmed that microscopic beings come into the world without germs, without parents similar to themselves. Those who affirm it have been duped by illusions."

Thus, before an audience as critical as any in the

world, this unassuming servant of science stood up and in a few quiet words, without eloquence or a trace of self-glorification, slew the false doctrine of " spontaneous generation," and slew it for ever.

He was attacked on all sides—attacked as being, among other things, an enemy of religion. " There is here," he answered, " no question of religion, philosophy, atheism, materialism, or spiritualism. I might even add that these do not matter to me as a scientific man. It is a question of fact. When I took it up I was as ready to be convinced by experiments that spontaneous generation exists as I now am persuaded that those who believe in it are blindfolded." He had been eager enough in the search ; he was careless now that the truth was discovered. Leaving his critics to dispute amongst themselves, he hastened back to his study of wine and fermented liquors. From this, just as he was starting on fresh discoveries, he was summoned to investigate a disease among silkworms which threatened to ruin the silk-growing industry in the south of France, and indeed over all Southern Europe. In the early days of Louis Philippe's reign this industry had been worth one million francs a year to France. Of a sudden all this prosperity fell away. Disease swept the mulberry tree—the " tree of gold," as it was called—of all its yield, and the plague spread everywhere, even to China. By 1864 healthy eggs could be found nowhere but in Japan. His old friend Dumas, now a senator, begged Pasteur to visit Alais, the silk-growing centre of Southern France, and attempt to stamp out the disease, which manifested itself in the form of tiny dark spots like a sprinkling of pepper grains. Pasteur obeyed, and set up a laboratory at Alais, where the cultivators grumbled, wanting to know why a " mere chemist " had been sent to them instead of an experienced silk-farmer. Pasteur answered, " Have patience." Those days at Alais were made sorrowful

(2,691)

by the death of his father and of his youngest child, his two-year-old daughter Camille.  He himself began to suffer from symptoms of failing health ; but he worked on, examining thousands of silkworms under the microscope, and gradually getting to the root of the " corpuscle disease," complicated though it was with another devastating disease known as "flachery."  During this time he was much cheered by the success of his old experiments in the preservation of wine by heating it, now that the government was putting his theories into practice on a large scale.  He found time to improve the vinegar industry at Orleans by teaching the merchants there to follow scientific principles ; and attacked the ministry in a pamphlet for cutting down the new laboratories at the École Normale—this at a time when millions upon millions of francs were being spent on the new Opera House !

" If the conquests useful to humanity touch your heart—if you are jealous of the share your country may boast in these—then, I implore you, take some interest in those sacred dwellings sneeringly described as *laboratories*. . . . Some nations have felt the wholesome breath of truth.  Rich and large laboratories have been growing in Germany.  At Berlin and at Bonn two palaces, worth four million francs each, are being erected for chemical studies.  St. Petersburg has spent three and a half million francs on a Physiological Institute.  England, America, Austria, Bavaria, have made generous sacrifices.  Italy has made a start.  And France ?  France has not yet begun."

He was approaching his conquest of the silkworm disease : he was sure of success.  He had separated the pure seed from the infected, and was growing healthy worms in distant " colonies " to restore the industry, when, on October 19th, 1868, paralysis struck him down, deadening the whole of his left side.  In the dark struggle before speech failed him he explained his own symptoms to the doctor, smiling, but with the brave smile of one who had no illusions. For a week he lay between life and death; and then, to the amazement of his pupil M. Gernez, who had scarcely left the bedside, started of a sudden to dictate a note on the silkworm disease quite clearly and concisely, in words which actually appeared in a memorandum to the report now ready for presentation to the Academy of Science. There were days of doubt after this. But his recovery was steady on the whole. On January 18th, 1869, exactly three months after his paralytic stroke, he insisted upon being carried back to Alais. On March 22nd the Lyons Silk Commission wrote to Alais, asking if it were possible to procure some guaranteed healthy seed. Pasteur's answer was to send four boxes of silkworms' eggs, with this message: "I have the honour to submit to you (1) one parcel of eggs which should succeed; (2) one parcel which should perish of the corpuscle disease; (3) one parcel which should perish of the flachery disease; (4) one parcel which should perish of the corpuscle and the flachery diseases combined." All happened as he predicted. Success was achieved. He spent the remainder of his convalescence at Villa Vicentina in North Italy, a silk-growing centre, spreading the good work, and in July 1870 returned by easy stages to Paris, making a detour to visit Vienna, and stopping a couple of days at Strasburg, his old home, soon to be lost to France. By the time he reached Paris the war had broken out.

Such, then, was the man—already, and in spite of his modest bearing, not undistinguished—who in the small cottage at Arbois swore to devote the remainder of his life to the uplifting of France. In his anguish he remembered the honorary diploma he had received two years ago from the German university of Bonn. From Arbois he returned the parchment to that university with a letter saying, " The sight of it is now odious to me, and I feel offended at seeing my name, with the qualification of ' illustrious,' placed under a name which is henceforth an object of execration to my country—that of your king, William." The protest or challenge may seem weak enough and undignified to us, whose patriotism has never known what it means to endure a helpless shame. Amid the brutalities of war the finest intellects that have lived for peace may find themselves helpless indeed. Even thus helpless was Pasteur when, having been for long without news of his son, who had been fighting before Héricourt, he with his wife and daughter started off on January 24th, 1871, in a broken-down chaise, along roads choked with snow, to search for the lad. After journeying for some hours in bitter weather the travellers found a wayside inn near Montrond, and spent the night there, the old carriage with its piled travelling boxes standing at anchor on the roadside like a gipsy's van. Next day they jolted through a pine forest, in a silence unbroken save by the masses of snow that dropped from the branches. That night they slept at Censeau, the next at Chaffois, and on the 27th reached Pontarlier. The town was full of straggling soldiers, some huddled around bivouac fires in the streets, others dying in the church on the very steps of the altar, others foraging for straw along the roads between the bodies of horses half snowed under. For long they could hear no news. "All I can tell you," reported one soldier whom they interrogated, " is that out of 1,200 men of that battalion there are but 300 left." As they were questioning another a passer-by stopped and said, "Sergeant Pasteur ? Yes, I know him. I slept by him last night at Chaffois. He is ill. You might perhaps meet him somewhere on the road thither." Back the Pasteurs started in their chaise, now almost a wreck. They had just passed through the Pontarlier gate when a rough cart met them. A soldier, wrapped in his greatcoat and holding by the edge of the cart, gave a cry of surprise. He clambered down, and mother and father embraced their son.

Such scenes were by no means rare in that winter of 1870–71, so terrible for France. Pasteur carried his invalided son off to Geneva and nursed him back to strength, so that in the early days of February the lad was able to get back to France and rejoin his regiment. The parents moved back to Lyons, where they lodged with Mme. Pasteur's brother, Dean of the Faculty of Science there. For Arbois had by this time been cruelly invaded, and was a Prussian depôt ; while Paris had passed from siege and bombardment to surrender and civil war. Amid these trials Italy remembered the man who had done so much for her peaceful industry, and offered him a professorship of agricultural chemistry at Pisa, with a high salary. Pasteur declined. " I should feel," he wrote in his letter of refusal, " that I deserved a deserter's punishment if I left my country in her distress to seek material gain better than she can offer me."

He accepted an invitation from an old friend and pupil, M. Duclaux, and became his guest at Royat, where the two set up a spare room as a silkworm nursery. This was in April 1871, and before summer was well advanced Pasteur had found a brewery hard by, and was deep in the process of brewing pure beer. He found the maltsters of this Chamalières brewery working by rule of thumb, ignorant of the science of their trade, and producing yeast pure and infected without knowing one from the other. Pasteur, as he taught them better methods, became as deeply interested in pure beer as he had been aforetime in pure wine. He resolved to visit England, the country of vast breweries, where surely, thought he, the principles of the manufacture would be understood. In London, where he came to learn, he was quickly able to teach. Our breweries, starting from his advice, underwent a great reform, particularly in the matter of cleanliness.   As Pasteur soon demonstrated, beer that contains no living germs will not decay, or " go bad " as we say ; it is only corrupted by infinitely small germs, which are the ferments of disease ; and these germs are brought to it in the dust of the air, in the ingredients, or by the apparatus used in the breweries.   Pasteur was a sworn foe of dust.   He never used a plate or a glass without inspecting it minutely and wiping it with his napkin—a habit that was often a sore trial to hostesses.

A study of beer does not strike one at first sight as a highly promising start towards restoring self-respect to a great nation.   But let us mark what followed.   The study of ferments in beer led to the study of virus ; that is to say, Pasteur asked himself the illuminating question, " *If germs are the secret of disease in wine and beer, may not germs also be the secret of much human disease ?* "

He regretted bitterly that he was not a medical man.   He foresaw, and accurately enough, that his further researches would arouse bitter criticism within the ranks of a close profession ; and it was mainly in the hope of arming himself against this opposition among men who spoke of him as a " mere chemist," a " poacher on the preserves of the physicians," that he consented in 1873 to be elected an Associate of the Academy of Medicine.   In his own mind he armed himself with the thought that to vanquish one disease was a nobler feat, and farther reaching, than to vanquish a whole army of Prussians.   It might be possible to save more lives than these enemies of France had ever destroyed.

Already throughout Europe earnest physicians were engaged in that study of contagion which in forty years has worked a complete revolution in medicine and surgery ; and already, though he had but faintly suspected it, some of the greatest had been working on lines suggested by Pasteur's researches.   That there may be no doubt of this let us quote from a letter addressed to him on February 13th, 1874, by our own great surgeon Lister, the discoverer of the antiseptic method :—

" I do not know whether the methods of British surgery ever meet your eye.    If so, you will have seen from time to time notices of the antiseptic system of treatment, which I have been labouring for the last nine years to bring to perfection.

" Allow me to take this opportunity to tender you my most cordial thanks for having, by your brilliant researches, demonstrated to me the truth of the germ theory of putrefaction, and thus furnished me with the principle upon which alone the antiseptic system can be carried out."

There were some indeed, who, when in 1874 the National Assembly voted a life annuity of 12,000 francs to Pasteur, supposed that the stricken man, always in danger of a second paralytic stroke, would now retire and end his days in tranquillity.    But Pasteur had no such intention : " he considered that not to work was to lose the whole object of living." He went back to his laboratory.    Our story cannot attempt to follow him through his researches into the causes of anthrax (that terrible disease of animals), bubonic plague, chicken cholera, yellow and other fevers ; but it may take as a sample of the whole the discovery by which his name is still most widely known—the preventive treatment of hydrophobia.

He had begun his experiments in 1880 ; and we must not hide the fact that from the first they involved vivisection.    Many of the best men and women in the world hate and denounce vivisection, and from the best motives.    Pasteur disliked it excessively, and his experiments, performed with the utmost gentleness, were only engaged in under a mastering conviction that by means of them untold benefit would result to the human race.

The problem of this horrible disease had haunted his mind for years, and by degrees came to occupy all his thoughts. The experiments, as may be guessed, were attended with no little danger. One day, for instance, Pasteur having wished to collect some saliva direct from the jaws of a rabid dog, two assistants undertook to drag a mad bull-dog, foaming at the mouth, from its cage. They seized it by a lasso and stretched the ferocious creature on a table, where they held it down while Pasteur, by means of a glass tube held between his lips, drew a few drops of the deadly saliva.

He located the seat of the disease in the nervous system. By a series of inoculations on rabbits he first learnt to predict with astonishing accuracy the time before, in each animal inoculated, the virus would take effect, and then set himself to decrease the strength of the virus—to reduce it to a *preventive*, as vaccine is a preventive of smallpox. Pasteur cut out a bit of the medulla (the lower part of the brain, where it meets the spinal cord) from a rabbit which had just died of the virus. This fragment he suspended in a dry phial, closed by cotton-wool to prevent the entrance of any dust. As the medulla shrank and became dry the strength of the virus in it gradually decreased until at the end of fourteen days it was quite gone. This medulla Pasteur crushed, mixed with pure water, and injected beneath the skin of several dogs. Next day he inoculated them in the same way with medulla which had been drying for thirteen days, and so on, until the medulla was used of a rabbit that had died the same day. These dogs not only escaped hydrophobia; they took no disease from the bites of mad dogs.

Pasteur repeated these experiments again and again, until absolutely certain that he had the cure of hydrophobia under his hand.

But a man may be a hundred times sure of such

a discovery by repeating experiments so hazardous upon animals. It yet requires a tremendous moral courage to put it to the proof upon a human being.

On Monday, July 6th, 1885, a little Alsatian boy, Joseph Meister, was brought by his mother to Pasteur's laboratory. The child, aged nine, had been bitten two days before, on his way to school, by a mad dog. The dog had rushed upon him, and he had fallen in the roadway, thinking only of covering his face with his hands and screaming. A bricklayer rushed up, beat the brute off, and picked up the boy, who was covered with blood and saliva. The dog's master, a man called Vone, came up and took the dog home, when it bit him in the arm. Vone at once shot it. Little Meister's parents carried the child off to a doctor, who cauterized the wounds, and advised his being taken at once to Paris. Vone, anxious on his own account as well as for the child, came also.

Pasteur reassured the man. His coat sleeve had wiped off the dog's saliva, and his shirt sleeve was hardly pierced. He might safely return to Alsace, and he promptly did. The child had fourteen wounds. Could Pasteur venture to risk on him the preventive treatment which he had tried again and again, and with steady success now, upon dogs? He suffered anguish of mind : but he reflected on the hideous death that almost infallibly awaited little Joseph, and he hardened his heart. Still he would not operate until he had consulted the wisest friends known to him in Paris. He made an appointment with the mother to call again at five o'clock, and went off to lay the case before these friends. They advised him to begin the inoculation at once.

At five o'clock he did so. It was a very slight operation—a mere pin-prick in the side, with an injection of a few drops of a preparation fourteen days old. The child, who had been crying bitterly with the fear of it, soon dried his tears on finding that this was all the pain he had to undergo. Pasteur in the course of the day had provided a comfortable room for mother and child, and the boy was soon happy playing with tame rabbits, guinea pigs, white mice. Further inoculations followed, with virus which steadily increased in strength. On the 11th Pasteur wrote, " The child sleeps well, has a good appetite, and the inoculated matter is absorbed into the system from one day to another without leaving a trace. It is true that I have not come to the test inoculations." As this time approached Pasteur's anxiety robbed him of sleep. At night visions haunted him : he saw this innocent child " suffocating in the mad struggles of hydrophobia." In such hours it was useless to tell himself that this would almost certainly have been the end had no treatment been attempted. The inoculations took ten days. After the final one, and when little Meister had been put to bed (first claiming a kiss from " dear Monsieur Pasteur "), the great healer broke down. Sleep would not visit him that night ; he felt sure the boy would die. But morning came, and little Meister, awakening without a trace of feverishness, began to call for his pets.

The cure was complete. Pasteur, having done all that his science could do, went off to take some needed rest at a quiet, almost deserted, country place in Burgundy, but within reach of the telegraph. Telegrams came, but all were reassuring. The boy returned to his home : still the news was good. By degrees all fear was at an end.

To me this vigil by the bedside of a waif of a boy— when we consider all it means, to what it has led, and to what it will continue to lead—appears the culminating point in the life of a truly heroic man ; a man, though modest, greater than famous conquerors who have founded empires. In his remaining years honours poured in upon him, as patients flocked to him, from every part of Europe. They were alike the tribute of the nations to France—his beloved France. He died—overtaken at length by his old enemy, paralysis—peacefully in his bed, his one hand resting in his wife's, his other on the crucifix. I, who write this poor account of him, came some weeks later in the great Church of Notre Dame upon a side chapel piled high as a man's waist with wreaths of immortelles. They had been piled on the grave of Pasteur. How many of them, one wonders, came from men and women whose lives he had snatched from torment and prolonged ?

He had accomplished his vow. He had turned the eyes of the world again upon France, for help. His own words rise up before me as this story concludes, words spoken by him to the Medical Congress of all Nations assembled at Copenhagen on August 10th, 1884 :—

" In the name of France I thank M. le President for his words of welcome. . . . Science is of no country. But though science has no country, the man of science must keep in mind all that works towards the glory of his country. In every great man of science will be found a great patriot. The thought of adding to the greatness of his country sustains him in his long efforts, and throws him into the difficult but glorious scientific enterprises which bring about real and durable conquests."

# GORDON

THE cartoons in *Vanity Fair* are famous, and the descriptions in letterpress which accompany them are as caustic as they are brief. Years ago, turning over a volume, I happened on the portrait of a shortish, pleasant-looking man with a stoop, and with short hair obstinately curling beneath the brim of a silk hat thrust well back on his head. Glancing at the letterpress, I was surprised and arrested by its unusual length ; and pausing to read it, received another shock. The conclusion ran :—

" He is now the grandest Englishman alive, and a Lieutenant-Colonel of Engineers in the English army, waiting for promotion.

" Colonel Gordon is the most conscientious, single-minded, unselfish, and honest of men. He has a complete contempt for money, and having again and again rejected opportunities of becoming rich beyond the dreams of avarice, he remains a poor man, with nothing in the world but his sword and his honour. The official mind, being incapable of understanding this, regards it as a sign of madness. And as it is found that besides being utterly without greed, he is also entirely without vanity or self-assertion, he is set down by officials as being ' cranky ' and unsafe to employ in comparison with such great men as ——, ——, and ——.

" He is very modest and very gentle, yet full of enthusiasm for what he holds to be right. This enthusiasm often leads him to interfere in matters which he does not understand, and to make in haste statements he has to correct at leisure. But he is a fine, noble, knightly gentleman, such as is found but once in many generations."

These words, written of Gordon before he sealed his greatness with his death, before he set out on his last mission, before even the mass of Englishmen of his generation knew of such a man in their midst, were prophetic if ever words were. I never pass Gordon's statue in Trafalgar Square without thinking of them. To me he is the noblest Briton of our times. With Lincoln we may dispute for him the title of the most absolute hero in this book—though it include Garibaldi. I think that others are of my mind, if one may judge from the wreaths laid and renewed by nameless admirers at the base of his statue where, in the centre of empire, his image seems to ponder and brood as the traffic of London roars by.

Charles George Gordon, fourth son of Lieut.-General Henry William Gordon of the Royal Artillery, was born at Woolwich, January 28th, 1833. His mother was Elizabeth, daughter of Samuel Enderby, a noted shipowner and merchant prince, whose whaling vessels, following the explorations of Captain Cook, opened up the South Pacific to British commerce, took out the first batch of British convicts to Australia, and (in the shape of runaways) planted the first seeds of British imperialism in New Zealand.

The Gordon family numbered five sons and six daughters. Three of the sons grew up to enter the army, and all three became generals. Of the boyhood of Charles, the youngest, little is known, and that little need not detain us. He was not strong, and he made no mark either at school at Taunton, or at the Royal Military Academy, which he entered in 1848, unless it were by a somewhat special aptitude for getting into scrapes. One characteristic story, however, is related of his cadet days at Woolwich. Having been rebuked by Captain Eardley Wilmot for incompetence, and told that he would never make an officer, he tore the epaulettes from his shoulders and flung them down at his superior's feet.

On the 23rd of June 1852, Gordon passed out of the Royal Military Academy, and was gazetted to the Engineers. In November 1854 orders came for him to proceed to Corfu, much to his disappointment; for the Crimean War was now in progress, and he had hoped for active service at the front. By the influence of Sir John Burgoyne, an old friend of the family, his route was changed. On the 4th of December he received orders to start for the Crimea, *and started that very day*. On New Year's Day, 1855, he reached Balaklava, and reported himself at headquarters.

By this time the battles of the Alma, Balaklava, and Inkerman had been fought, and the allies had settled down to besiege Sebastopol. The young subaltern's duties during that bitter Crimean winter consisted mainly in building new batteries in the advance trenches; and amid this wearying work he developed (as his superior officers testified) an extraordinary quick and seemingly intuitive knowledge of the enemy's movements and designs. "We always used to send him to find out what new move the Russians were making," writes Colonel Chesney. A small incident, which at the time merely illustrated Gordon's military thoroughness and his good-nature, was destined, as we shall see in due course, to give his career its first great opportunity. A keen officer, Colonel Staveley of the 44th Regiment, happened to say in Gordon's hearing that he had been given an awkward job for the morrow, having been appointed field officer of the day for the trenches, notwithstanding that he had just returned from sick-leave, and knew nothing of their geography. Now it was no business of a young subaltern of Engineers to instruct infantry field officers in their duties; and moreover Gordon, like every other man in the trenches, was well-nigh worn out with work. But throughout life he had no opinion of routine or etiquette when they stood in the way of helpfulness, and no idea of sparing himself while another man could be helped. "Oh," said he shyly, "come down with me to-night after dark, sir, and I'll show you over." "He drew me out," says Colonel Staveley, "a very clear sketch of the lines (which I have now), and down I went accordingly. He explained every nook and corner, and took me along outside our most advanced trench, the bouquets and other missiles flying about us in, to me, a very unpleasant manner; he taking the matter remarkably coolly."

Stray sentences in his letters from the Crimea seem

to show that the sense of an overruling Fate—the sense which in later years increased and wrapped him about as with a cloud, in which he walked apart from his fellows, protected, as he believed, and guided under God's unseen hand to further God's unguessed purposes—had already begun to give a cast to his mind. For example, referring to the death of a Captain Craigie, who was killed by a splinter from a shell, he writes : " I am glad to say he was a serious man. The shell burst above him, and by *what is called chance* struck him in the back, killing him at once." Some have suggested that Gordon learned his " fatalism " in later years from the Mohammedans in the Soudan, but it is certain, at any rate, that, though not yet " converted," he had in 1854, while stationed at Pembroke, begun to think seriously on matters of religion, largely through the influence of his elder sister Augusta. " You know," he wrote to her, " I never was confirmed. When I was a cadet I thought it was a useless thing, as I did not intend to alter (not that it was in my power to be converted when *I* chose). I, however, took my first sacrament on Easter Day (April 16th, 1854), and have communed ever since." On June 30th, 1855, he wrote home, " Lord Raglan died on the evening of the 26th, of tear and wear and general debility. He was universally regretted, as he was so kind. . . . I *hope* he *was prepared, but do not know.*"

The end of the war brought no promotion to Gordon ; but he was selected for the French Legion of Honour, a decoration conferred on very few subalterns. During the next year he acted as an assistant commissioner in marking out the new frontiers between Russia, Turkey, and Roumania. On his return home he was sent to perform a similar task in Armenia, where, with the interval of a six months' visit home, he remained until the autumn of 1858. On his return to England he was appointed to

Chatham as field-work instructor and adjutant, getting his captaincy in 1859.

By being employed in Armenia he had missed all chance of serving in India when the Mutiny broke out in 1858. But now (1859–60) we were at war with China, and he determined to see active service again, as a first step to which he resigned his appointment at Chatham, clean against the advice of his father and of many friends who prophesied that he was damaging his career. At one time this seemed likely enough, for irritating delays occurred. It was not until late in July 1860 that he started, and he reached Hong-Kong to learn that fighting had practically ceased with the capture of the Taku forts. Still he pressed on for Tientsin, a city below Pekin on the Peiho River, head-quarters just then of the French and English expeditionary force, and arrived to learn that the Chinese had reopened the quarrel, on the very eve of negotiation, by treacherously seizing under a flag of truce a number of officers and members of our diplomatic staff, and so barbarously using them that thirteen died of their maltreatment. To avenge this outrage, the allies marched on Pekin, and actually had their guns in position to blow in one of the great gates when the Chinese surrendered. French and English marched in to learn what had befallen their fellow-countrymen, and in his indignation Lord Elgin determined to teach treachery a lesson by burning down the famous Summer Palace of Pekin, the most splendid and wonderful treasure-house in the world. Its lawns, groves, and gardens, set amid exquisite scenery, with the snow-capped mountains of Tartary for background, covered an area of several miles ; and temples, pagodas, summer lodges, lakes, bridges, grottos, terraces, diversified the green enclosure. Into this fairyland and amid shrines of gold and silver, bronzes and ivory, lacquer and silks, the troops were let loose for two days to burn and pillage, destroying property

which it was estimated could not be replaced for four
millions of money. Gordon, who witnessed it, wrote
home :—

" You can scarcely imagine the beauty and magnifi-
cence of the places we burned. It made one's heart
sore. . . . Quantities of gold ornaments were burned,
considered as brass. It was wretchedly demoralizing
work for an army. Everybody was wild for plunder.

" The throne-room was lined with ebony, carved in
a marvellous way. There were huge mirrors of all
shapes and kinds, clocks, watches, musical boxes with
puppets on them, magnificent china of every description, heaps and heaps of silks of all colours, em-
broidery, and as much splendour and civilization as you
would see at Windsor ; carved ivory screens, coral
screens, large amounts of treasure, etc. The French
have smashed everything."

The allies went back to Tientsin for winter quarters,
Gordon returning with them as senior officer commanding the Royal Engineers ; and at Tientsin he
remained until the spring of 1862, varying his official
duties with many bold excursions into a country
almost unknown to Europeans, and in particular a
journey to the Great Wall of China.

In addition to her troubles with the " foreign
devils," China was suffering from an armed rebellion
in her midst, which at one time threatened to overthrow the emperor himself and his seat of government
in Pekin. This Taiping rebellion, as it was called, had
started in the southernmost province of Kwang-tung,
being headed by a schoolmaster named Hung-tsue-
shuen, who had failed to pass certain examinations,
and in consequence believed himself to be an object of
persecution. (Examinations are of such importance
in China that to pass in one or to fail is honour or indelible disgrace.) This disappointed examinee, having
met with a Christian missionary who gave him a
bundle of tracts, declared that he had been visited by

a messenger from on high, promising him omnipotence in China and the overthrow of the hated Manchoo dynasty. So boldly he preached his mission, and so hatefully had his race been oppressed by the ruling mandarins, that in a short while his little band of converts had swelled to an army of some hundreds of thousands. With this host, still gathering numbers as it went, the Tien Wang—or Heavenly King, as he now entitled himself—swept northward seven hundred miles, until he reached and took the great city of Nanking on the Yangtsze-Kiang, where he set up his throne, dispensing government and receiving worship, while five subordinate warrior-kings or Wangs ordered the movements of his vast forces.

Up to 1860 this insurrection had been solely directed against the Chinese Imperial Government, which had its hands full with its enemies the French and English. But now, flushed with success, the rebels threatened to attack from landward the consular port of Shanghai; and the European merchants there, finding that little help could be expected from Pekin, subscribed to levy a small army of their own, which they placed under the command of an American filibuster named Ward—a man whose history should be well worth writing if it be true that during his brief career he fought seventy actions and was never beaten in one. So brilliant indeed was his generalship that the Pekin Government bestowed on his troops the title of the Ever-Victorious Army, and the baffled " Heavenly King," in October 1860, sent forth four armies, under four of his terrible Wangs, to clear the country for his attack upon Shanghai. But at this point the British Government interfered, in the person of Admiral Sir James Hope. After visiting Shanghai and other Yangtsze ports which, by agreement with the Chinese Government, were open to our trade, the admiral in February 1861 sailed up the river to Nanking, interviewed the " Heavenly King," and persuaded him to proclaim a truce for one year. It was honourably kept ; but when its time expired the rebels refused to renew it. Early in 1862 they marched again on Shanghai. Backed by an allied force upon the coast, where Gordon was helping his old Crimean friend General Staveley to keep the country clear for thirty miles around the threatened port, Ward held the rebel forces gallantly at bay until September, when he was killed in action, and the command of the Ever-Victorious Army devolved upon another American free-lance—Burgevine, an able fellow, but a scoundrel.

Now steps upon the scene a personage whose name was at one time familiar—the famous statesman Li Hung Chang. Already in January 1863, when he arrived at Shanghai to take command in the name of the emperor, he was governor-general of the Kiang provinces, and had seen ten years' service against the rebels. He found affairs in this position :—On the one hand, General Staveley told him that though the French and English would continue to keep the country clear for thirty miles around, the actual sup- pression of the rebellion must be undertaken by the Chinese, and to this end Li Hung Chang at once set about training his native imperial troops. On the other hand, neither he nor any other Chinaman could reorganize the Ever-Victorious Army, which was entirely officered by European and American adven- turers, and had for some months, under Burgevine, been degenerating into an undisciplined rabble of freebooters. Burgevine himself, having to complain of some arrears of pay, had marched a hundred men to the local treasury, bullied the mandarin in charge, beaten him with his fist, and ordered his men to carry off 40,000 dollars. For this outrage Li Hung Chang promptly cashiered him ; and the scamp, after appeal- ing to Pekin without success, eventually went off and sold his services to the rebels.

Meanwhile, who was to command the Ever-Victorious Army? Among its 150 officers (of whom, by the way, no less than eleven died of drink in the course of one month) not one was capable of bringing it back to discipline. Li Hung Chang applied to General Staveley. "Give us an English officer," he entreated, "one upon whom you can rely."

Staveley thought at once of Gordon, who had lately been promoted to the brevet rank of major; but Gordon had one fault which made his friend chary of recommending him—an absolute recklessness in exposing himself to danger. It is no part of a general's business to court bullets; so Gordon was told when, getting wind of what was in Staveley's mind, he applied eagerly for the post. It was only upon a promise to take care of himself that he prevailed. He could not take up his appointment at once, for consent had first to be obtained at home, from the Horse Guards; and before confirmation could be received from England the Ever-Victorious Army had still further tarnished its laurels by two defeats in the field—at Fushan and at Taitsan, at which latter place, through mistaking a water-moat thirty feet deep for a dry ditch, several hundred men had fallen in a useless assault, leaving two guns in the enemy's hands.

On the 24th of March 1863 Gordon took command of this beaten army of 3,000 Chinese, to reorganize it and lead it against a foe of overwhelming numbers. "I am afraid," he wrote home to his mother, "that you will be much vexed that I am now a mandarin. I have taken the step on consideration. I think that any one who contributes to putting down this rebellion fulfils a humane task. . . . I keep your likeness before me, and can assure you and my father that I will not be rash."

The little army had its headquarters at Sung-Kiang, west of Shanghai, and close to the edge of the thirty-mile radius within which it could fall back for support. It was generally supposed that the new commander would first of all spend some time in getting his force under discipline, and then march it again upon Taitsan, to wipe out the late defeat. Instead, he organized it in haste and marched to relieve Chanzu, a town to the north-west of that place, where a starving garrison was holding out bravely against the rebels. To relieve it he had to begin by capturing Fushan, a post between Chanzu and the Yangtsze River. Having moved two-thirds of his army up to the south of the besieged town, he himself, with 1,000 men, steamed up the Yangtsze in a couple of boats, landed, battered down the stockades of Fushan with his artillery, and carried the position by assault ; whereupon the rebels, fearful of being caught between the two divisions of his force, hastily moved off, and the siege of Chanzu was raised.

After this brilliant exploit, for which the emperor made him a brigadier-general, Gordon returned to Sung-Kiang, and at once set to work to reorganize his army, purging his staff of incompetent officers, laying down strict rules of discipline, and generally repairing defects which his brief campaign had revealed. In this work, which occupied three weeks, he had the loyal support of Li Hung Chang, especially in the matter of securing regular pay for his soldiers, that they might be broken of their old habits of plunder. He fixed also a liberal scale of rations, and gave them a uniform of dark serge with green turbans, in which they were mistaken by the enemy for Europeans, and the more readily because he taught them to drill, deploy, and take order like European troops. At first the men disliked this innovation, and resented being called " imitation foreign devils " by their fellow-Chinese ; but in time, as the Ever-Victorious Army recovered the right to its title, they wore the uniform with pride. Finally he provided himself with stronger guns, gun-carriages, boats, and pontoon equipment, escalading ladders, planks for short tramways, etc., and on April 29 took the field again.

In a straight line, along a road stretching from due north to north-west of Sung-Kiang, lay three rebel strongholds—Taitsan, Quinsan, and Soochow, of which the last was the chief. Gordon's purpose was to cut this line in two by capturing Quinsan, the midmost, which, moreover, contained the rebel arsenal and shot factory. He was marching upon it when news reached him that the rebel commander at Taitsan, having inveigled some 1,500 Imperial troops into the city on pretence of surrender, had shut the gates upon them, taken them prisoners, and beheaded 300, including Li Hung Chang's brother. At once he turned aside to punish this crime, though he mustered but 3,000 men, and Taitsan was garrisoned by 10,000. Seizing a canal which entered the town on its western side, he used it to work up his guns to within 600 yards of the walls, and opened a hot fire, under cover of which he pushed some of the guns forward to within 100 yards. He now concentrated his bombardment on one spot until large masses of masonry fell, forming a slope for the assault. This slope ran down to the deep water of the moat. Steamers and boats were brought up the canal and steered aside into the moat, across which they were packed, to form a bridge for the stormers. After two assaults and a hand-to-hand struggle, the defenders were stampeded from the walls, and Taitsan surrendered (May 1, 1863).

The victory was marred, however, by the behaviour of his men, who fell to looting. Their indiscipline was such that he felt unable to trust them until he had obtained some good officers in place of those who had fallen in the assault. Reluctantly, therefore, he gave over his intention of turning at once upon Quinsan, and marched his army back to headquarters, where he was fortunate in obtaining the services of some officers of her Majesty's 99th Regiment, who had been allowed to volunteer. This, and the appointment of an English officer to superintend the commissariat, gave such offence to Gordon's majors that they resigned in a body. Gordon accepted their resignations. Next day the men refused to march. The situation was critical; but on second thoughts the majors fell in with their regiments, discipline was restored, and the army marched off to the attack on Quinsan. This fortress was reduced by bringing an armed steamer to bear upon the waterways between it and Soochow, and cutting the connection by road— Gordon having discovered that a Chinese army will seldom stand when it has once lost hold of its communications or finds that its retreat is in danger. Leaving his main body before the east gate of Quinsan, he shipped a small force of riflemen on board his little steamer, the *Hyson*, and took them by circuitous waterways around the city to Chunye, a village some eight miles to the westward, on the Soochow road. Here he easily surprised and made prisoners of a small outpost of the enemy, thus cutting the road; and having posted some 300 riflemen in the captured stockade, himself pushed on in the *Hyson* to reconnoitre in the direction of Soochow. He had steamed but a little way when he fell in with a large body of rebels marching up alongside the canal to reinforce Quinsan. The *Hyson* blew her whistle, and opened fire with such effect that the whole mass broke and fled back, jamming themselves in the narrow path, tumbling into the canal, and—to make matters worse —rushing into the arms of fresh reinforcements, with whom they became hopelessly entangled, while still the little steamboat followed them with a deadly fire. In this way Gordon drove the fugitives up to the very walls of Soochow, and then, putting about, steamed back to his riflemen at Chunye. He found them greatly alarmed, having received word that the whole garrison of Quinsan, 7,000 strong, in a panic that their retreat was cut, had abandoned that city, and were coming down the road in full flight for Soochow. On Gordon steamed—it was now 10.30 p.m., and the night almost pitch dark—and, sure enough, soon met the rebels in full retreat. Again the *Hyson* blew her whistle and opened fire. The mass wavered, yelled, and fled back, the shells mowing them down as they ran. Straight back to Quinsan Gordon pursued them ; and by two in the morning the city was in his hands, some three or four thousand of the enemy having been killed, drowned, or taken prisoners.

But many untoward events now combined to prevent his attacking Soochow, the third and by far the most important stronghold. For Burgevine had not only turned traitor in revenge for his dismissal and joined the rebels there, but had enticed men away from the Ever-Victorious Army, and spread disaffection throughout its ranks by promising the men free leave to loot every town they took, including Shanghai ; whereas under Gordon all plundering was punished, and they received only their just pay. The Imperialist general Ching, too, was afraid of attacking Soochow at once : so again Gordon fell back on the task of getting his troops into hand. So mutinous were they that the artillerymen threatened to blow their officers to pieces, and putting the threat into writing, sent it to Gordon, who now showed that he could be as stern as he had been kind. Summoning his non-commissioned officers, whom he knew to be at bottom of the business, he threatened to shoot every fifth man of them if the writer of the notice was not given up ; whereupon all fell to groaning, and protesting their innocence. Observing that one man groaned more loudly than the rest, the general, who no doubt had his suspicions, ordered a couple of infantry soldiers to seize and shoot him. It then came to light that he was the real culprit.

Burgevine, meanwhile, by his arrogance and dissolute habits, was making himself just as much a nuisance to the rebels as he had been to his old employers ; and after being somewhat ingloriously driven by Gordon from some stockades in front of Soochow, his military reputation began to be questioned. Before long he made secret overtures to Gordon, proposing that they should combine against rebels and Imperialists together, seize Soochow, lay hands on its treasure, and march on Pekin with 20,000 men. Gordon scornfully put aside the suggestion, which he probably attributed to the workings of a drunken brain. Burgevine, in short, was fast collapsing. In the end, after attempting to desert and throw himself upon Gordon's protection, he was packed off by Moh-Wang, the chief rebel general in Soochow, to the American consul, and allowed to leave the country.

In Soochow matters were growing desperate as, in addition to Gordon's little army, some 10,000 Imperial troops gradually invested it. For Nanking was already beleaguered, and the " Heavenly King " could send no help without endangering his capital. The end was that all the Wangs in Soochow, with the exception of Moh-Wang, their chief, were anxious to desert and surrender the city. They met Gordon and General Ching in secret interview, and promised, *on condition that their lives were protected afterwards*, not to defend the city against assault. Moh-Wang, getting wind of their parleyings, sent for his six brother Wangs, to remonstrate with them. They met in council ; a hot dispute arose, and Moh-Wang was suddenly set upon and stabbed to death. Soochow surrendered that same night.

Gordon had exacted from Governor Li Hung Chang a pledge that the lives of all the Wangs should be spared, including that of Moh-Wang, whom he held in deserved respect. To his horror, on entering the city he learned that Li Hung Chang had broken his word, and that all the Wangs had been promptly beheaded. Having perpetrated this abominable crime, the governor very prudently fled to a distance; for Gordon, mad with rage, was hunting for him through the city, revolver in hand. There is no doubt that had he fallen in his way he would have been shot like a dog. As a rule, throughout his Chinese campaigns Gordon carried no weapon at all but a small cane which the Celestials took for a wand of magic. This was, says a biographer, the only period during which the commander of the Ever-Victorious Army " burdened himself with carrying arms."

Happily Li Hung Chang kept out of the way until Gordon's first hot fit of passion had cooled. But his indignation remained so strong that when the rebellion was over, and the emperor sent him £3,500 as a personal gift, he returned the money with the following note :—

" Major Gordon receives the approbation of his Majesty the Emperor with every gratification, but regrets most sincerely that, owing to circumstances which have occurred since the capture of Soochow, he is unable to receive any mark of the emperor's recognition, and therefore respectfully begs his Majesty to receive his thanks for his intended kindness, and to allow him to decline the same."

He accepted, however, to please his parents, the high decoration of the Yellow Jacket—which almost answers to our Order of the Garter—and was glad enough, before disbanding his Ever-Victorious Army, to distribute among it a handsome sum of money sent from Pekin. He also received the title of Ti-tu, which gave him the highest rank ever conferred on a Chinaman ; but his dislike of being fêted kept him from accepting an official invitation to Pekin, where he would have been received with almost royal honours. Prince Kung, then Regent of China, called on our ambassador, Sir Frederick Bruce, who happened to be leaving for England. "You will be astonished to see me," said the prince, "but I could not allow you to leave without coming to see you about Gordon. We do not know what to do. He will not receive money from us, and we have already given him every honour which it is in the power of the emperor to bestow; but as he does not prize these, I have brought you a letter, and ask you to give it to the Queen of England, that she may bestow on him some reward that will be more valuable in his eyes."

Some months later, when "Chinese Gordon" returned to London and presented himself at the War Office, the officials there seemed hardly to have heard of his name. Prince Kung's letter may or may not have been delivered. At any rate, all the reward he received was a Companionship of the Bath!

He was the last man to complain, for he hated pomp and show. He had been glad to get away from the press eulogies and illuminated addresses in which the Chinese hailed him as the saviour of their country. He preferred such a tribute as this, written by a rebel chief in the midst of hostilities :—

"I have heard that Gordon grieved bitterly over cruelties which he could not prevent. It may gratify him to know that even amongst those who would willingly be his friends, but are forced to be his enemies, he does not receive the blame. . . . Would to Heaven some worthless adventurer might take his place, some one that could be slain without regret! Often and often have I seen the deadly musket struck from the hand of a dastardly Englishman (tempted by love of loot to join our ranks) when he attempted from his place of safety to kill Gordon, who ever rashly exposed himself."

Gordon arrived in England early in 1865. He refused to be "lionized," and after spending a quiet six months with his parents at Southampton, was appointed Officer Commanding the Royal Engineers at Gravesend, to superintend the construction of five new forts for the defence of the Thames. He had no sooner examined the maps and drawings of these forts than he plainly saw that to erect them was mere waste —and enormous waste—of public money; but having pointed this out and been snubbed for his pains, he took up his task and carried it through with the strictest attention to detail. It was a humdrum employment; to ninety-nine men out of a hundred it would have been felt as a sad " come down " for a Mandarin of the Yellow Jacket and a Grand Commander of the Chinese army ; and it lasted for six years. Gordon called them " the most peaceful and happy of any portion of my life." His religious convictions had deepened; he lived wholly for others, and, when released from his official duties, spent his daily leisure in visiting the sick or teaching in Sunday school or ragged school. The workhouse and the infirmary were his constant haunts, and of pensioners he had a countless number all over the neighbourhood. Many of the dying sent for him in preference to the clergy, and ever ready was he to visit them, no matter in what weather or at what distance. But he would never take the chair at a religious meeting, or be in any way prominent. His old-fashioned house at Gravesend " was school and hospital and almshouse in turn—was more like the abode of a missionary than of a Colonel of Engineers." He had a number of keys made for his garden, and distributed them among poor persons, who were thus made free to wander in it, and not seldom departed with a gift of vegetables. The boys of Gravesend (many of whom he rescued from the gutter, clothed, taught in evening classes, and started in life) adored him, and expressed their admiration in their own way—for example, by chalking up " God bless the Kernel " on his palings. With all this, it may easily be guessed that his money escaped as from

a running tap. " You and I," he wrote to a friend,
" will never learn wisdom in money matters." He
told another that he kept a silver tea-service simply
because it would be sufficient, when he died, to pay
for his burial without troubling his family. His
purse, in fact, was kept drained by his constant
liberality; and beyond paying for his own modest
needs, he had an equally constant disdain of money.
But it came hard when he wished to relieve some new
applicant, and found no money in the house. Among
the few possessions which he prized was a gold medal,
specially struck in his honour by the Empress of
China. One day it vanished. He had heard of some
poor people in Coventry suffering as the result of a
cotton famine; had dived his hands into his pockets,
to find nothing; and so, having first gouged out the
inscription, had packed off the medal anonymously as
his contribution to the relief fund. " Gordon," said
a brother officer, " is the nearest approach to Christ
of any man who ever lived." Of his tenderness of
heart one biographer, Mr. Boulger, relates the following story as typical:—

" A woman called on him one day with a piteous
tale. Gordon went to his bedroom to get half a
sovereign for her, and while he was away she took a
fancy to a brown overcoat, which she hastened to conceal under her skirt. Gordon returned, gave her the
money, and she left with a profusion of thanks. While
on her road home the coat slipped down and attracted
the notice of a policeman, who demanded an explana-
tion. She said, ' I took it from the colonel,' and was
marched back for him to identify his property and
charge her with the theft. When Gordon heard the
story he was far more distressed than the culprit, and
refused to charge her. At last a happy thought came
to his relief. Turning to the woman he said, with a
twinkle in his eye, ' You wanted it, I suppose?'
' Yes,' answered the astonished woman. Then turning

to the equally astonished policeman, he said, ' There, take her away, and send her about her business.' "

In the year 1871 the " authorities " remembered Gordon's existence, and appointed him British member of the European Commission of the Danube. He left Gravesend with regret, and departed for Galatz on the 1st of October. As a leaving gift he presented to the ragged schools a number of Chinese flags—trophies of his victorious campaigns—which are still treasured and annually paraded in his memory.

Of his work at Galatz (duller if possible than his work on the Thames) nothing calls to be said, except that during his residence there he was vainly recommended to command a British expedition against the Ashantees, as at Gravesend he had applied in vain to be employed on the Abyssinian expedition. Of all the criticisms that have been levelled against the methods of our War Office from the days of the Crimea to those of the South African War—and they have been innumerable—I know none so deadly as the simple statement of the simple fact that, from the time when he served as a subaltern before Sebastopol, the one Briton of our time fit to be reckoned as a military genius was never once allowed to fight for his country's cause. It is, in the light of recent history, a disquieting thought that England, which claims to rule over so many of the darker-skinned races of the world, should not only have waited upon China and again upon Egypt to read her a lesson in intelligence, but have obstinately refused enlightenment when it had twice been offered her.

In 1873 Ismail, Khedive of Egypt, asked Gordon to take service under him, and accept the appointment of Governor of the Equatorial Province. The government at home raised no objection, and early in 1874 he left London for Cairo. The Khedive had fixed his salary at £10,000 a year ; but characteristically he refused to accept a penny more than £2,000, the sum he had been receiving in British employ. " My object," he wrote, " is to show the Khedive and his people that gold and silver idols are not worshipped by all the world. They are very powerful gods, but not so powerful as *our* God."

The task that lay before Gordon was a truly formidable one, and the Khedive had turned to him almost in despair. The Equatorial Province lies some way south of Khartoum (where the White Nile and Blue Nile meet), and stretches southward to the Albert and Victoria lakes. As a matter of fact, it barely touches the equator, which runs through the north of the Victoria Nyanza ; and also, as a matter of fact, the Khedive's rule over it was of the loosest. Egypt, scarcely able to govern herself, had since 1853 been extending her nominal empire southward over vast tracts of country she could not pretend to police or to supervise. They had originally been opened up by Europeans in search of ivory ; but these traders were not long in discovering that " black ivory " (slaves) was a far more profitable game, and before long the country was infested by armed bands, captained by Arabs, who raided far and near, kidnapping the unhappy natives and driving them northward to be sold in the slave-markets at Constantinople and elsewhere. The traffic became a scandal to the civilized world ; an outcry was raised, and the Europeans were forced to withdraw. But before withdrawing they disposed of their slave stations (at a profit) to their late employés, the Arabs, who paid a tax to the Egyptian Government ; so that in effect the condition of the natives, left to the tender mercies of men whose cruelty only began where a bad European's ended, was worse than ever. On top of this the Arabs grew so powerful that in practice they defied the Khedive's commands and his taxes. One of them indeed, Zebehr Rahama—known as the

" Black Pasha "—defied him openly, and overthrew in pitched battle an officer sent to teach him better behaviour. The Khedive, alarmed at this defeat, truckled to Zebehr, and actually invoked his aid as an ally to conquer another province, Darfur, to the westward. This was done, the Sultan of Darfur slain, and his country subdued. Zebehr's claims grew with his success, and he now demanded to be made governor-general. This was too much for the Khedive, who promptly discovered that the slave traffic was a shocking business and ought to be suppressed, or at least regulated. As things were, the southern provinces, instead of filling his treasury, made a constant drain upon it : the taxes were unpaid, and the cost of government (mostly corrupt) made chaos of his annual balance-sheet. By a happy inspiration then, his chief minister, Nubar Pasha, advised him to form the Equatorial Province into a separate government, and while claiming a monopoly of the slave traffic, to appoint an Englishman as governor—the righteous rule of the English being proverbial. When Sir Samuel Baker, the first governor, threw up his task in disgust, Nubar was not disheartened. With unwearied craft he sought about, and his choice fell upon Gordon. When the world asked, " Who is Gordon ? " knowledgeable folk would answer, " The man who did wonders in China—a sort of Christian knight-errant too—the last fellow in the world to suffer slave-dealing, or to dip his hands in corruption."

Gordon had spent but a few hours in Cairo before he detected the game that was being played behind this mask. He liked the Khedive, whose detestation of slavery he believed to be honest ; but of the Khedive's adviser he wrote home, " I think I can see the true motive of the expedition, and believe it to be a sham to catch the attention of the English people ; " and again, " I thought the thing real and found it a sham, and felt like a Gordon who has been humbugged." But he determined to go on, for he felt also that the Almighty's hand was upon him to override these plots and bring good to the oppressed races. As he wrote two years later :—

" I do nothing of this. I am a chisel which cuts the wood ; the Carpenter directs it. If I lose my edge, He must sharpen me ; if He puts me aside and takes another, it is His own good will. None are indispensable to Him ; He will do His work with a straw equally as well."

Cairo, with its intrigue and ceremonial, vexed his spirit. Breaking away impatiently, he reached Suakim on February 25th, travelled across the desert on a camel to Berber, and then took steamer for Khartoum, where he arrived with his small staff on March 13th, to be welcomed with an effusive show of friendliness by Ismail Yakoob, Governor-General of the Soudan. Nominally, Gordon, whose province lay to the south, was subordinate to Ismail Yakoob, through whom he obtained supplies ; but—to anticipate somewhat—after many a squabble between them, by September he managed to get his command made independent, to receive his supplies direct from Cairo, and, better still, to present his accounts on a separate balance-sheet that satisfied his English sense of exactitude.

It seemed of happy omen that just before his arrival at Khartoum the " sudd "—a mass of aquatic plant and mould that chokes the upper waters of the Nile for leagues together—had suddenly given way, and the journey up-stream to his headquarters at Gondokoro was covered in twenty-four days, whereas it sometimes took as many months. He reached Gondokoro on April 16th. He had already issued his first decree, proclaiming that the traffic in ivory was a monopoly of the government, that all traders were to provide themselves with a written permit, and that the recruiting of armed bands was prohibited within the province, as well as the importation of firearms and gunpowder. From Gondokoro—where no one expected him, and where the garrison dared not, except in large parties, wander out of range of their guns—he sped back all the way to Berber to hurry up his supplies, pausing on his way at Khartoum to make it plain to Ismail Yakoob and the donothings there that he meant to stand no nonsense. Having collected his supplies, he started up the river again, planting a chain of forts on his way, and intercepting whole droves of slaves and cattle. The slaves he either freed or took into his service for pay ; the cattle he restored, where he could, to their rightful owners. Word spread across that desolate land that a strange, unaccountable pasha had arrived, apparently out of heaven ; an incredible ruler, who waged war on the slave-dealers, and moreover took no money for administering justice. As a result he became the ideal of these oppressed tribes, and his name a terror to the slave-traders, whose field of operations he had cut neatly in half by his line of posts guarding the river—a stroke of strategy which prevented the gangs from combining and allowed him to deal with them in detail, choosing the right or left bank at will, and delivering his attacks with unexpected swiftness. His European staff sickened in the oppressive climate, and at one time were in hospital to a man. His native officials either cared not a fig for suppressing slavery, or were in secret collusion with the traders. Gordon's way of dealing with these traitors was short and direct : he ordered them back to his base at Khartoum ; and as they could find no other shelter from his wrath—for the surrounding tribes would murder them if they tried to escape—they had no choice but to obey. For his soldiers he had a well-grounded contempt, finding them cowards in grain. To supersede them by Arabs, however, was dangerous; for an Arab soldiery, if numerous, would as likely as not seize an early occasion to mutiny, and wreck the very purpose they were enlisted to protect. Gordon therefore got together, little by little, a picked guard of Soudanese—stalwart fellows whose bravery he had tested. In the first year he enrolled 40; by the end of 1876 he had increased their numbers to 500; and these men, planted in small contingents along the river posts, held the thin but invaluable line of communication through the vast country he continually strove to open up. In the pauses of his expeditions he tried to teach the natives to till the soil, providing them with seed for that purpose, and also to accustom them to the use of money. But this was heart-breaking work: for men will not grow crops save on ground which is secured to them, so that they can be certain of reaping the harvest; and the Soudan and the equatorial provinces would never be thus secure until civilization had opened them up. As Gordon wrote:—

" I believe if the Soudan was settled the Khedive would prevent the slave trade, but he does not see his way to do so until he can move about the country. My ideas are to open it out by getting the steamers on to the lakes, by which time I should know the promoters of the slave trade, and could ask the Khedive to seize them. . . . God has allowed slavery to go on for so many years; born in the people, it needs more than an expedition to eradicate it; open out the country, and it will fall of itself."

In pursuance of this purpose, and not with any idea of winning fame by a geographical discovery, Gordon started to explore the seventy miles of unknown country between Foweira (his southernmost station) and the Albert Nyanza. As he curtly puts it:—

" It was contended that the Nile did not flow out of Lake Victoria and thence into Lake Albert and so northward, but that one river flowed out of Lake Victoria and another out of Lake Albert ; and that these two rivers united and formed the Nile. This statement could not be positively denied, inasmuch as no one had actually gone along the river from Foweira. . . . So I went along it with much suffering, and settled the question."

He reached the Albert Nyanza at the end of July 1876, and from that time until he left to return home he worked with feverish energy in the hottest season of one of the hottest climates on earth, mapping and surveying, in one day pushing eighteen miles through jungle, and fifteen miles on each of the four days following. He was worn thin with sickness. His heart, too, was bitter at the small help sent to him from Cairo, and desperate over a task which Cairo too plainly treated as a sham. He alone had treated it as practical business. The equatorial provinces were no longer a drain on the Khedive's exchequer. In 1875 the Treasury had received £40,000 from the country which Gordon ruled at a cost of £20,000, and £60,000 more had been put to a reserve fund. This man, so careless of riches for himself, was a true economist of public money. But it must be confessed that he liked to do things in his own way, and was impatient of being thwarted. He had already sent the Khedive his resignation. In October he returned to Khartoum ; left it on the 12th of November ; reached Cairo on the 2nd of December ; and by Christmas Eve was back once again in England.

He said to himself that he would not return, and he vowed that he would not unless appointed to supreme authority over the whole of the Soudan. But his resignation had never been formally accepted, and he had scarcely reached home before the Khedive Ismail wrote reminding him that he was not released from his old promise to complete what he had begun.

" I cannot, my dear Gordon Pasha, think that a gentleman like Gordon can be found wanting with regard to his solemn promise." For " a gentleman like Gordon " this was enough, and early in February he returned to Cairo, where Ismail conferred on him the government of the entire Soudan, especially commending to his efforts the two objects dearest to his heart—the suppression of slavery and the improvement of means of communication.

He left Cairo in the middle of February. " I am so glad to get away, for I am very weary. I go up alone, with an infinite Almighty God to direct and guide me ; and am glad so to trust Him as to fear nothing—indeed, to feel sure of success." Having made a detour on his way, to attempt to settle a dispute between the Khedive and King Johannis of Abyssinia, he arrived at Khartoum, and was installed as governor on the 5th of May. All expected a speech from him, and he made one, of eleven words— " With the help of God I will hold the balance level." It delighted his audience more than if he had talked for an hour. In private he said, alluding to the incoherent and futile orders that reached him from Cairo, " I will carry things with a high hand to the last."

He did both. His first act—after abolishing punishment by the *kourbash*, or cat-o'-nine-tails, remitting arrears of taxation, and sanctioning a scheme for supplying the town with river-water— was to suppress the misdeeds of the Bashi-Bazouks, or Turkish and Arab irregulars, who pillaged and oppressed the people. There were no fewer than 6,000 of these Bashi-Bazouks dispersed about in various small garrisons—an arrangement useless for any military purpose on a large scale, but extremely convenient for the surreptitious slave-driving to which these gentry were addicted. Fortunately, a nuisance thus scattered was the easier to handle.

Gordon moved swiftly from garrison to garrison, "holding the balance level," and woe to the petty tyrant whom he caught in his tyranny! "In one month," he wrote, "I have turned out three generals of division, one general of brigade, and four lieutenant-colonels."

In the midst of this beneficial work he was called away, early in the summer, to Darfur, where a revolt had broken out, and the Khedive's garrisons at Dara, Kolkol, and Fascher were held at siege and in danger of starving. So, having collected 500 men, off he rode into that perilous country. From the frontier of it he wrote,—

"I have a splendid camel—none like it ; it flies along and quite astonishes the Arabs. I came flying into this station (Fogia) in marshal's uniform ; and before the men had time to unpile arms I had arrived with only one man with me. . . . The Gordons and the camels are of the same race—let them take an idea into their heads and nothing will take it out."

Thus, riding far ahead of his men, he released garrison after garrison. The rebels, who had been hideously maltreated by the Bashi-Bazouks, came in to make submission, ask his pardon, and lay their troubles before him. "Nay," said Gordon, when he had heard their story and cross-questioned them, "you ought rather to pardon *me*."

We have already spoken of the great slave-dealer, Zebehr Rahama, the "Black Pasha." He had incautiously gone down to Cairo to bribe the government, and the Khedive had seized the opportunity to hold his old enemy captive. Zebehr no sooner found himself tricked and held prisoner than he telegraphed in cipher to his son Suleiman to rise in revolt ; which Suleiman promptly did, taking the field with some 3,000 warriors as bold as Gordon's were cowardly. Gordon thereupon played one of the boldest strokes of his life. Riding on ahead of his untrustworthy troop, and covering on camel-back eighty-five miles in a day and a half under an August sun, he dashed straight into Suleiman's camp and summoned him to an interview. The young robber chief was dumbfounded. He could not believe the truth, that he had, if he minded, the terrible Gordon Pasha at his mercy. " I will carry things with a high hand," Gordon had promised, and now, if ever, he kept his word. He even made a difficulty over granting Suleiman an interview, on the ground that he had not made proper submission. And all the while he was helpless, in the midst of a splendid army. For the time Suleiman submitted, but in the end revolted again, and was finally subdued by Romulus Gessi, a daring Italian, the one man of Gordon's staff who ever learned to combine something of his chief's daring methods with his chief's whole-hearted abomination of slavery.

Gordon's busy administration of the Soudan was now interrupted by a telegram from the Khedive, summoning him to Cairo to help Egypt to put her finances in order. He went willingly enough, but only to find his master surrounded by the representatives of foreign bondholders, and too much terrified of them to listen to advice and insist on Egypt holding an independent commission to inquire into her own affairs. Gordon insisted on an independent line. The Khedive, who at heart agreed with him, weakly threw him over and, like many another man ashamed of himself, avoided the company of his better adviser. Gordon shrugged his shoulders, bowed to fate, and went back to his province. " I left Cairo," he wrote, " with no honours, by the ordinary train, paying my own passage. . . . I calculate my financial episode cost me £500. His Highness was bored, and could not bear the sight of me."

Ismail would have done better to listen to Gordon's

strong advice.    He shirked it, bought himself a short respite from worry, and in the end lost his throne. At Fogia, where he was still hunting the slave-hunters, on the 1st of July 1879 Gordon received a telegram announcing that the Khedive had been deposed, and that Tewfik, his son, reigned in his stead.    " I am one of those he fooled," he commented ;   " but I bear him no grudge."    But he had no mind to serve under a new khedive, and having tried Tewfik with a request, to which no answer was sent, for a regiment to back him on a most dangerous embassy to Abyssinia, he returned to Cairo, gave the new Khedive a piece of his mind, laid down his governorship, and returned to England in January 1880, little guessing that Egypt was to claim him yet once again, and for the last time.

His life moves restlessly, feverishly now ;   and maybe he, being a fatalist in the last days, smiled to remember its aimless oscillations before fate shook it back on its pivot, to point finally to Khartoum and the end.    He who had been dictator over a land as wide as Germany, France, and Spain put together found it not beneath him to accept the post of private secretary to Lord Ripon, the new Viceroy of India. But he had no sooner reached Bombay than he threw up his post, and hastened on to China, where his old friend, Li Hung Chang, stood for the moment almost alone against all the imperial court in opposing the empress regent, who was anxious for a war with Russia.    " My fixed desire," he wrote, " is to per- suade the Chinese not to go to war ; " and the word of Gordon still carried such weight at Pekin that he prevailed, and saved China from a monstrous folly. He used such extremely outspoken language that the interpreter refused to repeat it ;   whereupon Gordon seized the dictionary, looked up the Chinese for " idiocy," and waved it under the high potentates' noses.

He returned to England in October 1880, and after

six months' leave offered to go out to the Mauritius to plan some fortifications, after two officers had declined the task on account of the climate.

> " Lord, even so
> I ask one prayer,
> The which if it be granted
> It skills not where
> Thou plantest me, only I would be planted."

After ten months of quiet work, being now promoted to major-general, he received a telegram from the Cape Government to come and help them to terminate war in Basutoland, and persuade the Basutos to accept a peaceful British administration. With the assent of the War Office he sailed. But this mission did not succeed, the reason being that he was not given the full powers promised to him. " God judges by motives, men by actions," commented Gordon. " When I went to the Cape I prayed for glory to God and the welfare of the people, so I am glad I got no glory out of it." The year 1883 was spent in Palestine, where he had a great desire to identify the " holy places " of Jerusalem.

" The ravines round Jerusalem are full of the dust of men, for over a million bodies must have been slain there. What a terrific sight the resurrection there will be ! . . . Scenes of days gone by—real scenes, actions on the stage of life—all gone ! It quiets ambition.

" I came back from Gaza yesterday. . . . Like all the coast, it is most dreary ; yet one sees that all the country was once thickly populated. Sand from the shore is creeping in steadily, and makes it mournful. Napoleon, Alexander the Great, Sennacherib, Nebuchadnezzar, and a host of great men passed by this route. Titus came up by Gaza to Jerusalem ; Richard Cœur de Lion was years at Askelon. All gone, these old familiar faces."

The time was drawing near for *his* dust to be one with the dust of these great commanders, and *his* memory to blossom from the dust.

At the close of 1879, as he left Egypt, Gordon had been able to say : " No man could lift his hand or his foot in the Soudan without me." But the good administration he had brought required a good and just ruler to continue it ; otherwise the Soudan was a house swept and garnished, inviting devils. And unhappily just such an evil spirit succeeded him in the person of Raouf Pasha, whom Gordon had twice turned out of subordinate posts for playing the tyrant. " As soon as I had gone the Turks and Circassians returned in full force ; the old Bashi-Bazouk system was re-established ; my old employés were persecuted ; and a population which had begun to appreciate something like decent government was flung back upon the vast excesses of Turkish rule."

Among Mohammedans there was a widespread expectation, almost a belief, that in the year 1882, which closed the twelfth century of their religion, there would arise another prophet, or mahdi, to regenerate Islam and rescue the poor and oppressed. In the autumn of 1881 a dervish of Dongola, Mohammed Achmet by name, began to rally the religious about him in the southern Soudan. At his ear he found a counsellor, so well known to us after as the Kalifa, and this man soon taught the prophet politics. Summoned by Raouf Pasha to Khartoum to give account of himself, Mohammed Achmet boldly refused to obey. " I am the Mahdi," he proclaimed ; " by the grace of God and His prophet I am the master of this country." Small expeditions were sent against him ; he destroyed one after another. With each successive victory the Soudanese flocked to his banner by the thousand. Finally an army marched to crush him, under the command of Colonel Hicks, a retired Indian officer. The Mahdi lured it into a defile on the road between Khartoum and El Obeid, and annihilated it. Of more than 11,000 men not eleven escaped back to Eygpt. The whole Soudan lay at the Mahdi's mercy.

Let two points here be made plain—the first, that the Mahdi's rebellion was a rising against horrible misrule by "a people rightly struggling to be free." Those were Mr. Gladstone's words, and Gordon is just as emphatic. " Something like decent government " had since his departure been " flung back to suffer the vast excesses of Turkish rule. The inevitable result followed ; and thus it may be said that the egg of the present rebellion was laid in the three years during which I was allowed to govern the Soudan on other than Turkish principles."

Secondly, the possession of the Soudan had hitherto been a calamity to Egypt, with the brief exception of Gordon's rule. It was more than she could govern ; and now, with the Mahdi in triumphant revolt at the head of some 30,000 men, it was more than she could hope to reconquer. No one saw this more clearly than did Gordon. The Egyptian troops had proved themselves quite valueless against the Soudanese. Every wise counsel was for withdrawal.

Unfortunately the business of evacuation was not easy, because, in mere humanity, it meant extricating the Egyptian garrisons scattered about the immense Soudan and besieged by the Mahdi's triumphant and relentless hordes. How could this be done ? A cry arose that Gordon was the only man capable of doing it. Sir Evelyn Baring (later Lord Cromer), our representative in Egypt, was at first unwilling ; finally he agreed that Gordon would be the best man if he would pledge himself to carry out the policy of withdrawal as quickly as possible. " Whoever goes," he wrote, " will undertake a service of great difficulty and danger." On January 16, 1884, Gordon received a telegram from the Ministry. He was in Brussels,

**where** King Leopold had made arrangements to employ him as governor of the Congo ; but he returned to London forthwith. On the 18th he called by appointment at the War Office, and was ushered into the presence of four of her Majesty's ministers. The question was put to him by Lord Wolseley in the anteroom : " Government are determined to evacuate the Soudan. Will you go and do it ? " Gordon said, " Yes." He went in, and they said, " Did Wolseley tell you our orders ? " " Yes. You will not guarantee future government, and you wish me to go up and evacuate now ? " " Yes," they agreed. At eight o'clock that evening he took the train at Charing Cross Station. The banks were closed, and Gordon, of course, had no money. Lord Wolseley ran about and managed to raise £200 in hard cash. At the station Lord Granville took Gordon's ticket, Lord Wolseley carried his bag, and the Duke of Cambridge held open the carriage door. The train was delayed for some while for their final instructions, and so Gordon went off on his last mission.

His instructions were " to report to her Majesty's Government on the military situation in the Soudan, and on the measures which it might be deemed advisable to take for the security of the Egyptian garrisons still holding positions in that country, and for the safety of the European population in Khartoum." Appended to this was a small clause, of which nobody thought much at the moment, though it afterwards became very important : " You will consider yourself authorized and instructed to perform such duties as the Egyptian Government may desire to entrust to you, and as may be communicated to you by Sir E. Baring." Here is no place to discuss who was most to blame for a series of misunderstandings in which no one concerned was wholly blameworthy or entirely guiltless ; but certain it is that as Gordon was on his way to Port Said he had suggested that it would help the evacuation if the Khedive made him again governor-general of the Soudan, that the British Government assented, and that Baring gave the authority " for the time necessary to carry out the evacuation." Thus the little clause had become a very important one even before Gordon left Cairo.

He had brought with him a single staff-officer, Colonel Stewart, of the 11th Hussars—a trustworthy helper, who knew Egypt well. The two proceeded from Cairo to Korosko, where on February 1 they took to their camels and plunged across the Nubian desert, travelling at Gordon's old unrivalled rate. " Gordon," wrote Mr. Power, correspondent of the *Times* (the only British subject left in Khartoum), " Gordon —sword and Bible—travels like a whirlwind. No Arab of the desert could vie with him in endurance on camel-back. . . . I don't believe the fellows in Lucknow looked more anxiously for Colin Campbell than we look for Gordon." And that eager expectation was— for what ? For a commander marching to their relief at the head of a victorious army ? No ; but for a man riding, with one comrade, merely to share their privations and perils. If there be a more striking example on record of the confidence a thoroughly good and thoroughly brave man can put into the hearts of his fellows, I do not know of it. *" And a man shall be as a hiding-place from the wind, and a covert from the tempest ; as rivers of water in a dry place, as the shadow of a great rock in a weary land."*

He arrived, and the people of Khartoum received him clamorously. " I come," he said, " without soldiers, but with God on my side, to redress the evils of the Soudan ; " and with the old calm-eyed courage, quite as though no horrible danger threatened, went about his work of dealing justice, remitting iniquitous taxes, hearing petitions, fascinating (one may say) the people back to confidence, while his mind worked incessantly on the problem of saving the distant garrisons surrounded, as he already was almost surrounded, by hordes of foes.   Power writes :—

"Gordon is a most lovable character—quiet, mild, gentle, and strong.   He is so humble, too.   The way he pats you on the shoulder when he says, 'Look here, dear fellow, now what would you advise?' would make you love him.   When he goes out of doors there are always crowds of Arab men and women at the gate to kiss his feet. . . . It is wonderful that one man could have such an influence on 200,000 people. . . . He is indeed, I believe, the greatest and best man of this century. . . . One day of his work and bother would kill another man, yet he is so cheerful at breakfast, lunch, and dinner; but I know he suffers fearfully from low spirits.   I hear him walking up and down his room at night (it is next to mine).   It is only his great piety carries him through."

His first decision was that all pretence of suppressing slavery in the Soudan being for the present ridiculous, it should be frankly abandoned; his next, that the one man who could cope with the Mahdi and extricate the garrisons was the great ex-slave hunter, Zebehr!   "Send me Zebehr," was his message back to Cairo; and it made all men wonder, for Gordon and Zebehr had always been deadly enemies.   There was even a blood-feud between them; for under Gordon's orders Zebehr's son Suleiman, who had persisted in rebellion, had been taken and shot by Gessi. Yet Zebehr was a great man and a master of men; and Gordon, himself without a trace of vindictiveness, calculated—rightly, as it appears—that Zebehr, if asked, would rise above personal hatreds and come. Only the great can properly understand the great. To people in Cairo it appeared incredible that these two could ever work together to save the almost desperate situation; and then there was the scandal of condoning slavery.   Though all depended upon instant action, Gordon's request was refused.   "Send

up Zebehr," he persisted.  " He will run straight, for
that is his interest.  If he be dangerous, the Mahdi is
ten times more dangerous, and there is no one to cope
with him but Zebehr."   At home the Cabinet met and
considered the request.  It was refused.  To be just
to the Ministry, it should be said that even had the
Cabinet consented Parliament would probably have
declined to sanction what was called " a gambler's
throw."  Zebehr was not sent.  " Come home," was
in effect the message sent instead—" come home, and
leave Senaar "—the farthest garrison—" to its fate."
" Were the road open," was Gordon's answer, " the
people here would not let me go.  *Leave Senaar to
its fate!*  I would sooner die!"  On April 16th he
managed to get a telegram through to Cairo.

" You state your intention of not sending any relief
up here or to Berber, and you refuse me Zebehr.  I
consider myself free to act according to circumstances.
I shall hold on here as long as I can, and if I can suppress the rebellion I shall do so.  If I cannot, I shall
return to the equator, and leave you the indelible disgrace of abandoning the garrisons of Senaar, Kassala,
and Dongola, with the certainty that you will eventually be forced to smash up the Mahdi under great
difficulties, if you would retain peace in Egypt."

Prophetic words !  After this no message came except that the Nile was beginning to rise : the water
had hitherto been too low for him to retreat and carry
his Khartoum garrison down the Nile, even had he
wished it, or to allow a relief expedition to come up
by steamer.  Then the telegraph operated no longer,
and for more than five months a curtain fell over
Khartoum and the little pin-point garrisons, each
smothered in a cloud of Arab spears !

Fatal weeks of delay followed at home, while military authorities urged on a distracted Cabinet their
various opinions as to the best route for the relief
expedition, which all now agreed to be necessary.  It

was not until August that the Nile route was chosen
and Lord Wolseley placed in command.  He reached
Cairo on September 9th, Wady Halfa on October 5th.
At Korti he received a message with a note in Gordon's
handwriting, " Come quickly, come together."  The
messenger reported that Khartoum was starving, and
the Mahdists knew it ; there was not a moment to be
lost.  At once Lord Wolseley sent a small force, under
Sir Herbert Stewart, to dash on across the desert
towards the doomed garrison.  The force, after san-
guinary fights at Abu Klea and Metammeh, reached
Gubat on the Nile on January 20th, and there found
four steamers which Gordon had sent down.  Sir
Herbert Stewart had been mortally wounded on the
way ; and Sir Charles Wilson, upon whom the command devolved, started up the river on the 24th.  It
was not until the 28th that they passed the Sixth
Cataract and steamed into easier water.  As they
neared their goal, solitary voices from the river bank
called to them that Khartoum had fallen and Gordon
was slain.  By-and-by the officers on deck, scanning
the country through their field-glasses, perceived the
square roof of the palace above the walls of Khartoum.
But no flag flew above it, and the building was in
ruins.  The place had fallen—two short days before
—and Gordon was slain.

It had fallen after a defence which—as the story
can be pieced together from Gordon's own journals—
is one of the marvels of military history.  Almost to
the end he could have won his way out with a few
fighting men ; but it would have meant abandoning
the poor half-starved inhabitants who had trusted
him, and to this he could never have brought himself.
The journal ends on December 14th : " Now mark
this—if the expeditionary force (and I ask for no
more than two hundred men) does not come in ten
days, *the town may fall* ; and I have done my best for
the honour of our country.   Good-bye."

Precisely how the end came is not known ; but all the evidence shows that the garrison, by Gordon's skill, held its own, and could have held it, under direction of the same skill, for months to come, had food lasted.   It was only when the famished soldiers could not crawl to their posts that the Mahdists broke in, and Gordon fell among the remnant he had devoted himself to save.

As every one knows, his death has been avenged ; and now, in a Khartoum recovered and prosperous, his image on camel-back gazes out over the land across which his living eyes so often sought to the horizon for the purposes of God, as from the pedestal, in Trafalgar Square, his statue broods on the feverish traffic of London.   He " who at all times and everywhere gave his strength to the weak, his substance to the poor, his sympathy to the suffering, his heart to God," asked no reward in this life, and received none beyond the joy of a good heart.   But where his blood was shed the African desert has blossomed, and at home, in Trafalgar Square, there never lacks a wreath laid, by unknown hands, at the feet of this hero of heroes.


# FATHER DAMIEN

JOSEPH DE VEUSTER was born on January 3, 1840, in the small Belgian village of Tremeloo, some six miles north of Louvain, pretty close to Malines, and not far from Brussels.   Twenty years later, on his entrance into the religious life, he took the name of Damien, choosing for his patron saint, as if by prophecy, one of the two brothers and good physicians, SS. Cosmas and Damien, whose feast falls on September 27th ; and it is as Father Damien that the world remembers him.   But his baptismal name was determined for him by a cousin of the family, an honest soldier, who happened to visit the house where the newly-born child lay in its cradle. The parents asked him to stand godfather. " With all my heart," said the soldier, " but only on condition that you call him Joseph, after the head of the holy family, who has always been a favourite of mine."

In the long family were three children—a sister and two brothers—not far removed in age. Pauline, the eldest, was two years older than Auguste, Auguste two years older than Joseph. The good father and mother—devotedly pious Catholics, but by no means affluent—also found room in the household for an orphan cousin Henri, of the same age as Auguste. As he grew up, but before he was old enough to go to school with the others, the small child Joseph spent much of his time in wandering solitary about the fields. He had an especial fancy for trotting after the sheep to their pastures and making friends with them; so that the neighbouring shepherds learned to nickname him " the little shepherd " (*le petit berger*). One day when he was four (it reads curiously like a famous passage in St. Luke), on the occasion of a kirmess, or fair, in a village close by, his parents missed him. They searched in vain amongst the crowds, and as evening fell were at their wits' end ; until at last his old grandfather suggested looking for him in the church. Accordingly he set off, and found the small wanderer at the foot of the pulpit, praying, all alone in the dusk of the deserted building.

" There was in the house," writes his brother Auguste, " a collection of *Lives of the Saints*, written in old Flemish, and printed in black letter, a book two feet long and a foot and a half broad. Our mother could read through old type fluently, but we children, accustomed to the modern printing of our school-books, could not decipher a word. She used, therefore, to read it to us, while we listened with intense delight. We often insisted on her giving up her

**FATHER DAMIEN.**

*From a pen-drawing by
E. Heber Thompson.*

work and reading to us ; especially the accounts of martyrdoms, and of the ancient hermits, such as Paul and Antony ; and the old-fashioned woodcuts were a great attraction for us. . . . We all used to walk to school together, and carried our slices of bread and butter in a basket for our dinner. One day, on our way to the school, we took it into our heads to be hermits. It was half-past eight in the morning. We pushed our way into a copse by the side of the road, and put ourselves on our knees in solitude and silence. At noon our basket was opened, and we each took our share, but without a word spoken. So we remained, crouching down in silence. Evening came on ; it was nine o'clock when a passer-by, catching sight of us, gave notice at home, and a servant was sent to fetch us in. I was not then quite ten years old, and I perfectly remember the spot, and the determined way in which my brother Joseph took to the character of hermit." What view the schoolmaster took is not recorded.

Of these three strange little Flemings, Pauline in 1858 entered a convent ; Auguste, who from the first had been destined for the priesthood, left home for Paris to become a student under the Society of the Sacred Hearts of Jesus and Mary, better known as the "Picpus Fathers," from the name of a house in the Faubourg St. Antoine, where they first set themselves up in 1817. As for Joseph, his father and mother intended him for business, and sent him to a middle-class school at Braine-le-Comte, to learn French and receive a commercial education.

He learned his French assiduously enough ; but his letters home proved that his thoughts were ever harking back from the path of business proposed for him to that which leads aside from the world, and along which his sister and brother had preceded him. In his eighteenth year, while he was still at school, the Redemptionist Fathers held a mission at Braine-

le-Comte. Joseph attended it. He returned to the
school, and spent a great part of that night on his
knees. He had heard a clear call to the religious life,
and in the first flush of enthusiasm desired to join
the Order of Trappists, but abandoned this for a project of journeying to Paris to the Picpus Fathers, and
joining his brother, who had by this time exchanged
the home name of Auguste for that of Father Pamphile. *

In a letter dated from school, July 17, 1858, we
find him writing :—

" I was very glad, my dear parents, to receive the
parcel you sent me, and also a letter from Pauline.
You sent me the very clothes I wanted. I was more
anxious to read the letter than I was to look at the
clothes. She told me she had left you on June 8th.
What a happiness for her ! She has had the happiness
of having fulfilled the most difficult task on earth
(that is to say, of renouncing the world to become a
nun).

" I hope my turn will come to choose the path I
ought to tread. Will it be impossible for me to follow
my brother Pamphile ? "

Five months later, on Christmas Day, he writes
more firmly, yet still respectfully :—

" This great feast has brought me the certainty that
God has called me to quit the world and embrace the
religious state. Therefore, my dear parents, I ask you
again for your consent ; for without it I cannot venture
to enter on this career. God's command to obey our
parents does not apply only to childhood. Do not think
that in choosing the religious state I am guided only by
my own will ; I assure you that I do but follow the will
of Divine Providence. I am not afraid that you will
refuse me, since it is God who calls. . . . Auguste writes
me that I should certainly be admitted in his congre-

* It is customary in France to call the young religious by the
title of Père even before they become priests.

gation as *Frère de Chœur*, that I should not fail to speak
to the superior at the New Year, and should begin my
novitiate a little after.—Hoping for this great happiness,
I sign myself, your obedient son,

"JOSEPH DE VEUSTER."

Quite early in the New Year, on his nineteenth
birthday, his father took him to pay a visit to Pamphile, and having some business to transact, left the
two brothers to dine together.  Here was the opportunity for the step which Joseph had long been de-
siring to take ;  and when his father came back that
evening it was to be told that his son would return
home no more, and that it would be better thus to
avoid the pain of farewells.  The good man was not
altogether unprepared for this ;  his cab was waiting,
at any rate, and there was no time for demur.  They
parted at the railway station, and Joseph went back
to be admitted to the brotherhood.

The superior received him gladly.  He was at this
time a singularly handsome lad, with crisply waved
hair and the face of a Greek god.  Later, the priesthood robbed him of this young beauty, as it is apt to
do ;  gave an ugly positiveness to the chin, and clapped
still uglier spectacles upon the visionary eyes.  Later
still the leprosy ate away the last of his good looks.
But at the age of nineteen he was winning to look
upon and exceptionally stalwart—the right build for
a missionary.  Years after, in Hawaii, the natives
marvelled at his strength.  " What a man ! " they
would cry when they saw him shoulder and carry, for
church building, a beam of timber which three or four
of them could scarcely lift.  For long he had been
secretly hardening himself for the life of austerity.
At home, as his brother relates, " he kept hidden
under his bed a long board ;  at night he slipped it into
his bed and lay upon it.  But one morning he forgot
it, and great was our mother's surprise to discover the
plank.  A severe reprimand put an end, for a time at

least, to this practice." Another anecdote must be told of that love for all suffering creatures which he took into Christ's ministry. His brother takes it down from the lips of an old woman of eighty.

" We had a sick cow, and the farrier left us no hope of saving her. We were in despair." (Here it should be said that a good cow was worth a fortune to these poor folk.) " But Joseph, hearing of our misfortune, installed himself in the stable and insisted on dismissing the butcher who had come to slaughter her. In fact, he took such tender care of the poor beast, sitting up all night in her stall without closing his eyes, that the next morning the danger was past, and in a few days she was quite cured. Joseph saved her."

He was modest and gentle withal during his term of novitiate. (We may likely enough set it down to his modesty that he chose the second of the two saints, Cosmas and Damien, when choosing his patronymic name as priest.) But the trouble was that, having been trained for a commercial life, he knew no Latin at all. Pamphile, half in joke, taught him a few disjointed words and sentences. Damien caught them up so eagerly that the lessons were continued in earnest. In six months he could translate Cornelius Nepos fluently. His superiors saw that the lad was not only earnest but capable. They sent him to Paris to pass his novitiate. From Paris in January 1861 we find him writing home : " We live happily and peacefully. I study Latin and Greek from morning till evening. Every Wednesday we have a walk. To-day, I believe, we are going skating. I must ask Gerard to lend me his skates, because they don't know how to skate here." Again in April he writes :—

" Of course you are anxious to know how things are going on in Paris. It is very seldom I go out in the town. Every Wednesday we go for a walk in the

wood at some distance.   About this wood I could say
a great deal, as I know every avenue in it.   About a
thousand men are always at work there, in order to
make it more and more pleasant.   They make new
roads and dig small water-courses.   But unfortunately, whereas before one could be quiet and enjoy
the pleasures of a walk, now we see nothing but
gentlemen and ladies, riders and carriages, at every
turn, which are a great distraction and very annoy-
ing.   What walks there are in the town have now no
attraction for me as they had at the outset : to
my mind there is something very melancholy about
them. . . . In our community everything is going
on splendidly.   We are all active as hares, and get
on capitally.   The arrival of one of our missionary
bishops has given me an occasion of having Pontifical
Mass in our chapel. . . . I believe he will shortly
return to his mission in Oceania, and may possibly
take some of us with him.   Would you not be happy
if I were one ? "

Here again is unconscious prophecy.   His novitiate
over, Damien returned to Louvain to study, living in
the same house with his brother Pamphile.   Here he
withdrew himself more and more from the world.   It
is recorded of this time that there were two things
Damien could not abide—discussion among religious
brothers and criticizing of superiors.   " Are these the
Children of the Sacred Hearts ? " he exclaimed one
day, upon two quarrelling brothers, and flung out
of their presence.   On his desk he cut with his knife
these words—*Silence, Recollection, Prayer.*

Now, in 1863, while he was yet in minor orders,
came the crisis of his life and as if by hazard.   His
brother Pamphile, already a priest, was ordered by the
superiors to prepare for an early departure to the
Sandwich Islands, which, so far back as 1825, had
been assigned to the Picpus Fathers for missionary
work.   Pamphile was eager, but almost on the eve of

sailing was laid low by an attack of typhus. Damien over his bedside asked, " Brother, will it console you if I go in your place ? " Receiving an eager " Yes," he wrote off at once to the superior-general in Paris, asking for his brother's place, and entreating that the passage-money should not be wasted. To the surprise and slight annoyance of the local superior— without whose cognizance no such letter should by rule have been written—the permission came.

The local superior walked into the refectory and tossed it to him, saying, " You silly boy ! You are impatient—you that are not yet a priest. But you are to go, it seems."

Damien caught up the letter and ran out, waving it. " Is he crazy ? " asked his fellow-novices. He rushed in upon his brother's sickroom, still waving the letter and crying, " I am to go instead of you ! "

Without waiting for dinner, he set off to bid good-bye to his father and mother ; for there was no time to lose if he would catch the ship, which was almost due to start from Bremerhaven. In the next few agitated days he parted from all his kinsfolk, never, as it proved, to see them again ; yet found time, with his mother, to pay a visit to the shrine of Our Lady of Montaigu, near Tremeloo. By October 30th he had reached Bremerhaven, and wrote : " At noon on Saturday we shall leave the harbour. . . . My dear parents, do not trouble in the least about us. We are in the hands of God. Good-bye ! "

The ship was only a sailing vessel, and took over five months on the passage. Off Cape Horn she came near to foundering. This gale lasted for several days, and they encountered another vicious but shorter one in mid-Pacific. But at last they made the Sandwich Islands, and came to port in Honolulu on the feast of Damien's patron, St. Joseph, March 19, 1864.

The Hawaiian or Sandwich Islands lie out in the

North Pacific Ocean, almost 2,000 miles from the nearest mainland. They are eight in number—if we omit to count uninhabited islets—and have been formed by volcanoes, the fires of which appear to have died down one after another, following a south-easterly curve to Hawaii, the largest and southern-most island, where they are yet active. (Travellers speak of its boiling lake of lava under Mount Kilauea as one of the wonders of the world.) This pent-up volcanic heat, for ever palpitating beneath the earth's crust, quickens and pushes the growth of vegetation through every crevice of dead lava, and has clothed the islands in green tropical beauty. Mr. Edward Clifford, who made a pilgrimage to them in 1888, to visit Father Damien, quotes a passage from Tenny-son's " Lotos-Eaters " as exactly descriptive :—

> " A land
> In which it seemed always afternoon. . . .
> A land of streams ! some, like a downward smoke,
> Slow-dropping veils of thinnest lawn, did go ;
> And some through wavering lights and shadows broke,
> Rolling a slumbrous sheet of foam below.
> They saw the gleaming river seaward flow
> From the inner land : far off, three mountain-tops,
> Three silent pinnacles of aged snow,
> Stood sunset-flushed.''

" The mountains and the river are there," writes Mr. Clifford, " and the delicious streams are for ever falling by scores down the green precipices of Hawaii into the blue sea. How lovely that sea is can scarcely be told. One puts his hand in, and all around it is the softest and most brilliant blue ; below are growths of pure white coral, and among them swim fishes as brilliant as paroquets. Some are yellow like canaries, some are gorgeous orange or bright red. I tried to paint a blue fish, but no pigment could represent its intensity. The loveliest of all was like nothing but a rainbow as it sported below me. Groves of coco-nut trees rise from the water's edge. The gardens are rich with roses, lilies, myrtles, gardenia, heliotrope, and passion flowers. Near by is a great tropical forest, which I always feared as I entered ; for there is an element of the terrible in this tremendous vegetation, and in the perfect silence of it all. The trees are wreathed with humid creepers ; the ferns are fourteen feet high ; even the stag's-horn moss grows taller than a man."

The islands, if we read their names along the curve north-west to south-east, are—Nihau, Kauai, Oahu, Molokai, Lauai, Maui, Kahulaui, Hawaii ; the capital, Honolulu, is in Oahu, nearly midway in the curve. They were discovered in 1778 by the great navigator Captain Cook, who, on his return visit in the following year, met his death from the natives, through a miserable misunderstanding. As a rule, these natives are of the gentlest and sunniest disposition. They received Christianity in 1820 from some American missionaries, and the tale has often been told how a chieftainess Kapiolani, one of their first converts, mounted the slope of Kilauea (supposed home of the terrible goddess Pelè), and broke the spell of the old bad religion, casting into the fiery lake a sprig of the scarlet-yellow ohelo berries, Pelè's sacred plant, and defied the goddess to hurt her. " If I perish by her anger, then dread her power. But see, I live and am safe, for Jehovah the Almighty is my God. O all ye people, behold how vain are the gods of Hawaii, and turn and serve the Lord ! "

Unhappily, other white visitors came and brought evils to outweigh the good—drink, for instance, and terrible diseases ; among these leprosy, now the scourge of the islands. It is not certainly known how the leprosy came to Hawaii some sixty years ago ; but according to general belief, some ill-fated foreigner brought it over from Asia. Once introduced, it spread far and wide, helped by the sociability of the natives. They are hospitable to the last degree ; all they have is yours. The sick and the sound would eat from the same dish, sleep on the same mat, even smoke from the same pipe. By 1865 leprosy had taken such a hold on the people that the Hawaiian Government determined to isolate the infected, and an Act was passed that all lepers should be deported to a settlement on the north coast of the island of Molokai.

Father Damien, when his ship dropped anchor in Honolulu harbour on March 19, 1864, if he knew of these poor lepers, probably thought little about them. His whole soul was bent on preaching the faith to the heathen. The bishop, Monseigneur Maigret, received him paternally ; but before he could actually set out to evangelize the natives it was necessary that Damien, still in minor orders, should be ordained priest. Ordained he accordingly was, after two months' preparation, at Whitsuntide, and after visiting one or two of the islands in company with the bishop, was assigned to the district of Puna, among the volcanoes of Hawaii. He wrote home :—

(1) " I am sorry I am neither a poet nor a writer, to send you a good description of my new country. . . . The climate is delightful, so that strangers easily become accustomed to it, and generally enjoy better health here than in their own country. The archipelago is made up of eight islands, four of which are large and four small. Hawaii, the one on which I am stationed, is larger than all the others together. It is as large as Belgium, if not larger. In the centre are three volcanoes, two of which appear to be extinct. The third is still active, and it is in the neighbourhood of this that Providence has destined me to be placed. From one end of my district to another you have to walk on lava. . . . I think I shall require fully three days to get from one end to the other. In every

direction there are little villages scattered about, and
for seven or eight years there has been no resident
priest. Before leaving, the bishop told me that I
must remember the mission was quite in its infancy.
Indeed, I found no church in which to say Mass,
but two are now in course of construction. . . . I
want you, dear father, to buy two bells for my two
new churches; they must be smaller than the one at
Louvain which Mgr. d'Abierie blessed."

(2) " March 1865. Our bishop has just made over
to me a new parish, a little larger than that of Tremeloo ! It takes me quite a month to get round it.
Here we cannot travel by rail, or by carriage, or on
foot. How then, think you, do we perform these long
journeys ? Well, we have mules here and horses. I
have just bought two—a very good horse for 100
francs and a mule for 75. Sometimes I shall have to
go by boat. The poor islanders rejoice when they
see me coming. I like them immensely, and would
willingly give my life for them, like our Divine Lord."

" Truly," he writes again to his brother Pamphile
(now a parish priest at home), " I ought to be proud
of my district, for it is as large as the whole diocese of
Malines." With his superb bodily strength he accomplished wonders in traversing it. One day, it is related, he arrived at the foot of a steep mountain, somewhere behind which there lay a Christian settlement
not yet visited by him. Determined to visit it now,
he tethered his horse and began the ascent, climbing
on his hands and feet, so precipitous was the track.
The summit gained, he could discern no habitation,
but, in the distance, a second mountain as high as
the first. Undaunted, he covered the intervening
valley and climbed the second slope. Again on the
farther side no sign of a church or village met his eye to
encourage him. Below him lay a wide flat country,
and still beyond that another hill. Commending
himself to God, he persevered over the third mountain

and across another ravine. Fatigue overcame him for a while; his boots were cut, his feet bleeding, his hands lacerated. He looked on them and cried "Courage! the good Lord also has shed His blood for those souls yonder!" He reached the settlement, more dead than alive, to be repaid by the joy of the Christians there, who welcomed for the first time their new-found apostle.

In a later letter occurs the entry: "Leprosy is beginning to be very prevalent here. There are many men covered with it. It does not cause death at once, but it is very rarely cured. . . . Do not forget, my dear parents, to pray for me every day; there are so many dangers here both for one's soul and one's body."

We have seen that in 1865 the Hawaiian Government had passed a law to segregate the lepers in the island of Molokai. But to pass a law and to enforce it are two very different things. The lepers were scattered over the islands, and their friends and kinsfolk clung to them with truly Hawaiian tenderness. They hid them in their houses, and even deep in the woods. The law worked slowly for some years, though many men were taken to the leper island; but in 1873, under a new king, it began to be rigorously enforced. Then the ports of embarkation became constant scenes of the most tragic partings. Let Mr. Clifford describe one as he witnessed it, some years later, on his way to Molokai.

"The little steamer *Mokilii* leaves Honolulu, the capital of the islands, on Mondays at five o'clock for Molokai, and on the 17th of December I took my passage and went on board. The sunset was orange, with a great purple cloud fringed with gold. It faded quickly, and by the time we reached a small pier-head outside the town it was dark, and the moon was casting a long greenish light across the sea. From the pier came a continuous tremolo wail, rather

mechanical, but broken by real sobs. I could see a
little crowd of lepers and lepers' friends waiting there.
' O my husband ! ' cried a poor woman again and
again. Thirteen lepers got into the boat, and were
rowed to the steamer. Then we sailed away, and
gradually the wailing grew fainter and fainter, till
we could hear it no longer.''

Such scenes coming under Father Damien's close
observation—for he had to comfort wives, husbands,
fathers, mothers, who had lost their dearest—pierced
him to the heart. His thoughts began to detach
themselves from the spiritual welfare of his healthy
parishioners, and to follow the poor lepers across the
sea to Molokai, where was no priest nor shepherd of
those souls that, more than any on earth, needed
consolation.

A day came when he happened to attend the
dedication of a chapel recently erected on the island
of Maui. The bishop, Monseigneur Maigret, was
there, and in his address lamented that, owing to the
scarcity of missioners, he was unable to do anything
for the poor lepers on Molokai, and especially did
he regret that he was unable to send them a fixed
pastor. Some young priests from the Picpus Congregation had just arrived for mission work, and before
them Father Damien instantly spoke.

" Monseigneur," said he, " here are your new
missioners. One of them could take my district ;
and if you will be kind enough to allow it, I will go
to Molokai and labour for the poor lepers, whose
wretched state of bodily and spiritual misfortune has
often made my heart bleed within me."

Thus simply was made, by an obscure priest on a
far-away island, an offer of which the heroism, when
the world came to know it, made cowards shudder
and brave men wish they had been braver. It was
accepted, and that same day, without any farewells,
Father Damien embarked with the bishop on a boat

that was taking some fifty lepers to Molokai. On arriving, the bishop assembled the lepers and said, " My children, you have been left alone and uncared for. You shall be so no longer. Behold, I have brought you one who will be a father to you, and who loves you so much that for your sakes he does not hesitate to become one of you, to live and die with you." So the bishop departed, and Damien was left to his mission.

From the first he never doubted that he would take the leprosy in time, as how—constantly living with the contagion, dressing the patients' sores, washing their bodies, even digging their graves—could he escape it ? But he fell to work with a cheerful heart. He was now about thirty-three years old, of unusual physical strength, hardened by much exercise and spare living. He had come in such haste that he had brought not even a change of linen. Since there was no house for him, and he could not herd with his lepers at night, for some while his only shelter at night was a pandanus tree in the churchyard. There was no time to build a hut ; for Molokai never saw the face of a doctor, and of his flock from eight to twelve were dying every week. In the midst of this first terrible business Father Damien found time to " do things." The lepers, though better lodged than he, were living pell-mell under booths constructed of rough timbers " covered with ki leaves or with sugar-cane leaves, the best ones with ' pili ' grass. They passed their time with playing cards, native dances, drinking fermented ki-root beer, home-made alcohol, and with the sequels of all this. Their clothes were far from being clean and decent, on account of the scarcity of water, which then had to be brought from a great distance. Many a time I have been compelled to run out of these domiciles to breathe fresh air. To counteract the stench I accustomed myself to the use of tobacco. The smell of the pipe preserved me somewhat from carrying in my clothes the noxious odour of the lepers." He sent word across to Honolulu, and by-and-by several schooner-loads of scantling arrived, to build decent frame-houses. Friends sent rough boards, shingles, flooring. Some of the lepers had a little money, and hired carpenters; for those without money Father Damien built with his own hands, helped by a little gang of leper boys. He sent requisitions across, and obtained warm clothing for his flock. He looked up at the cliff—the leper settlement lay under the shadow of a cliff—and wondered how to obtain a supply of water. Until now the lepers, when they wanted water, had to carry it from a distant gulch in pitchers on their sore shoulders; also they had to carry their filthy infected clothes to a considerable distance to wash them. Damien explored the stream, and, some way up its valley, came to a deep basin of ice-cold water. The natives informed him that in the severest droughts this basin never ran dry. He applied to Honolulu for water-pipes, which were sent, and with his lepers he piped a steady stream of clear water down to the settlement. He built chapels and a dispensary. Hitherto the lepers had dreaded the very name of hospital; and small wonder, for the same cart that brought a patient for admission brought his coffin also! Father Damien changed all this. He did not rest until the hospital was supplied with a resident doctor and nurses. He provided for the decent interment of the dead. Since the government did not supply money to buy coffins (the price of a coffin was two dollars), those who died penniless were buried without them. Damien formed a " coffin association," and also made a large enclosed cemetery, adjoining one of his churches. Before 1879 he had buried sixteen hundred lepers, and often had to act as undertaker and sexton as well as priest. " I dig the graves," he wrote home, " and if time allows I

make the coffins." He set himself a far harder task—
to fight the despairing vice that had taken for its
motto, " In this place there is no law." He found
this vice to be fed by a drink which the lepers dis-
tilled from the root of a plant called " ki." The
law forbade this distillation, and in enforcing the
law Damien learned what it means to be hated for
righteousness' sake. He earned unpopularity. His
enemies were obstinate, his supporters were indolent;
nor did the tide turn until both discovered that he,
their best friend, had become a leper even as they.

He had lived with them about ten years when he
began to suspect it. He quietly consulted the doctors
who came over to Molokai, and they reassured him.
But one day, feeling unwell, he took a foot-bath. The
water brought him was scalding, but he plunged his
feet in it, and did not discover that it was over-hot
until he saw the effects of the scald. Then too well
he knew. This deadness of feeling is one of the first
symptoms. " I have seen," writes Father Albert, a
missioner who laboured at Molokai for some years,
" the lepers sometimes take a knife and chop off their
dead fingers and toss them away, just as if they were
pieces of wood." Damien asked the resident doctor
to examine him carefully. " I cannot bear to tell
you," said Dr. Arnim, " but what you say is true."
" It is no shock to me," said Damien, " for I have long
felt sure of it."

In his letters home he made no mention of his fate,
but to his bishop he wrote :—

" I cannot come to Honolulu, for leprosy has
attacked me. There are signs of it on my left cheek
and ear, and my eyebrows are beginning to fall ; I
shall soon be quite disfigured. . . . The good God knows
what is best for my sanctification, and I say gaily,
*Fiat voluntas tua*, with a ready heart."

Henceforward, in preaching to his flock, he no
longer said " My brethren," but " We lepers." By

this time the tale of his self-devotion had travelled among many nations of men; but their wonder and pity could not help him. "He saved others; himself he could not save." He went steadily forward to the end, instructing his fellow-outcasts, receiving their confessions, binding their sores, even feeding them, putting the food into their mouths when the leprosy had eaten away their hands—all the while facing the sight of that to which he must surely come. Mr. Clifford thus describes a meeting with him in these latter days, and his appearance.

"At dawn we were opposite Kalaupapa. Two little spired churches caught my eye first, and around them were dotted the white cottages of the lepers, who crowded the pier to meet us. But the sea was too rough for us to land. . . . We went on to Kalawao, but were again disappointed; it was too dangerous to disembark. Finally it was decided to put off a boat for a rocky point about a mile and a half distant from the town. Climbing down this point, we saw about twenty lepers, and 'There is Father Damien!' said our purser; and slowly moving along the hillside I saw a dark figure with a large straw hat. He came rather painfully down, and sat near the waterside, and we exchanged greetings across the waves. . . . At last all was ready, and we went swinging across the waves, and finally chose a fit moment for leaping on shore. Father Damien caught me by the hand, and a hearty welcome shone from his kindly face as he helped me up the rock. He immediately called me by my name, 'Edward.' . . . He is now forty-nine years old—a thick-set, strongly-built man, with black curly hair and short beard, turning grey. His countenance must have been handsome, with a full, well-curved mouth and a short, straight nose; but he is now a good deal disfigured by leprosy, though not so badly as to make it anything but a pleasure to look at his bright, sensible face. His forehead is swollen and rigid, the eyebrows are gone, the nose is somewhat sunk, and the ears are greatly enlarged. His hands and face look uneven with a sort of incipient boils, and his body also shows many signs of the disease, but he assured me that he felt little or no pain."

Towards the end his noble spirit at times came near to breaking down. Reports of his disease found their way into the Belgian newspapers. Some one imprudently told the news to his old mother, and it hastened her death (1886). In 1887 he writes home : " My dear brother, having been informed that some of the Belgian papers had stated the death of your exiled brother, I suppose that is one reason why you do not write to me any more. Unfortunately, Almighty God has not yet called me out of this miserable world." That is the one and only querulous passage to be discovered in all his correspondence ; and the letter promptly goes on : " I have accepted this malady as my special cross, which I try to carry, as Simon the Cyrenian, in the footsteps of our Divine Master." In a letter to Mr. Clifford (February 21, 1889) he repeats this image—" My love and good wishes. . . . I try to make slowly my way of the cross, and hope to be soon on the top of my Golgotha."

On Thursday, the 28th of March, he took to his bed, having first arranged his temporal affairs. " How happy I am," he said, " to have given all to Monseigneur ! Now I die poor, having nothing of my own." On the 30th he made his general confession to Father Wendelin, who ministered to him. " Look at my hands," he said. " All the wounds are healing, and the crust is becoming black ; that is a sign of death, as you know very well. Look at my eyes. I have seen so many lepers die that I cannot be mistaken. Death is not far off. I should have liked to see the bishop again ; but the good God is calling me to keep Easter with Himself."

" My father," said Wendelin, " will you leave me
your mantle, that I may inherit your great heart ? "

" Fie ! What would you do with it ? " said
Damien. " It is full of leprosy."

He also said, after receiving extreme unction :
" How good God is to have preserved me long enough
to have two priests by my side at my last moments,
and also to know that the good Sisters of Charity are
at the *léproserie*. This has been my *Nunc Dimittis*.
The work of the lepers is assured. I am no longer
necessary, and so will go up yonder."

" When you are there, father," said Wendelin,
" you won't forget those whom you are leaving
orphans ? "

" Oh no," he answered ; " if I have any credit with
God, I will intercede for all who are in the *léproserie*."

After this he rallied a little, but on April 13th
became much worse, and on the 15th died without a
struggle, as if falling asleep. Towards the end he had
a vision of two figures continually standing watch—
one at his bed's head, the other at his feet. Who
they were he did not say.

In accordance with his own wish, his friends buried
him beneath the pandanus tree whose boughs had
been his roof when he first came to Molokai. He had
lived in Molokai a little over sixteen years.

" *I was sick, and ye visited me. Come, ye blessed of
my Father, inherit the kingdom prepared for you from
the foundation of the world.*"

**THE END**

# HORIZON BOOKS

### Edited by Dr. G. B. Harrison

*Fully illustrated.*               *Each 3s. 6d. net.*

An entirely new series of books for boys and girls—" answers worth hearing to questions which were worth asking." They are concerned alike with the past, the present, and the future : with science and the modern world, with ancient times, the lives of great people, and adventure throughout the ages. They are exciting books—simple, vivid, and accurate, and all have been written by authors of high reputation who have a genuine enthusiasm for their subject.

It is a special feature of the Horizon Books that they have all been planned and discussed in committee by their authors and Dr. G. B. Harrison. The Committee consists of Miss Eleanor Farjeon, Miss Helen Simpson, Miss Lorna Lewis, Mr. John Hampden, and Mr. L. A. G. Strong—names which are ample guarantee of the books' quality, accuracy, and literary distinction.

DIGGING FOR HISTORY, by G. B. Harrison
CONQUERING SPACE AND TIME, by A. M. Low
THE MAN WHO ASKED QUESTIONS (SOCRATES),
by L. A. G. Strong
PALADINS IN SPAIN, by Eleanor Farjeon
LEONARDO THE INVENTOR, by Lorna Lewis
LIFE AND ITS STORY, by A. M. Low
THE WANDERINGS OF ULYSSES, by G. B. Harrison
HENRY OF AGINCOURT, by L. A. G. Strong
NANSEN, by Lorna Lewis
THE WONDERS OF HERODOTUS,
by Eleanor Farjeon
MUSSOLINI—HITLER—STALIN. (In preparation)
MARY KINGSLEY, by Helen Simpson. (In preparation)

*Full descriptive catalogue post free from Nelsons*
35–36 Paternoster Row, London, E.C.4
Edinburgh : Paris : Melbourne : Toronto : New York